Office Automation

A User-Driven Method

APPLICATIONS OF MODERN TECHNOLOGY IN BUSINESS

Series Editor: **Howard L. Morgan**
University of Pennsylvania

COMPUTERS AND BANKING: Electronic Funds Transfer Systems and Public Policy
Edited by Kent W. Colton and Kenneth L. Kraemer

DATA COMMUNICATIONS: An Introduction to Concepts and Design
Robert Techo

DATA BASE ADMINISTRATION
Jay-Louise Weldon

OFFICE AUTOMATION: A User-Driven Method
Don Tapscott

Office Automation

A User-Driven Method

Don Tapscott

Trigon Systems Group
Toronto, Ontario, Canada

PLENUM PRESS • NEW YORK AND LONDON

Library of Congress Cataloging in Publication Data

Tapscott, Don, Date-
   Office automation.

(Applications of modern technology in business)
   Bibliography: p.
   Includes index.
   1. Office practice—Automation. I. Title. II. Series.
HF5548.2.T28 1982   651.8′4   82-15133
ISBN 0-306-41071-0

© 1982 Plenum Press, New York
A Division of Plenum Publishing Corporation
233 Spring Street, New York, N.Y. 10013

Printed in the United States of America

Foreword

Every pioneer takes large risks, hoping that the new frontier he seeks will provide the benefits of independence and good fortune. Don Tapscott is such a pioneer in the area of office automation. He has been a true pioneer, having entered the field in its early days and taken the risk of working not in technology, which was fashionable, but in the field of the problems of organizations, which was less fashionable, but in many ways more important.

The utilization of computers for data processing, accounting, inventory, and other "bread and butter" applications is now well entrenched in our society and culture. The process of designing such systems tends to focus on the needs of the company and the constraints of the equipment, leading to efficient systems with little tolerance for the variety of people who must use or interface with them. Within the office automation area, these methods do not work nearly as well. The frequency and amount of human interaction in the office environment, and the wide variety of situations and reactions therein, demands a different design methodology.

Don Tapscott has shown the way for this new method, through the user-driven design techniques described in *Office Automation*. It is, after all, the user who must be happy with a system in order for it to function well in an organizational setting. Some of the success of the word processing and early office automation systems came about because they freed users from the grasp of the data processing department. The ability to use a word processor with records processing as a simple data processing system was a godsend to many user departments for jobs that were otherwise too small for DP. As these users learned, they often came into conflict with data processing, which created organizational stress. For many similar reasons, office automation has more serious organizational and systems problems than technical ones.

The methods presented in this book for studying one's own organization should prove invaluable to those starting on the road to office automation. I have often been called upon to consult for companies which have never been very introspective. All seem to want the same thing—a priori proof that office automation will save them money. None wants to trust in the words of experts or the often overblown claims of vendors, and rightly so. Yet performing the detailed activity analysis, communications analysis, and systems design in a large organization is very costly when done by outsiders. The user-driven methodology discussed in this book, if properly applied, will permit your organization to generate its own analyses, and determine for itself where or whether the new technologies can be best utilized.

Don Tapscott has not only learned through his consulting and research activities over the years. He has also been an early and constant user of the technologies. By working with the most advanced systems of the day, and living with terminals at home and office, he has seen some of the more subtle benefits of office automation. These are reflected in several of the chapters in this book.

Office automation has the potential truly to reshape the world in which we work and live. Transportation/telecommunication tradeoffs, more flexible organizational structures, far better user interfaces through voice and graphics, and focus on easing the communications and information retrieval bottlenecks are all reasons these techniques will inevitably touch those of us who work over the next few decades. The ever decreasing costs of hardware also contribute to the wide coverage which the technology will have. Yet change of this magnitude will not come without many social and organizational difficulties. New power structures, shifting control of technology from an elite to the masses, and the young generation of managers, trained in and expecting computers on their desks, will create problems.

I am pleased that this book may help those of you who read it and who apply its methods to attenuate the problems. Its message is that users can control their own destiny in office automation, and that exercising such control is better not only for them, but for their organizations as well. Heed the message!

Villanova, PA, 1982
Howard Morgan

Preface

The three technologies of computers, communications, and the office are converging to bring about integrated office systems. These systems address pressing needs of today's organizations for better information management, improved communications, and more effective office administration. These cornerstones of productivity and growth are centering on "electronic workstations." Typical tools include electronic mail, decision support systems, interactive information retrieval, text processing, enhanced telephony, and personal support tools. When combined to directly support professionals, managers, and other office workers, these systems are making profound improvements in productivity, effectiveness, and quality of work life.

However, while there are far-reaching opportunities, there are many obstacles. The technology, while cost–beneficial today, is still embryonic and evolving. Determining system requirements has proven to be more complex than ever before. It has been difficult to measure the impact of these systems on productivity and to develop a solid cost justification. Implementing systems for nontechnical users and managing change have posed unanticipated challenges. New planning methodologies are required along with new organizational structures to oversee system design, implementation, and evolution.

The overall problem is one of a "gap" between the users and providers of the new technologies. Office system vendors are having to modify traditional approaches in order to close the gap between themselves and the users. New methods of product planning, evaluation, marketing, and implementation are required to correspond to the new complexities of user requirements.

This book is aimed at closing that gap. It outlines a method for "user-driven design" of integrated office systems. This method can be used by both the users and the providers of technology to design systems that better meet the needs of people and organizations.

Chapter 1 overviews the technology; it explains the origins of these new systems and discusses their potential to improve the effectiveness of organizations and quality of work life in the office.

Chapter 2 discusses the problem of "technology-driven" systems and explains the need for a user science, a new method for determining user requirements and for designing office systems.

Chapter 3 explains the different ways of looking at office systems. Five conceptual approaches are reviewed: Organizational Communication, Functional, Information Resource Management, Decision Support, and Quality of Work Life.

Chapter 4 develops a conceptual model of the office and, using it, critiques the five conceptual approaches outlined in Chapter 3. By understanding the office we can better understand how to improve its function.

Chapter 5 explains the concepts of efficiency, effectiveness, and productivity as they pertain to the office. The problem of measuring productivity and organizational performance is presented and the "office model" is used to illustrate an approach to solving the problem.

Chapter 6 outlines the process of "user-driven design" in some detail. Assessment of user needs is seen as: participative, multidisciplinary, ethically acceptable, evolutionary, and a process of change. Contrasts with previous approaches to design (as with data processing or Management Information Systems) and one contemporary approach called "Applications Development Without Programmers" are explained. The specific phases in the design process are described with the recommended output from each.

Chapter 7 discusses the importance of having a controlled evaluation of the office system and its impacts. Different research designs and the use in evaluating office systems are discussed along with the utility and limitations of Action Research.

Chapter 8 talks about measurement. The key categories of measurement instruments are reviewed: survey questionnaire, diary or log, activity sampling, network analysis, content analysis, observation, critical incidents, secondary sources, tests, and system monitoring. Criteria for evaluating instruments are presented.

Chapter 9 describes how information from the requirements analyses can be translated into a pilot systems design. Twelve areas of assessment are discussed: communication opportunities, information requirements, decision support, document production, administrative support, data processing, new procedures, job design, environmental design, implementation needs, categorization of current in-house technologies, and vendor evaluation.

Chapter 10 presents a method for conducting a cost–benefit analysis for various system alternatives.

Chapter 11 outlines some practical guidelines on planning and implementation of pilot systems.

Chapter 12 is a case study, showing one experience evaluating an integrated office system pilot. Some of the key issues in the transition from pilots to fully operational systems are explained.

Chapter 13 stands back from the process and reviews some of the broader issues that increasingly face designers of these new systems. These issues include the impact of the new technologies on work, employment, the nature of organizations, and on the future of our society.

This book was written for a wide group of people with diverse interests, needs, and objectives. With this in mind, a detailed table of contents is provided to enable the reader to skip from one topic to another. Rather than going from cover to cover, you may benefit from designing your own "user-driven" manuscript.

Toronto, Canada   DT
December, 1981

Acknowledgments

The author gratefully acknowledges Bell Canada and Bell Northern Research Ltd. (BNR). Many of the ideas in this book were developed during my work with the Office Information Communications Systems (OICS) program at BNR, and Bell-Northern Software Research (BNSR), the predecessor of BNR's Toronto lab. In particular, thank you to Dave Sadleir who initiated the OICS group and who, as a Bell Canada executive, continued to support it, and to Dick Cuthbert, my former boss at BNR for his support of the group's work and his contribution to my understanding of office automation.

I also express my deep gratitude to colleagues at BNR during that period for their insights, critiques, and assistance on the manuscript. This book would not have been written without them. In particular, thanks to Jim Bair, Mark Graham, Morley Greenberg, Del Henderson, Ingrid Lebolt, Joanne Licursi, Angela Macrae, David Macfarlane, Laura Oda, Loris Sartor, Bharat Shah, and Glenda Thompson.

Also, many thanks to colleagues Mary Baetz, Terry Burrell, Dave Conrath, Douglas Englebart, Michael Hammer, Tom Lodahl, Dean Meyer, Howard Morgan, Dave Potter, and Norman White for their assistance in developing the ideas contained herein and/or critical comments on the manuscript. And my sincere thanks to David Droeske, illustrator for the volume.

Finally, my gratitude to Del Henderson for pointing me, years ago, in the right direction, and to Ana Paula Lopes for her ongoing insights and encouragement.

Contents

9. Assessing the Organization: System

10. Assessing the Organization:

11. Getting Going **187**

List of Illustrations

The Advent of Integrated
Office Systems

*One of the tool's that shows the greatest immediate promise is the computer, when it
can be harnessed for direct, on-line assistance, integrated with new concepts and
methods. . . . Every person who does thinking with symbolized concepts (whether in
the form of English language, pictographs, formal logic, or mathematics) should be
able to benefit significantly.*

(Douglas, Englebart, *Augmenting Human Intellect: a Conceptual Framework*, 1962.)

1.1. INTRODUCTION

The 80s is a decade that is bringing about very profound and far-reaching changes in the office. These changes are beginning to transform many of
the ways in which people and organizations work.

Many terms are used to describe the phenomenon—office automation,
the office of the future, integrated office systems, office information communication systems. Douglas Englebart, who in many ways is the father of the
new field, has referred to it as one of the most significant industries of the
century.[1] With hindsight it appears that even Englebart understated the
scope and significance of the revolution which he was precipitating. Toffler
describes it as part of "The Third Wave"—the first being the development of
agriculture and the second being the industrial revolution.[2]

The industrialized world is moving into a period in which most office
workers will be supported directly through a personal computer terminal by a
set of integrated communication and information handling tools. The widespread proliferation of "integrated office systems" designed to augment the

effectiveness of office workers has become quite astounding. New industries are being born with a rapidity which few anticipated. Many existing vendors of computer, communications, and traditional office technologies—who are eager to capture a part of the gigantic and exploding market—are on fast migration paths towards an integrated system product line. User organizations, who more and more realize that their ability to succeed, and even survive, will depend on their ability to become part of the "third wave," are beginning to undertake massive change. The "winners" in this race are, in general, prospering.

However, the picture is not all rosy. While many vendors have made substantial progress, many others have become marginalized or have disappeared. For many user organizations, the first steps on the road towards the office of the future have been frustrating. Many more organizations have been reluctant to take the first steps. And while the opportunities are great, evolution towards the future has been fraught with problems which no one anticipated.

This book is an attempt to provide both user and vendor organizations with guidelines on avoiding and handling some of these key problems.

1.2. THE ROOTS OF AUTOMATION

Why is all this happening? What are the major factors propelling us into this stormy sea of change?

The momentum towards the office of the future is rooted in recent significant technological developments which have occured simultaneously with an acute need to augment the productivity of the white collar worker. That is, a "technology push" and a "demand pull" provide the driving forces behind the changes which we are experiencing.

1.2.1. Technology Push

Technology is developing at a furious rate. Recent technological developments in two main areas have provided the basis for office automation.

The first area is chip technology. Moore's law states that the number of electronic components that can be placed on a single silicon chip doubles each year. We are now employing at least a thousand times more computing power than we were 12 years ago. Twelve years from now we will be using a thousand times more computing power than we are using today. Large mainframe computers of the mid-1970s are now contained on a single chip. Integrated wafers contain microcode which knows where impurities on a chip lie and bypass them. In 1981, one third of a million components were contained on a chip. By 1990 a single chip will contain hundreds of millions of components. Such explosive growth is changing economics of data processing beyond recognition. Moreover, the continuing gains in microprocessor technology and microelectronics in general are now providing the processing capacity required for office automation, at a cost which enables that capacity to be beneficially applied. For example, the cost of main memory has decreased 10 times in the last four years. (See Figures 1.1 and 1.2.)

The second area is telecommunications. There is a rapidly growing trend to interconnect various kinds of computer and other office hardware with the new generation of telecommunication systems. Relatively primitive data communications facilities of the 1960s have evolved today into communications network architectures which make it easy to connect various pieces of equipment to a communications network. These network architectures and the resulting capacity to move electronic information easily, quickly, and inexpensively are leading to entirely new uses of computing and electronic communications.

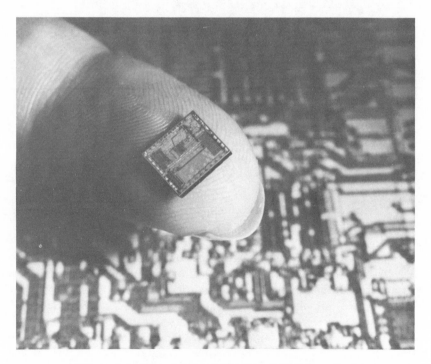

Figure 1.1. Microprocessor (Courtesy Intel Corporation).

Figure 1.2. 32-Bit Micromainframe (Courtesy Intel Corporation).

Developments in switching technology, including the wide use of intelligent digital switching systems, have transformed the capacity of a network to route information. Another set of developments is related to the growing capacity of transmission media. One is fiber optics. Using a lightweight flexible cable and sophisticated interface electronics and laser light, extremely large amounts of data can be transmitted with very low loss and distortion. Satellite systems are enabling organizations to have their own ground stations that can connect them into a worldwide transmission/broadcast networks. In one example of things to come, the U.S. Navy is developing a transmission device that would be capable of directing a signal through the middle of the earth with only a 1% signal loss.[3]

The 1970s was a decade of pioneering in networks. The 1980s have become a network of mass production.

Technological developments provide only the material basis for office automation. It is because these developments correspond to a growing need for the fruits of technological change that office automation has flourished. There are several aspects to this need.

1.2.2. Demand Pull

Paul Strassman, one of the pioneer researchers in the area, has explained that in the past 20 years white collar labor has been the fastest-growing component of the work force in every industrialized country. Yet this sector shows tiny increases in productivity compared to the industrial and agricultural sectors of the economy where the need to make appropriate capital expenditures has been understood.[4]

One of the most popularly quoted arguments for spending money on office systems is that the office is a place where little capital expenditures have been made. Estimates, according to Michael Zisman of MIT, for average capital investment per office worker range from $2,000 to $6,000. By comparison, the average capitalization per factory worker is $25,000.[5] At the same time, according to a Stanford Research Institute study, between 1960 and 1970, industrial worker productivity in the USA rose 83% white collar productivity increased only 4%.[6]

It is important to note that such estimates are not based on valid data. Zisman, more recently, has partially withdrawn his previous argument.[7] However, the fact remains that the office is a very labor-intensive environment which can be improved through the judicious application of the new technologies.

Over the past decade, written communications and related cost increases have combined to push office costs from 20–30% to 40–50% of the total costs of most businesses. If current trends continue, by the mid 1980s the number of secretaries/typists will have tripled since 1960. And by 1985 it has been estimated that the knowledge worker will outnumber the production worker by 3 to 1.[8]

The bottom line of all this is that a lot of money is being spent on a lot of people (a growing proportion of the work force) who now need tools to be more productive.

Managing the information resource, both in terms of information-cost management and enhancing access to pertinent information, is moving into focus for more and more organizations. This is especially true of information-intensive organizations like insurance companies, banks, credit card organizations, governments, research organizations, unions, political parties, and corporate head offices. Some kinds of operating information lose their value over time, and a delay in assembling the right proposal, the complete answer, or the appropriate files can mean a missed opportunity.[9]

As organizations have grown and become more complex and data processing has enabled rapid measurement of performance from various sources, the need to *decrease* the amount of data and *increase* the amount of usable information which the knowledge worker is exposed to has never been greater. Moreover, this information must be communicated. The problem of information management can be summarized as the activity of getting the right information to the right people at the right time in a cost-effective manner.

A new field of management/behavioral science known as *decision support systems* (DSS) focuses on managers' decision-making activities and the use of computer-based technology to support them in complex and unstructured tasks.

Peter Keen and Charles Stabell explain decision support this way:

> It has been recognized for some time that systems to assist managers in relatively complex and nonprogrammable activities are different from the structured decision systems that have been developed for the more operational tasks in the organization. There has been relatively little exploration of the implications of these differences. The Management Information Systems field is technical and presciptive. Decisison Support requires a behavioral and descriptive grounding.[10]

In the work of most office workers there are activities which require judgment to be exercised. If this judgment involves data, especially data in complex arrays, a decision support system may be extremely useful. Examples are a manager formulating a budget; a purchasing agent attempting to determine an appropriate mode of transportation, a doctor diagnosing a patient; an oil explorer analyzing geological data; or a union negotiator attempting to determine the consequences of various wage settlements on union membership.

A worker uses a DSS by constructing a model of his/her decision problem. Models may be analytical, such as a linear model for resource allocation, tabular, such as in budgeting and financial planning, or more complex, such as in simulating the effect of a certain government policy on inflation.[11]

The decision maker then interacts with the model by asking, for example, "what if" statements. Other uses include risk analysis, through the quantification of uncertainty and goal seeking, applicable when the decision maker has data but is not clear what his/her goals are.

Linking both areas of information management and decision support is communication effectiveness. Most knowledge workers spend a majority of their time communicating.

Henry Mintzberg of McGill University, who conducted one of the most thorough and complete investigations of managerial work, found that managers spend 66–80% of their time in oral communications.[12] A study performed at Bell-Northern Research (BNR) had similar results. Both technical–professional and managerial staff spent a majority of their time in oral comunication—on the telephone, and face to face in meetings.[13] Harvey Poppel reported that 40% of a typical manager's time is spent on mail processing, telephone calls, and business travel. Activities like this are all forms of relatively unstructured person-to-person communication, which, as Poppel says, has been virtually unaffected by previous technological advances.[14]

Mintzberg was inspired during his study. . .

> . . . by the fact that the executives I was observing—all very competent by any standard—are fundamentally indistinguishable from their counterparts of a hundred years ago (or a thousand years ago, for that matter). The information they need differs, but they seek it in the same way—by word of mouth. Their decisions concern modern technology, but the procedures they use to make them are the same as the procedures of the nineteenth-century manager. Even the computer, so important for the specialized work of the organization, has apparently had no influence on the work procedure of general managers. In fact, the manager is in a kind of loop, with increasingly heavy work pressures but no aid forthcoming from management science.[12]

Mintzberg's observations summarize the problems of information management, decision support, and communications effectiveness which confront the contemporary manager, and more generally, knowledge worker. These problems and the urgent need to ameliorate them are propelling more and more organizations towards the office of the future.

A 1978 study performed for Steelcase Inc. by Louis Harris and Associates indicated the remarkable changes in office work. Of the national American sample, 54% of office workers now use some kind of data-processing, telecommunications, or electronic equipment on the job. In the last 5 years, 54% have seen their offices redesigned; 57% have changed jobs within the organization; 72% have acquired new jobs or responsiblities; and 73% have had to learn new skills on the job.[15] This gives just a taste of the massive changes that are beginning to take place.

1.3. INTEGRATED OFFICE SYSTEM TECHNOLOGY

There are a number of methods of describing the new technologies. For example, products provided by each vendor could be summarized. Systems can be described according to their applications (for example, electronic mail, text editing, decision support systems). Or systems could be summarized according to *functions* or the *type* of office worker they address. One useful framework views office systems from the perspective of the capture, storage/processing, retrieval, and communication of information.

1.3.1. Information Capture

A number of new input tools facilitate the creation of information, its storage, processing, retrieval, and communication. Key punching was the main entry device for data processing (DP) and management information systems (MIS). Word processing, which was viewed in the 1970s and early 1980s as primarily a device for improving typing efficiency, has become one of the central tools for generating textual data bases.

Keyboards were initially used exclusively by secretaries. Now the ability to use, or willingness to try using, a keyboard is a prerequisite for many senior jobs. Many vendors have developed modified keyboards, more suitable for some managers and executives who are reluctant to use a full alphanumeric keyset. Although voice input and other input devices are being produced for those who prefer to avoid typing, there is a general trend for individuals at all levels of an organization to acquire some keyboarding skills. For example, it has been noted that increased use of a keyboard can be coupled with increased use of machine dictation.[16]

While dictation is an appropriate input tool for some kinds of textual material, there has been a trend for professionals and managers to use a keyboard and word processing as a *thinking tool*, rather than a tool to improve typing efficiency. Powerful text manipulation systems can dramatically facilitate the thinking processes involved in constructing complex textual material. By interacting with text on a screen, an author can organize her or his ideas, formulate and reformulate thoughts, and produce clearer, better-structured text than using a pen and paper. This is especially true when the text processing system is integrated with other communication, information retrieval, and analytical tools.

One system uses a chord keyboard with five keys and a mouse positioning element which the operator uses to point to parts of the screen. This concept is possibly the precursor of the Xerox "CAT"—a small round touch-sensitive tablet on the keyboard to control the cursor on the screen. Other pointing devices include the joystick, the light pen, and touch sensitive screens. Handwriting input devices such as communicating notepads or communicating electronic blackboards have some limited applications, but will likely be replaced by more advanced tools and concepts, just as the "horseless carriage" was replaced by the automobile.

Undoubtedly the most exciting new technology for capture of information is voice input. Voice messaging systems now enable the storage, editing, and forwarding of spoken information. Voice information can be appended to textual messages or files for distribution or to be keyed by a word-processing operator. Because speaking is normally faster than typing, there is an ongoing market for dictation systems which send spoken words to operators for transcription.

Most significantly, the speech-processing revolution promises to greatly enhance workers' abilities to use intelligent systems by providing an unrestricted, real-time, interaction—based on voice—between people and machines. By the end of the 1960s computer scientists had succeeded in establishing the first person—machine voice communication. By the beginning of the 1980s there were commercially available systems with a programmable vocabulary of over 300 words. The main application for these systems was voice activation of processes, for example on an industrial production line where the worker's two hands were occupied. Other applications included aids for the handicapped, quality control inspection, order entry systems, and real-time investment quotations. With the exponential growth in microprocessor power, the capability for large vocabulary recognition of continuous speech is in the foreseeable future. The relationship between different types of voice input is depicted in Figure 1.3.

Through optical character recognition (OCR) equipment typed material can be converted to digital form for further action by data-processing or word-processing systems. In the 1970s OCR was limited to a few specific fonts, but the capability now exists to read a wide variety of type styles and even handwriting.

Once information is captured in digital form it can be stored, processed, retrieved, and communicated.

1.3.2. Information Storage and Processing

The speed with which the new storage and processing technologies are developing is staggering. These include both hardware and software.

Hardware advances fall in the categories of main memory, auxiliary memory, and micrographic and video disk technologies. The changes in chip technology have resulted in plummeting digital main memory storage costs and skyrocketing storage capacities. The age of ultra-large-scale integration means that the office worker of the mid 1980s will have private access to the storage and processing power of the large mainframe computers which served entire corporations of the mid 1970s. When one considers the differences between an optical microscope and an electron microscope it is different to imagine the impact when chips are etched with an electron beam as opposed to a light beam.

Another development is Josephson technology. With it, information is

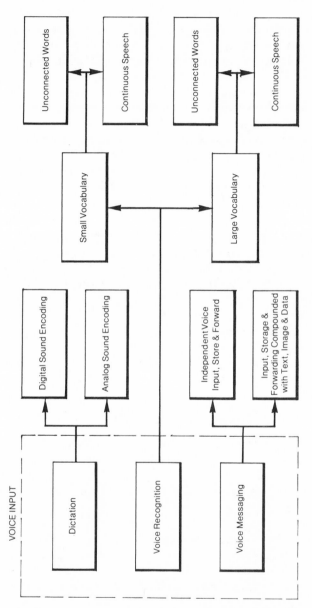

Figure 1.3. Voice input technologies.

1.3.4. Information Communication and Distribution

In the early 1970s only a handful of communications tools were used with any degree of frequency in the office: the telephone, the public post office, private mail services, telex, and the telegram. By the end of the decade, facsimile systems, communicating word processors, teletypewriter networks, synchronous teleconferencing systems, public and private computer-based message systems, and computer conferencing systems were added to this list. We have now entered a period where the list includes videotex systems, voice messaging systems, and systems which communicate integrated voice, data, text, and image forms of information.

Public dial-up and private line telephone networks allow one piece of equipment to enable various pieces of equipment to communicate with each other. Private line networks such as those used by banks, airline, or rental car reservation systems, are more costly than dial-up networks but are faster and easier to access and can be more secure. The key office system vendors will be engaged for some time to come in a fierce battle over the "local area network" (LAIV) market. One approach to local networks is indicated in Figure 1.5.

There have been many traditional "networks" within offices. These were networks which a) attached all devices to a central hub (computer or PABX), and b) were single vendor. However, with the proliferation of independent computing devices such as word processors, small computers, display telephones, intelligent copiers, etc., the issue became posed very sharply: "How do we enable these various tools to talk to each other?"

With the Xerox – DEC – Intel accord and the announcement of Ethernet, local area networks became one of the hottest topics in the office automation field and also one of the most complex. At the end of 1981 there were over 150 vendors of LAN market.

The main varibles distinguishing LANs are topology (bus, ring, star, hybrid); transmission medium (coaxial cable, twisted pair telephone wire, fiber optic cable, infrared light, radio transmission, etc.); multiplexing method (time division and frequency division); and access method (contention methods like CSMA/CD or token passing, reservation methods, polling, etc.). The key to selecting a network as with any technology is to first access what you want the network to do.

Local networks internal to an organization may also link with external networks. Examples are IBM's Satellite Business Systems (SBS), AT&T's Advanced Communication Service (ACS), Xerox's Telecommunications Network (XTEN), and the Canadian TCTS' Datapac Network. Recently there has been a rapid growth in value added networks, which provide access to a variety of network services. Examples are Bell Canada's iNET (Intelligent Network), GTE's telenet, Tymshare's Tymnet, MCI's execunet, and CN/CP's Infoswitch.

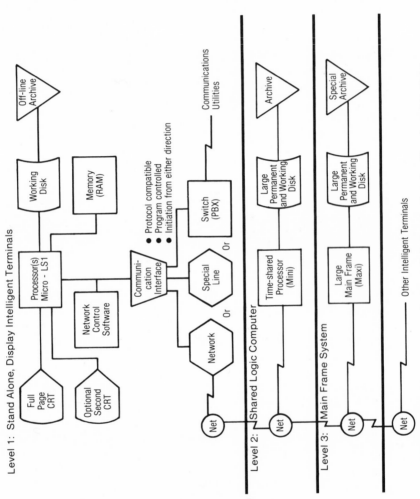

Figure 1.5. One conceptual approach to local networks (Courtesy J.H. Bair).

1.4. CONVERGING TECHNOLOGIES

Before the 1980s there were three traditional technologies in the office which were relatively separate and independent. *Data processing technologies* included computers, storage devices, output devices, etc. *Office technology* included typewriters, copiers, adding machines, dictation machines, etc. *Communications technologies* included telephones private branch exchanges (PBX), telex machines, etc.

These traditional technologies have been converging to the point that it is becoming impossible to view them as distinct technologies. The computer and communications technologies have converged to produce distributed data processing, intelligent switching devices, etc. The computer and office technologies have converged to produce the pocket calculator and computer, COM, CIM, and smart copiers. The office and the communications technologies have converged, resulting in dial dictation, communicating copiers, facsimile, and teleconferencing.

All three technologies are converging to produce tools such as computer-based messaging systems, portable intelligent terminals, communicating word processors, intelligent communicating copiers, compound document (voice, text, image, data) storage, intelligent PBX's linked to desk-top terminals, etc. This convergence is depicted in Figure 1.6.

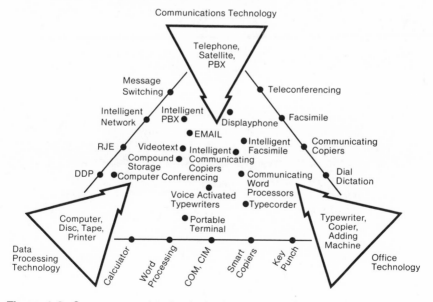

Figure 1.6. Convergence of technologies in the office (Courtesy Bell Northern Research Ltd.).

1.4.1. Integration

The great potential of these systems, lies not simply in the power of their individual applications, but in the *synergy* resulting from increasingly profound *integration* of various system components. We can see this integration beginning to take place on a number of overlapping levels.

(1) Integration of Tools. The integration of various tools such as electronic mail, voice messaging, voice and text editing, decision support, information retrieval, administrative tools, and teleconferencing results in a whole which is much greater than the sum of its parts. For example, two authors of a report, one in Toronto and the other in Denver discuss a piece of text on a screen. There are two versions of the chapter contained in two windows on the screen. One author questions a statistic in the paragraph so she accesses a numerical data base using an interactive statistics package. The Toronto author, who is watching, notes that a graph would give a more balanced view and inserts it in the new version of the text. The graph appears to be different from previous research on this topic so the Denver author accesses a bibliographic information system and adds some additional information from another author. A reference is automatically entered in the report's bibliography. Both authors agree that it would be good to get the opinion of the previous researcher on this matter and they send him a message requesting an audiovisual teleconference. The administrative support system is accessed for available times to have a conference. It is decided, owing to busy schedules, to discuss the matter using a written "computer conference." A conference is established to end in 10 days. A chairperson and list of "attendees" is chosen. The conference proves to be so valuable that its entire contents are inserted as an appendix in the report.

While the individual technologies are very useful, a greater order of utility is obtained because of their integration. More and more, such integration of tools is taking place, both in terms of the underlying architecture and data base structure of the system, and also in terms of the interface presented to the user. That is, the user can easily switch from tool to tool, taking information obtained from one source and using it with another.

(2) Integration of Media. The direction of the new systems is to integrate the four media of voice, text, data, and image. In the 1970s there were separate and isolated systems for voice (telephone, teleconferencing, etc), text (word processing, computer based text messaging, etc.), data (decision support tools, MIS, traditional data-processing systems, etc.), and image (graphics systems, video conferencing, etc). Now these media are being integrated to produce capabilities such as appending voice messages to text messages; dictation which permits on-line editing for authors; graphic output for elec-

tronic work stations; video projection for face-to-face meetings; and voice recognition for commands, eg., "scan inbox."

(3) Integration over Distance. Access, independent of location, is proving to be an important feature of the new systems. As office workers become more dependent on electronic tools it is important that these tools are available wherever s/he is, whether at one's desk, someone else's desk, at a meeting in a hotel room in another country, on a commuter train, stuck in traffic, at home, or at the cottage. The telephone and public data networks provide the central vehicle for such integration across geography. Other contenders include the television cable networks, radio, and satellite transmission.

(4) Integration over Time. For some time users have been attracted to products which can evolve and be integrated with new products over time. Because of the explosive developments in technology one of the greatest concerns of decision makers in user organizations has been "How will I be able to still make use of this product once it becomes obsolete?" In a period where many products become obsolete within a year or two, this is no moot point. As a result, systems which are "forever upgradeable," and integratable with an evolving product line have tended to have a better chance of success.

(5) Integration with Other Technologies in the Office. The new systems draw upon traditional computer, communications, and office technologies. Because the new systems are in their infancy, they do not yet encompass or subsume these traditional technologies. There are still many computer, communications, and office tools and applications which are outside the purview of the new integrated systems. As a result, the direction of many new systems is to be able to hook up with the traditional technologies. Some examples are decision support systems which access corporate data bases; word-processing systems which hook up with the telephone for dial dictation; computer-based messaging systems which can output to a laser copier for distribution to individuals who do not have messaging accounts; graphics systems which link with traditional teleconferencing systems to provide graphic displays; and messaging applications which enable a switchboard operator to easily inform system users of telephone messages.

(6) Integration of Orgware with Hardware/Software. Unlike previous data-processing systems, integrated office systems include not just hardware software but what can be called *orgware*. An office system is a sociotechnical system containing both technical and social subsystems which must be jointly optimized for the system to achieve maximum success. Orgware consists of the procedures, workflow, job redesign, training strategies, implementation plan, educational activities, system responsibilities, and so on which optimize the social component of the new work system. In the late 1970s little attention was given to this issue as systems were generally viewed to consist of

technology only. However, with experience, much of which has been negative, practitioners, users, and vendors alike have begun to consider more carefully what changes to the social system must be implemented concommitantly with changes to the technical system.

(7) Integration With Manual Information Systems. Paper records continue to be an integral part of the office and it is anticipated that this trend will continue in the foreseeable future. While the new systems cannot *replace* all paper records, they can provide improved management of existing paper and other manual files. Examples are computer systems which provide pointers to microform systems, or computer record management systems which enable an on-line index of paper records. Such systems are useful not simply for archived records which are physically remote from the office worker, but ongoing operational records, including access to one's personal files.

(8) Integration of User Interface. Users need an integrated interface with their office system. This has several aspects. The user must be able to move easily from one subsystem to another, applying the information derived through one to another. A simple example is messaging systems which enable a message to be filed in the "tickler" file of an administrative support system to remind the author to act on the message at a certain specified time(s).

Interfaces are being standardized *between* various components of a system. One example is the use of the same text editor for document composition, altering messages, or changing an entry in an information retrieval system. Interfaces are also becoming evolutionary for individual users. There is no one "best" interface for all users for any time in a user's development. Novice users may prefer a very simple menu interface where they can perform various activities on the system by simply pressing one number key. More sophisticated users may prefer a terse command-oriented interface using a "natural language." Highly technical users may prefer to navigate through the system and execute programs using highly technical interface language. Thus the user interface must be evolutionary over time, enabling the user to migrate from one to another.

An early example of an integrated office system workstation is Displayphone—shown in Figure 1.7. It integrates the technologies of data processing, communications, and the office with the media of voice, text, image, and data.

Englebart, through his experience with the most advanced integrated office system available during the 1970s (Augmented Knowledge Workshop), noted multiple levels of synergism at work. It is useful to quote him at some length:

> The synergistic effect of integrating many tools into one coherent workshop makes each tool of considerably more value than if it were used alone—for instance, the

Figure 1.7. Displayphone—an integrated workstation (Courtesy Bell Canada).

value of teleconferencing is very much greater when the participants are already doing a large proportion of their everyday work on line, so that any of the working material is available for selective citing and accessing, and when the users are already at home with the basic techniques of preparing and studying on-line material and of organizing and finding related passages.

And at another level, the synergistic effect of integrating many augmented individuals into one coherent community makes each element of augmentation of considerably more value than if it were applied just to support its one individual—this is derived from the collaborative communication capabilities as applied through extended organizational methods to integrate the augmented capabilities of individuals into augmented teams and communities.

And finally, for any application of significant power—of which augmentation of (a) ... project would be a good example—the adaptability and evolutionary flexibility of the computer communication system is extremely important. The working methods of individuals will shift markedly as they settle into use of a comprehensive workshop, and with these new methods and skills will come payoff potential for changes and additions to their workshops—a cycle that will be significantly active for many years to come. A similar cycle will be even more dramatically evident at the organizational level.[1]

1.5. THE POTENTIAL: AUGMENTATION OF KNOWLEDGE WORK

Depending on whom you talk to, office automation holds different possibilities. Major vendors of word-processing hardware emphasize the savings to be made through increased clerical efficiency. Some management scientists hold that the office of the future will bring about increased productivity of managers.

A more comprehensive view is that the greatest contribution of the changes beginning to occur will be the *augmentation of the abilities and effectiveness of the knowledge worker*. This refers to the application of computer power and telecommunications to help those who work with their minds process, manage, retrieve, and communicate information.

Such an emphasis has until recently been at variance with the industry trends, which have centered on cutting costs through the application of word-processing technology to typing. More and more, however, leaders in the field of office automation are coming to the conclusion that the quest to reduce the number of keystrokes by an organization's secretarial staff is basically a wild-goose chase. As Howard Anderson, President of the Yankee Group recently put it: "Word processing is the silliest form of office automation."[18] Or as James Carlisle, President of Office of the Future Inc. put it: "Word processing is to (office) automation what key punching was to management information systems—only the tip of the iceberg."[19] The reason for this is simple. Word processing addresses itself to less than *five percent* of total office costs.

The most often cited proof for this was formulated in the mid-1970s by Alan Purchase and James Bair, who examined U.S. white collar labor costs. They showed that the secretary-typist's costs amounted to only 6% of total labor costs. They then examined the distribution of daily activities for secretary-typists and showed that the actual time spent typing was approximately 20% of the seven on-the-job hours. Thus, typing accounts for approximately 1.2% of white collar labor costs of U.S. businesses. Their conclusion was that the leverage for office automation is not in typing.[20] (See Figure 1.8.)

Three-quarters of total office labor costs are spent on the knowledge worker.[20] It is the managers, administrative support personnel, engineers, scientists, operational researchers and other professional and technical people working with their minds, who are the fastest-growing sector of the overall labor force. And it is in the augmentation of their abilities and effectiveness that the greatest potential of office automation is contained. Meyer, who takes a similar view, looks back over the previous waves of innovation in business management.[21] He concludes that the 1940s might be viewed as the age of industrial engineering. The 1950s brought operations research, and the 1960s data processing. The major innovations of the 1970s were word processing, management science, and distributed processing. And now the

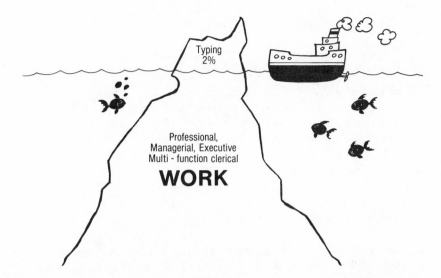

Figure 1.8. Word processing—tip of the iceberg (Courtesy Bell Northern Research Ltd.).

1980s have brought the era of integrated systems designed to improve productivity through providing personal information and communication tools for professionals and managers.

1.5.1. Information Access

Office automation provides more effective media for storing, organizing, and managing information. It can be the central thrust of a strategy for the rationalization and control of the information resource which is consumed by the knowledge worker. Pertinent information can be more accessible, in greater quantity, increased variety, higher quality, more usable in a "live" form, and more timely. Time, especially "critical time" like the day or hour or 5 minutes before an important meeting can be saved. Individuals will be able to interface more effectively with the knowledge base to access, reorganize, and capture pertinent information. And, in general, through the use of office technology, the ability of the human intellect to process information rapidly and effectively can be extended.

In the 1970s those data base installations which were successful have been useful primarily in routine processing of corporate information. However, they were not very useful in providing flexible access to information by decision makers and knowledge workers in general. The new data base management strategies which are increasingly used in conjunction with integrated systems have a different emphasis: the goal is to provide personal interactive access, from many different points to both common and individual data bases.

The new approaches to word processing emphasize the value of text editors in enabling authors to construct ideas and translate them into text. Hierarchical file structures such as Hypertext provide a powerful tool to organize thoughts and interact with them. "Textual data bases" are now being formed in many organizations, where previously entered text can be recalled, modified, used as boiler plate, or dissected and merged with new material. It appears that the quality of textual information has also been improved through the use of the new tools. Automatic spelling checks, easier modification of drafts, puntuation tools, flexible and fast standardization of text format, easier multiple authorship of documents, etc., have contributed to this.

Personal information management tools have been found to be very popular and were one of the first applications to entice managers to use a terminal on their desks. Diaries, to-do lists, scheduling tools, ticklers, automatic follow-up, administrative lists, etc., help a knowledge worker maintain better management over his/her personal information resource.

1.5.2. Communication

Moving information electronically at the speed of light as opposed to the speed of paper-based mail systems has advantages which are usually raised in any discussion on office automation. Certainly it seems a bit absurd that the majority of paper communication is now generated by computers, and moreover in a large number of cases, computers are used to generate a reply, or even to input and store the original information. Still, one cannot help but comment that the emphasis on the "paperless office" is likely analogous to previous discussions of the "horseless carriage" or to "wireless telegraphy."

All were narrow and limited views of major changes in the making. In fact, it has been found that often the main advantage of a computer-based messaging system is not in replacing *paper*, but in replacing and augmenting *other* forms of communication.

By enhancing communication among people and organizations, the productivity of the knowledge worker can be augmented in striking ways.

In addition to more and faster communication tailored to the needs of users, office communication systems can stimulate the metabolism of an organization in ways which are not yet fully understood. Bair attempts to show how electronic mail can save a knowledge worker two hours per day by reducing shadow functions, notation time, media translation time, and interpretation, wait, and recycle time. A number of writers have discussed the communication benefits of computer mail.[19, 20, 22-24]

A by-product of existing electronic mail systems appears to be the growth of communications infrastructures within the organization. Communications become more structured and planned. Carlisle has shown how communications can become "nonsimultaneous." A recipient of a communication sitting at his/her terminal will be able to hear or see, and respond to, a message when it is convenient to do so. This has a number of benefits. Fewer interruptions increase worker's control; employees can receive a message when they are in frame of mind to give it a better, more reflective response; the quality of messages improves over less structured verbal communications; shadow functions caused by things such as busy telephones can be reduced; the office becomes less of a *place*, and more of a *system* as people can send messages to one another at any time and often at various locations. As a result there can be greater flexibility in where and when people work.[19] Electronic mail also provides a permanent, searchable stored record of all communications to appropriate persons. The list goes on and on.

1.5.3. Improved Procedures

It appears that a well-designed office system can improve and/or go hand-in-hand with important improvements in the overall office procedures. Although much of the activities of knowledge workers are somewhat unstructured, much of the day is still spent in more-or-less well defined procedures that have an associated purpose.[25] A procedure specifies the order in which various activities are to be performed, the persons involved, the actions to be taken, and so on. An office system implemetation can help rationalize and streamline office procedures, resulting in faster information flow, faster decisions, more output, fewer bottlenecks, improved structures, and responsibilities, better specification of procedures, etc.

1.5.4. Decision Support

Office automation can enable the construction of a supportive systems environment in which decision making and problem solving can be transformed.

Decision support systems enable decision makers to examine more alternate solutions to a problem, hopefully resulting in better quality solutions and a reduction in wrong solutions or errors. They can also save time. Anyone who has manually prepared a reasonably complex budget knows what a time-consuming and painful process that can be. This is especially true when new variables are added which necessitate a modification of previous calculations. Less tangible, but no less important, benefits include the improved sensitivity of analyses, and user confidence about the decisions s/he has made.

1.5.5. Quality of Work Life

Often when the idea of office automation is introduced in an organization it conjures up notions of people being replaced, or at best harmed, by machines. Computers are often thought to make life more miserable for people, resulting in more structured, rigid, and less enjoyable jobs. Early research indicates that well-designed and implemented system can do the opposite.[26] These systems can result in improvements in the design of jobs and the quality of work life in general. Work can become more interesting, challenging, and fulfilling. Because an employee spends less time doing nonuseful, frustrating work s/he can simply do more of what is important and, hopefully, rewarding. These systems can provide new career paths, especially for women. In one implementation, three of the four secretaries placed on the system acquired new skills and were promoted to the professional staff. The new communications tools can improve organizational communications relationships, resulting in better collaboration between employees and fewer isolates, cliques, and antagonisms. Improvements of this kind are not inherent in the technology, just as the technology is not inherently bad or injurious. Whether or not such benefits are derived will depend on how the system is designed and implemented.

1.5.6. Profound Changes in the Making

The end result of the augmentation of knowledge work can be an increase in organizational productivity. However, as automation is introduced we are beginning to see many more far-reaching changes.

An enterprise's entire organizational structure may be modified. One example is the company which discovered regional offices were unnecessary once a communication system enabled the head office to communicate directly with branches. New functions and activities are being created. Career paths are changing. Reporting structures are changing. The nature of knowledge work is starting to be transformed. Even goals and objectives of organizations are changing, as companies find their office information and communications systems open up new markets. One example is the evolution of credit card companies into the mail order business.

All of this sounds quite euphoric. No review of the potential of office automation would be complete without showing the dark side of that potential. Office automation holds the potential for better information management, communication, and decision making along with increased job satisfaction, quality of work life, opportunities for growth, and freedom for millions of people. But, as Carlisle has pointed out, it also holds the potential of alienation, the stifling of creativity, job fragmentation, dehumanization of communications, regimentation, and the 1984 horror of monitoring all electronic communications. [19]

Burns has added another cautionary note:

> ... The associated risk is that these systems [office of the future] tamper with the most sophisticated process I know of—the office. Although we take it for granted, it is the product of 200 years of development and refinement, and changing it will require our best systems planning skills. [27]

On a broader scale, the office of the future poses very profound questions regarding the nature and the future of Western society. Bair notes the effect of increased white collar productivity and possible labor reduction on unemployment. "If increased productivity means unemployment, we have a 'Catch 22' effect." On the other hand he suggests there are problems with a shorter work week. "If increased productivity can support a shorter work week, what will happen to inflation?" He concludes that the social and economic implications of office automation may outstrip the ability of contemporary society to deal with them. [20] The implications of office automation for transforming the quality of work life for women have been discussed by numerous authors. [6, 28] Other writers have suggested that office automation will lead to a massive rise in unionization of white collar workers, as workers organize to protect themselves from the harmful effects of technological change.

In one very articulate and coherent paper which argues the case against office automation, "Working Women, The National Association of Office Workers" notes some of the dangerous trends some of these systems have taken. The organization cites cases of office system implementations where jobs were degraded, deskilled, and devalued and where the fruits of office automation for some of the users was unemployment. They note discrimination against women in employment within the newly emerging system occupations, in which women tend to be streamlined into the low-level entry and clerically related occupations and men receive the more interesting and highly paid technical and professional positions. They argue that the evidence regarding the safety of VDTs is, at best, inconclusive. For them, office automation has a number of potential benefits, which are being undermined by current management approaches which focus on cost displacement and work simplification.

The character and results of office automation will depend on who is driving it and what generalized design methodology and implementation strategy they employ. Which brings us to the main problems which must be confronted.

The Problem: Technology-Driven Systems

If Office Automation is the answer, what is the question?

2.1. UNDERSTANDING NEEDS, PEOPLE, AND ORGANIZATIONS

The main obstacle to the office of the future over the past period can be summarized as follows: there has been no adequate methodology or way of assessing the system needs of an organization, designing and implementing comprehensive sociotechnical systems which correspond to those needs, and measuring the effects of the system, once implemented. In other words, many of the main difficulties of this "third wave" in the office have not been technological. Rather, they have focused on our ability to understand system requirements, psychological needs, and organizational factors. More and more it appears that the biggest challenges are in making systems appropriate, and dealing with the many complex human and organizational issues in system design and implementation.

This problem has been reflected in many ways. The science of measuring managerial effectiveness, office communication, and the augmentation of knowledge work is in its infancy. Howard Anderson put it well some time ago: "How do you measure management effectiveness? In decisions per fortnight?" [1] Because of this, office automation was for years derailed into the limited domain of word processing, where lines per hour could easily be counted. Most organizations will not make investments in technology which cannot be cost-justified in hard dollars. As a result, the marketing strategy of all the major vendors of office automation focused on selling word processing hardware which could be cost-justified on a short-term basis. Because of this the office of the future took a full-scale *detour* away from the technologies and applications where the really substantial benefits are to be found.

It was quite remarkable to watch how this dilemma was posed concretely at conferences on the office of the future at the beginning of the 1980s decade. Researchers and behavioral and management scientists tended to speak of the advantages of electronic mail, office information systems, and so on. The vendors on the other hand extolled the virtues of stand-alone word processors as a way of cutting costs. In the middle were bewildered users, inundated on the one hand by scores of vendors with iron to sell, and scolded by consultants and researchers on the other, saying word processing is a waste of time.

Most organizations, in the search to cut costs, ended up relying on the word-processing vendors and purchased hardware which often became an expensive obstacle to office automation in the high payoff areas. For years few organizations were willing to go beyond word-processing systems. It was only the corporate giants like Exxon or Citibank—all of which could afford to make a risk investment in the hope of making qualitative gains—or research/consulting companies which had an interest in selling expertise and experience in this area who made the plunge.

Another way the lack of a comprehensive office systems methodology is reflected is that there is little understanding of the human element or "people issues" of office automation. In a recent survey by the Diebold Office Automation Program, the researchers found that this was the most frequent concern of organizations which were venturing into the new technology.

Carlisle put this well:

> Too many computer-based systems have already been designed on the basis of technological breakthroughs and innovations which were insensitive to the limit of man's rationality and the social needs which must be met within organizational structures.[2]

At the 1981 Office of Tomorrow Conference in Toronto, one speaker made a stunning comment that is typical of those who approach office automation from an exclusively technological perspective. He said people in the office "will have to adapt to the technology and not expect the technology to adapt to them." The truth, of course, is precisely the opposite. Technology must be humanized. It must be built, interpreted, organized, and introduced in such a way that it meets the needs of people and organizations. It must not only make organizations more productive, but must improve the working lives of those in them. If this cannot happen, experience has indicated that there will be no office of the future. A few examples are illustrative:

One technologically perfect word-processing system crashed because the operators could no longer take coffee breaks together. They became hostile to the system and through lack of motivation and cooperation they sabotaged it.

It has been found that many managers, for example data-processing managers who were former programmers, or administrative managers who were formerly secretaries, resist having an electronic mail terminal on their desks. Lack of understanding of the psychological issues in problems such as this and how to resolve them has obstructed automation programs.

Centralized word-processing systems have been found to increase typing efficiency. But in many cases the increase in shadow functions and other wasted time of knowledge workers getting material in and out of word-processing centers resulted in a decline in productivity. Lack of appreciation of the "people issues" led to a system which *increased* efficiency while *decreasing* the organization's overall productivity.

A group of practitioners laid out a complete action plan to move their organization into the era of integrated systems. However, they paid inadequate attention to the problem of winning and sustaining top management commitment. Because rational, appropriate plans tend to be counterpolitical the plan was never implemented.

An automated system was introduced in one department of a company and readily and enthusiastically accepted by the workers. The same hardware never got off the ground in another department of the same company because of the way in which it was presented to the workers.

A company was able to "unfreeze" an office and successfully introduce a system. But they did not know how to institutionalize the change, or "refreeze" the new system. They did not know that a system is most vulnerable once it is running. The system failed.

One multidepartmental team of data-processing, administration, and communications professionals were successful in getting the go-ahead to implement a value-added pilot office system. The pilot was judged by all who used it to be a success, but because the implementors failed to situate the pilot within a controlled evaluation plan they were unable to provide hard data regarding the impact of the system. Lacking convincing evidence that the system had caused measurable productivity improvements the executive terminated the project and the pilot was never extended to an operational system.

These are just a few of hundreds of examples which make the point: office systems must be designed and implemented in such a way that they can measurably meet user needs and take into full consideration the human and organizational factors and constraints of the situation. If not, the result will be inappropriate or inflexible system designs; unrealistic expectations; worker perceptions of a "hostile" rather than a "friendly" system; inadequate procedures, guidelines and system controls; unprovable benefits; and in general, system failure.

2.2. TECHNOLOGICAL IMPERATIVES AND FAILURES

The essential problem of office systems design has been the gap between the providers and users of these systems. The conception, design, marketing, and implementation of office systems tends to be driven in very few ways by valid information from the user. This problem affects just about everyone touched by the new electronic office systems:

- Product designers, who need better user data to resolve the many issues of product concept, features specification, system functionality, and user interface.
- "Choosers" of electronic office systems in user organizations, who need data regarding their requirements and opportunities for systems. They also need user-based data to enable cost–benefit analyses for alternate system designs.
- Vendors, who need data to better understand the user environment and the impact of various office systems on productivity in order to segment intelligently the market and develop product strategies.
- Designers and implementors, who need better information to customize systems for specific user situations.
- Users, who need a vehicle to express their needs—needs which they usually cannot articulate and are not equipped to understand fully.

Both generic system designs and specific systems designed within a given user environment are not driven by the user, but by technologists working in a vacuum. This problem, that office system design is "technology driven" rather than "user driven" has been discussed by many authors. For example, Bair writes

> The traditional design is driven by the highly technical, precise and demanding computer and engineering sciences. . . In this culture the questions posed do not arise from user needs for the most part, but rather from technological potential: "What neat thing can I get my software to do?" The result of competent effort is a system design that functions well for the programmer-designer. Of course, accommodating the user is merely a matter of adding some user support—documentation, training, and an introduction to computers for good measure. The end result typifies message systems and other office systems today: a *working nonsolution.*[3]

Or as Morton et al. put it:

> What we know above all is that the new user is most emphatically not made in the image of the designer.[4]

2.3. SOCIOTECHNICAL ANALYSIS—SYSTEM CUSTOMIZATION

2.3.1. Design Levels and Corresponding Measures

The many different types of user measurement and data collection have design implications at several levels. One is system conceptualization. User measurement here includes market research, evaluation of the effects of systems, etc. A second is specific product feature design. User measurement includes ergonometric studies, user acceptance investigations, etc. A third could be called system customization to a given user environment. User assessment in this case includes systems analyses, cost benefit analyses, etc.

While the methodology described in this book can provide data relevant to all levels of the design process, the book focuses on the third level—system customization. The investigation of the user environment to enable system customization is called sociotechnical analysis.

Typically, with traditional word-processing systems, and now with more advanced office systems, vendors "install" standard products in customer environments. The large body of failure literature indicates that such an approach has not and will not enable the successful implementation of integrated office systems.

Lodahl makes the case that customization of office systems to the specific user environment is necessary.[5] He argues that production style approaches of "installing" standard products do not work in the *custom* office environment, for a number of reasons. In the custom designed office there can be no "one best way" because things are constantly changing and because different subgroups have different needs. Standard designs have also failed to solve the problem because all offices are mixed, with some custom and some production elements. The task is to identify where and how much of each exists in an office and to design a subsystem for each subgroup with appropriate perfomance characteristics. Also, organizational analysis is in its infancy and it is difficult at this stage to get adequate information about an organization to enable the effective implementation of a standard design. Furthermore, vendors have made little effort to do this. Finally, standard design approaches have made no provisions for the human problems in managing change. Office automation deeply affects every aspect of office life: ways of doing work, work flows, the distribution of work, and the quality of relationships among workers, to name a few. The far-reaching change introduced by office systems must be carefully designed and managed.

To get a better idea why customization in general, and user-driven customization (or design) in particular, are necessary, it is useful to examine some differences between electronic office systems (EOS) and data processing (DP) or management information systems (MIS).

2.3.2. DP/MIS versus EOS: Pertinent Differences

Electronic office systems are different from traditional DP or MIS systems in ways which have important implications for the design methodology to be used.

Traditional systems focused on automating manual processes and/or providing management information. The new office systems more and more focus on providing an individualized tool for the gamut of office workers to enable them to work more effectively and efficiently. EOS users will tend to be generalists without the technical backgrounds found in the MIS or DP departments. EOS users range from office clerks to corporate presidents.

The scope of electronic office systems is much greater than traditional systems. Office systems are beginning to transform the ways that people and organizations work. Initial research has indicated far-reaching changes in how people spend their time, how they communicate with whom, the design of jobs and organizational structures, and the quality of working life.[16] Whereas previous systems consisted primarily of hardware and software, office systems have both technical and "social" components. The technical subsystem includes the tools, techniques, and methods involved in doing office work, while the social subsystem includes the people with their job responsibilities, communications patterns, attitudes, etc. Any significant change in any part of this sociotechnical system will affect other components of the system, as has been shown with numerous office system implementations. The task before the designer is therefore to design the overall work system, jointly optimizing social and technical sides. On the other hand, the task of the designer of a traditional (DP/MIS) system is to configure a technical solution that satisfies precisely described problems.

Office system technology is still in its infancy. Typical integrated system products are primitive in their functionality, person–machine interface, and general compatibility. This immaturity of the technology suggests the need for more careful investigation into the user environment than in the case of long-standing DP and MIS packages which have been tested and refined over the years.

The diversity of office system application is enormous. A typical integrated office system can encompass a wide range of traditional DP and MIS systems and to these add a decision support system, electronic messaging, administrative support subsystems and computer conferencing, to name a few. Which components will comprise any particular integrated office system will depend on information from the user environment.

Little is known about the human and organizational factors involved in designing and implementing systems. To successfully plan and manage the organizational, procedural, attitudinal, and other changes involved, there is a need for valid information from the user environment.

Finally, it is more difficult to cost-justify office systems, compared to traditional systems. There is little information about the impact of integrated office systems on how people work. These systems also have their greatest potential in *adding value* to work, rather than *displacing costs*, as in the case of traditional systems. Moreover, there are very few implementations, and even fewer within a controlled research design, which can enable quantification of benefits. As a result, most organizations will become involved only through experimentation with small pilot systems, through which they can evaluate the system effects and proceed on a basis of knowledge about likely outcomes. Such evaluation requires careful and controlled measures, before implementation, during system use, and after the system has been up for some time.

The conclusion to be drawn from these differences is that for the foreseeable future the investigation required into the user environment will be much greater for electronic office systems than for traditional systems. The process of selection of applications, customization of existing products, cost-justification of solutions, and their implementation must be propelled by valid information from the user environment.

2.3.3. Why Is a Methodology Required?

It is not possible simply to ask users what they need. Users may have valuable insights into their own problems. However, they are usually not able to identify the system solutions to these and other problems they face, let alone to specify in detail, cost-justify, and plan an implementation strategy for the solutions.

Vendors, on the other hand, while often adept at cost-justifying their latest product line, are also poorly positioned to assess user requirements adequately. Typically they start with a solution in search of a problem. Investigations into the user environment, then, tend to serve the function of providing ammunition for the sales team, rather than enabling the design and implementaion of the truly appropriate systems solutions. Moreover, in the highly competitive marketplace, vendors simply do not have the funds to allocate to careful analysis of user requirements for complete sociotechnical systems.

The inability of both users and vendors to obtain required user-based data points to the need for a user science and for user-oriented teams equipped with the methods and tools for valid user measurement. That is, there is a gap between the providers and users of office systems. The conception, design, marketing, and implementation of office systems tends to be driven in very few ways by valid information from the user.

Both generic system designs and specific systems designed within a given user environment are not shaped by the user, but by technologists working in a vacuum. The results are often technically good systems which do not correspond to the requirements of users. Often these systems do not adequately take into account the many complex human and organizational factors involved in systems design and implementation. A brief review of the failure literature helps substantiate this point.

2.4. THE NEED FOR A USER SCIENCE

Because of these problems it is popular to speak of "involving the user" in the process of system design. But few practitioners have addressed the question: "How can this be done?"

It is not adequate to ask users what they need. Moreover, it is not adequate to simply use subjective measures to evaluate the user organization and user requirements. One classic example is time estimation. Office workers who are asked to estimate how much time they spend in various activities such as typing usually give grossly inaccurate responses.

Rather it is necessary to develop a "user science" which enables the scientific investigation of the user organization and the translation of user data into meaningful information for the system designer.

2.5. PERSPECTIVE ON OFFICE AUTOMATION

To avoid the trap of "technology-driven" systems it is vital to take an overall User-Driven perspective on the design and implementation of integrated office systems.

This User-Driven perspective for office systems places emphasis on augmenting the knowledge worker rather than on increasing typing efficiency. To this end, the needs of the user are considered before the technology. The user's information and communication needs should drive office automation.

In order to meet the user's needs, this perspective emphasizes the user's participation and involvement from the onset and incorporates human factors into the design and implementation of office systems. And, because users are vital to an office system's success, the User-Driven perspective requires carefully planned education and training of users along with continuing sys-

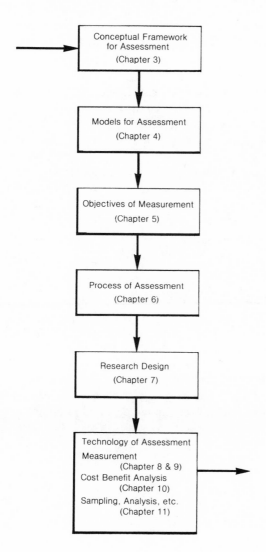

Figure 2.1. Integrated office system design: User-Driven Design methodology.

tem review and refinement as users become more experienced and their needs change and evolve.

Being multidisciplinary in nature, a User-Driven perspective must take into account factors such as computer and information sciences, management, education, and interior design. The User-Driven methodology is not purely empirical, but draws upon theory in areas such as organizational development, sociotechnical systems theory, industrial psychology, strategic planning, and operational research. Technologically it must maintain an ongoing evaluation of the myriad of office system and local network vendors to ensure adequate data for vendor selection.

Practitioners of the User-Driven school seek to develop tools and analytical procedures to obtain valid and reliable measures of pertinent activities, functions, processes, and attitudes in the office milieu. The approach also calls for the utilization of experimental procedures, statistical analyses, modeling, and simulation techniques.

And finally, a User-Driven perspective takes an evolutionary approach to implementing office systems which are based on small, manageable, and measureable pilots which can grow into full operational systems. Such an evolutionary approach must appreciate the symbiotic relationship between ongoing strategic planning and practical experience with implementation to ensure continued success in all phases of an office system's evolution.

2.6. DESIGNING INTEGRATED OFFICE SYSTEMS

This book outlines a methodology for User-Driven design of integrated office systems. Such a methodology is one component of an overall comprehensive approach to office systems implementation. The methodology contains a number of components which are discussed in the book. These components, and their relationship to the ongoing processes of strategic planning, vendor evaluation, and user education, are depicted in Figure 2.1.

Chapter 3

Conceptual Approaches to Electronic Office Systems

"Would not a rose, by any other name smell as sweet?" Whether it is called distributed processing, office automation, the wired society or the interconnected future, the basic elements have been shown to be feasible. It is now only a matter of time before the economics brings the technologies onto most of our desks.

(Howard Morgan, 1979)

There are a number of different conceptual approaches regarding where the main opportunities for integrated office systems lie. It is important to understand the main types of frameworks which are currently in use so that the implementor can adopt or synthesize an appropriate approach for his/her organization. The conceptual approach selected will shape the objectives of the office automation project, the measures for determining requirements and selecting a system, and the measures for evaluating the impact of the system. Five approaches are reviewed below. Each has relative strengths and weaknesses which are descibed below and summarized in Chapter 4.

(1) Organizational Communication Approaches. These approaches view the organization as a communication system. The objective of office systems, for those holding this view, is to improve communications, resulting in time savings, increased collaboration, better access to information, improved organizational relationships, and more control, etc.

(2) Functional Approaches. Functional approaches emphasize the impact of office systems on the underlying functions which the office exists to fulfill. To the functional practitioners, other approaches mistakenly confuse the ends (functions) that the office is realizing with the means (e.g., communica-

tions) used to achieve them. To improve office functions, the designer should focus on improving office procedures using the new technology.

(3) Information Resource Management Approaches. Information system approaches go beyond traditional MIS approaches to view office systems as enabling effective management of the information resource. Like money, people, facilities, and materials, information should be viewed as a resource which can be better managed through use of the new systems. Quantifying the value of information is central to this approach.

(4) Decision Support System Approaches. These approaches situate office system design and measurement in the context of supporting the judgement of managers and other workers who make decisions. From this framework, the objective of office systems research is to study the effects of systems on the performance of complex, unstructured, or semistructured activities.

(5) Quality of Work Life Approaches. Quality of Work Life (QWL) approaches emphasize the impact of office systems on the nature of work, the motivation of the worker, and the design of jobs and organizations. QWL contains an intervention strategy called *sociotechnical systems analysis and design.* This strategy can be used in office system research, design, and implementation to jointly optimize the effectiveness of both the social and technical components of any work system.

3.1. ORGANIZATIONAL COMMUNICATION APPROACHES

> The essence of the concept "organization" is to be found in the interpersonal communication networks which exist within any defined organizational boundaries.[1]

Organizational communication researchers and theorists view an organization primarily as a communication network. This approach is not new. Barnard argued for the centrality of communications in understanding organizations as far back as 1938:

> In an exhaustive theory of organization, communication would occupy a central place, because the structure, extensiveness and scope of the organization are almost entirely determined by communication techniques.[2]

In the early 1950s Deutch presented a more elaborate view:

> Communication and control are decisive processes in organizations. Communication is what makes organizations where control is what regulates their behaviour. If we can map the pathways by which information is communicated between different parts of an organization and by which it is applied to the behaviour of the organization in relation to the outside world, we will have gone far toward understanding that organization.[13]

Communication approaches hold that if organizational communication is poor an organization is likely to have problems, and if it is good, an organization's performance and overall effectiveness are also likely to be good. It follows that computer systems which can improve organizational communication in an office can improve the effectiveness of knowledge workers and organizations.

Most individuals taking a "communications" approach to organization have not yet concerned themselves with computer communications tools. Rather, most research methodologies and intervention strategies focus on auditing and altering communications networks, styles, behaviors, relationships, information flows, etc., independent of the new technologies.[4] However, some leaders in the field have made substantial progress in conceptualizing the problem and developing methodologies to study the effects of office systems.

There is a massive body of literature regarding the role of communication within organizations. The American Business Association in conjunction with the International Communication Association publish an annual *Organizational Communication Abstracts* surveying the research. The 1979 volume alone contains 768 abstracts and reference 947 works published in 1977.[5] Table 3.1 illustrates the frequencies of publications by topic area that year.

There are differences among those people taking the Organizational Communication approach as to what type of variable "Communication" is. This debate is summarized by Goldhaber.[4] Likert describes communication as an "intervening variable" affected by such "casual variables" as leadership behaviors and organizational climate, and affecting "end result variables" such as job satisfaction and productivity.[6] Correlations have been found between communication indices and performance measures, job satisfaction,

Table 3.1. 1977 Organizational Communication Abstracts*

Major literature classification	Quantity
Interpersonal communication	74
Intergroup communication	53
Intergroup communication	69
Communication factors and organization goals	214
Skill improvement and training	70
Communication media	74
Communication system analysis	77
Research methodology	71
Texts, anthologies, reviews, and general bibliographies	66
Totals	768

* Source: Greenbaum and Falcione, 1979.

perceived organizational effectiveness, and absenteeism, grievances, and efficiency to name a few.[7-11]

On the other hand, many researchers have found that good organizational communication does *not* appear to correlate with such variables.[12-15] Others still argue that communication should be viewed as a casual or dependent variable which is not only *correlated with,* but *causes* variation in effectiveness, job satisfaction, and so on. For example, Goldhaber writes that communication can be a causal *or* intervening variable *or* both simultaneously.[4] Communication is central to everything because it is the process which connects the parts of an organization to each other and the system itself to its environment. It has, he argues, a direct impact on interactive patterns, behaviors, attitudes, and effectiveness.

Communications researchers who are concerned about the impact of computer systems on knowledge workers come at the problem from different angles. Hiltz and Turoff focus on computer conferencing essentially from a social-psychological perspective.[16-22] They have explored the impact of computer-mediated communication on factors such as interaction patterns, communications styles, group dynamics, decision-making processes, problem solving, managerial and organizational styles, job satisfaction, and organizational effectiveness, to name a few. This work is summarized in *The Network Nation: Human Communication via Computer.*[3] In addition to outlining their perspective, this book is one of the most comprehensive texts to date overviewing the topic of office communications systems.

Bair has outlined a methodology for conducting "Productivity Assessments of Office Automation Systems." [24-27] The approach views the organization as a communication system. Office automation can speed up and otherwise improve communication, resulting in *payoffs* (direct dollar savings) through the reduction of labor required to process information and *benefits* (less tangible results of office automation that can be identified but do not show a direct dollar saving).

Potential payoffs–benefits can result from reducing *media transformations* (changing the medium of the message); reducing *shadow functions* (unforeseen, unpredictable, time consuming activities that are associated with any task but do not contribute to productivity); *automation of manual processes; improved timing;* and *increased control.*

Bair's complex methodology, he argues, enables a comparison between the labor expended in an organization's current communication activity, and the labor expended once an appropriate office automation system had been selected and implemented. It would also enable the evaluation of alternate system designs and the identification of what conditions are needed to attain the payoff–benefits that have been identified within previous experiences with office automation.

Conrath has come at the problem from the perspective of organizational behavior.[1, 28-31] He argued that an organization's communications environment and structures will significantly affect its performance.[30] However, rather than proceeding from a theory of organizational communications behavior, he set out a research methodology to collect the empirical data required to construct such a theory. He was among the first to probe the problem of measuring the computer's impact on organizational structure.[28] Initial research indicated that the pattern of written communication most closely paralleled the formal authority structures. The pattern of telephone communication most closely paralled the task or work flow structures; and the face-to-face mode was most influenced by physical proximity. However, computer communications had not been probed.

In 1974 Conrath and Bair presented an evaluation of the Augmented Knowledge Workshop (AKW), the pioneering office system developed by Douglas Englebart at Stanford Research Institute.[32-35] The evaluation centered on measuring the frequency of communications by various modes (including the AKW and by other organizational variables (e.g., authority, relationships, intra/extraorganizational status, etc.).

Several of the findings, while limited in scope, are noteworthy. The AKW was used heavily as a communications device, replacing some face-to-face and telephones interactions; and superior/subordinate communication was facilitated.

Another investigator who has focused on the communication impacts of integrated office systems is Edwards.[36] In a study for Bell Canada she surveyed about 100 users of the Natural Language System (AKW) system. She notes how the system altered both work modes and work hours and location. She found that "remote" management, joint authorship of documents, file sharing, and communication over distances were reported as having been facilitated. Face-to-face communication, in particular routine administration meetings, decreased. The user's working day was extended, and working at home increased. As well, productivity (self-reported) increased.

Two other organizations which have conducted extensive research from a communications perspective are Communications Studies and Planning Ltd. (CS&P), London, England, and the Institute for the Future, Menlo Park, California.

CS&P has conducted communication studies, in particular evaluations of telecommunications systems and programs for a broad range of major international corporations and governments. More recently it has undertaken explicit office automation projects covering all areas of the needs analysis, design, and implementation phases. Key authors from CS&P have included Roger Pye, Barry Stapley, and Michael Tyler.

The Institute for the Future is an "independent, nonprofit, research organization founded in 1968 ... dedicated exclusively to systematic and comprehensive studies of the long-range future." As such, it quickly became involved in studying the effects and implications of office system technology. The focus has been computer conferencing and its impacts on interpersonal communication. To conduct this work the FORUM system was developed. Key authors include Robert Johansen, Hubert Lipinski, Kathleen Splanger, and Jacques Vallee.

The main technologies which are discussed by those taking a communications perspective are electronic messaging (text and voice), teleconferencing (voice and video), and computer conferencing. It is argued that the integration of these tools with others in the office can fundamentally alter the communications environment and structures of an organization in such a way as to significantly improve the performance of that organization.

While these technologies, the communications process which they address, and their embryonic methodologies for assessment are very important, they are not adequate as a comprehensive framework for office system design. The main weaknesses arise when one considers the Functional and QWL approaches.

3.2. THE FUNCTIONAL APPROACH

Hammer and Zisman, and later, Hammer and Sirbu, have developed a Functional approach to office systems which provides a unique conceptual approach for determining user requirements and evaluating the impact of integrated office systems. For Hammer and Zisman, most researchers and practioners in the field make the mistake of focusing on superficial *processes*, such as communications, rather than the more important underlying *functions* which office work exists to fulfill. Offices, they say, do not exist to "communicate," "use information," or "push paper." Consequently any approach to office automation measurement, design, and implementation which concentrates on these activities or processes is missing the mark. Rather, an office exists to meet certain functional needs of an organization. And the goal of office automation must be to improve these basic business functions.

> The difficulty with both the standard view of offices and the conventional approach to office automation is that they are too *general* and do not relate to the *purpose* for which the office exists. They focus on the *form* rather than on the *content* of office work. There are many different kinds of offices, performing many different kinds of activities. We are suspicious of any perspective which glosses over these differences. An office does *not* exist to enable its inhabitants to engage in paper-pushing. *An office exists in order to meet certain business needs of an organization.* [37]

Hammer and Sirbu explain the point by noting the difficulties one has attempting to explain to a child what people do in an office. To the child office work appears comprised of activities such as typing, talking on the telephone, shuffling papers. Yet this does not capture the essence of the office, which has more to do with making payments, scheduling production, or negotiating contracts. [38]

Hammer and Zisman define office automation as "the utilization of technology to improve the realization of office functions." This definition is viewed as deliberately broad and inclusive, focusing on no particular mode of technology, single kind of office work, or particular kind of office. In order to automate an office, it is necessary to understand what the office is doing. They therefore argue for a holistic perspective which focuses on the office as a functional system rather than on the individual workers, tasks, activities, or processes within it.

This approach makes an important distinction between *task* and *function*. A task is seen as a narrowly focused activity, usually performed by a single worker. A function is an end to be realized by means of task performance. A given function may be realized in many different ways, by means, of different task structures. True automation (the use of technology as a substitute for human labor) can only be implemented for the highly structured tasks. These tasks can be so well understood that an automatic system can be accomplished to perform them, as the process by which the job is done is embedded in the device. On the other hand, activities which are not sufficiently structured to allow for automation may nonetheless be subject to *mechanization*, which means the augmenting of human workers with improved tools for performing these activities. From this general perspective two approaches to office system design can be isolated.

The first is based on the use of generic tools to perform general office tasks. These tasks include document preparation, communication, numerical computation, filing and retrieval, and the like. The corresponding tools are word-processing systems, electronic mail and facsimile systems, calculators, information storage and retrieval systems, etc. These tools can be used in many different environments. To Hammer and Zisman they address the lowest common denominators of office work, that is those tasks which occur in a wide range of offices. Even in their most sophisticated and advanced forms such as "electronic work stations" these generic tools are viewed as maintaining the traditional task orientation to office work. "The assumption is that the office worker will continue to perform the same activities that he currently does, but that he will perform them with the aid of computer based tools." [37]

The second approach to office automation is based on the use of functional and application specific systems that are composed of high-level tools. Such a system would address not the actions of the office workers but the larger issue of the functions that require the existence of the office in the first place. "Such a system is conceived in terms of an overall picture of the operation and goals of the office, rather than in terms of the low level tasks which with office workers occupy themselves." [37] It follows that to measure the effect of a system one would attempt to measure the impact of the system on office functions, rather than on activities, processes, etc., taking place within the office.

Hammer and Zisman polemicize with James Bair and his approach to measuring the effects of office systems on productivity:

> If the goal of an office system is to improve office productivity, then this productivity must be measured in terms that relate to the purpose of the organization, rather than purely by means of "information" measure.

To those who would attempt to cost-justify office systems using "information and communications audits" of how an organization creates, transmits and stores information they argue:

> All too often office automation efforts based on these approaches end unsatifactorily; the reasons are that they take no recognition of the business function of the organization and that they confuse the ends that the office is realizing with means used to achieve them. [37]

Implications of this approach are that to determine user requirements, it is prudent to begin with an examination of the overall business goals of the office, the functions that are to be improved, and the entire office procedures which are used to execute those functions. [38]

Those holding a functional framework have developed methodologies for determining user requirements which focus on identifying opportunities for improving office procedures. For example, Hammer and Zisman outline 10 steps for the design and implementation of a functionally oriented office system:

1. Conduct a functional analysis of the office's operations, expressed in business terms. Indentify the procedures being performed and their purposes.
2. Construct a specification of the existing procedures.
3. Analyze these specifications for their inefficiencies and bottlenecks. Analyze them in the context of the kinds of office equipment available for use.
4. Redesign the procedures in the context of existing office structures and the analysis of Step 3.
5. Identify the critical steps of the new procedures and abstract the fundamental issues involved in their implementation.

6. Specify the objectives and the functionality to be designed by the results of Step 5.
7. Design and implement a system to meet these objectives.
8. Develop an introduction path for the new system.
9. Install the new system.
10. Enhance and maintain the system.[39]

Tsichritzis has also developed an approach to office systems which centers on the specification of office procedures.[40] Business forms are seen as tools to tie many media and office information objects together. A prototype form management system was built. An employee uses office specification tools to initiate operations using the facilities of the system directly or to carry out prespecified office procedures.[40] With such a system, actions can be triggered automatically when forms or combinations of forms arrive at particular nodes in the network of stations.[41]

To specify office procedures adequately, it has proven necessary to develop a language to describe the office. Hammer and Zisman lamented the fact that there was no suitable linguistic mechanism to describe what takes place in an office. English suffers from ambiguity and imprecision. Existing attempts at a taxonomy of office functions are unsatifactory, being either too general or too far removed from the English language to be comprehensible to the office worker.[37]

There have been a number of efforts to construct an office specification language. The most ambitious to date is the Office Specification Language (OSL) developed at MIT.[42, 43] OSL is designed to enable the description and specification of office procedures. It is based on the notion that there is considerable commonality of structure and activity among procedures in different offices. Given this, at a certain level of abstraction the specification of the new system can be the same as that of the old. The two are distinguishable only at the level of the actual system implemented. The language can be used as a guide for analyzing system requirements, detailing software specification, and also simply as a tool for documenting office procedures.

A functional approach to designing systems must contain a methodology to analyze the office. A good example is the work done at the Xerox Palo Alto Research Center on office modeling. Ellis and others on a research team developed a mathematical technique to model office procedures and streamline information flow. The technique derives a "normal form description" of any office and then uses this description to derive other forms of the office which are minimal in certain well-defined ways. These minimal forms of the office description show the basic necessary information flows and the invariant information requirements that must be met in the realization of a given set of office functions. The technique is supported by a rigorous mathematical model called *information control nets* (ICN). Throught the ICN model, the researchers attempt to yield a comprehensive description of activities within existing and hypothetical automated offices. In doing so, they attempt to test the underlying office description for flaws, inconsistencies, to quantify certain aspects of the information flow, and to suggest possible office restructuring permutations. Examples of office analyses that can be performed via the model include detection of deadlock, analysis of data synchronization, and detection of communication bottlenecks. Restructuring permutations that can be perfomed using the model include streamlining and automation.

The Xerox researchers believe that there are compelling arguments in favor of analytic modeling: the technology of these systems is still in the formative stage; office systems cause and are often accompanied by large-scale changes in office procedures, personnel, and office requirements; and there is no comprehensive theory of office systems which could obviate the utility of modeling:

> Indeed, there is strong reason to believe that the office of the future will need to lean heavily on modeling and theoretical analysis. And since the office can be viewed as a network of highly interactive parallel processes, models and analyses used in studies of computer systems are highly applicable.[44]

Another example of a functional methodology which focuses on office procedures is the office analysis methodology developed at MIT by Sirbu, Schoichet, Kunin, and Hammer.[45] With this methodology the analyst examines not just the business objectives, functions, and procedures of the office, but also reporting relationships, key interfaces, communications patterns. However, the goal is to derive a valid and detailed understanding of office procedures.

While the development of a functional research methodology to measure user requirements and the effects of systems is clearly in its very early stages, this functional perspective can be isolated as one conceptual framework from which to approach the problem of measurement and design.

The strength of the approach is its insistence on "getting to the heart of the matter"–office functions. However, doing so is not a simple matter. Clearly those who hold a functional orientation have not yet developed an adequate methodology to measure opportunities for the improvement of office functions, nor to measure the impact of systems in making such improvements. Rather, they have stopped short at the level of office procedures. Improvements in the latter may cause improvements in the former, but the two cannot be equated. The conceptual gap between the overall business functions of the organization and a given set of procedures, which may or may not be related, has not been bridged.

Another limitation of the approach is that it mainly concerns itself with relatively routine office work which is highly proceduralized. Half to two-thirds of the white collar workforce are multifunction clerical, professional, or managerial employees, whose work does not fall into this category. It is true that there are certain procedures involved in the work of just about every office employee, and if not there should be. However, numerous studies have indicated that the bulk of this is relatively unstructured and not addressable by procedure-oriented systems.[25, 46–48]

Moreover, there is more to office work than procedures, even for employees involved in routine work. The single-minded pursuit of office procedures becomes less admirable when critical processes, and human considerations, are excluded. A system designed to simply improve procedures is vulnerable to failure if issues such as the human communication network, user attitudes, job design, and decision making are ignored. Because of this the functional school is vulnerable to charges that it constitutes another narrow extension of traditional data-processing approaches to systems.

3.3. INFORMATION RESOURCE MANAGEMENT APPROACHES

A third contender framework for approaching integrated office systems and their measurement comes from the data-processing (DP) and management information systems (MIS) community. This approach emphasizes the importance of information to the organization. Originally, information systems could be grouped into two categories. One was systems for data processing. These automated clerical functions such as payroll, accounts payable, acounts receivable, inventory control, etc. A second category was management information systems, which were designed to aggregate data to aid managers in budgeting, planning, etc.

Both DP and MIS are becoming terms of interesting historical significance, having given way to new approaches on information. Information became viewed by many in the DP and MIS professions as a *resource*, which like other resources—people, money, materials, and facitilities—must be managed. Information resource management (IRM) became a cause célèbre in the early 1980s as DP/MIS managers, with the support of corresponding vendors, attempted to respond in theory and practice to the integration of computer, communications, and office technologies taking place around them.

As early as 1977, practioners in the field of computer technology, seeing that the distinctions between different areas of sophisticated computer and communications technology were becoming less distinct, began to write about the concept of (IRM).[49] Various early definitions of IRM share the same theme: the concept of information resource management as managing the integration of the information processing technologies:

> Image, voice, text, and data will no longer be the separate disciplines that we have all known, but they will blend into a new hybrid technology called the management of the integrated information resource.[49]

Oplinger defines it as follows:

> An organizational and policy framework to assure that information is available to whom it is needed, at the time and place needed, and in the form needed. . . . Information which is today being mobilized by data, text, voice, image and other [media], and is managed by data processing, administration, communications, office services and libraries will be managed by IRM tomorrow.[50]

IRM proponents argue that the blurring of traditional distinct lines between computer, communications and office technologies has resulted in a need to centralize control. New organizational forms and positions should be created to enable this. The notion of ther information services group was developed by the Diebold Group in 1979:

> Helping . . . realize the potential of the emerging information systems technology is the most important product of today's MIS/IRM organization. Your organization is providing services which are rapidly becoming more pervasive in the corporate operating and decision-making processes. If corporations are to capitalize on the potential of information technology, a businesslike approach needs to be taken for the management of all information resources. In fact, we should think in terms of a broad-base corporate Information Services Group which deals with data processing and information resource management.[51]

It is argued that such a group should be headed by some new type of information executive who, naturally should be today's MIS manager. Leading IRM spokesman James Martin views the new office systems as being a logical extension of data processing and MIS.[52]

There are a number of thorny problems regarding IRM's bid to be the leading approach to integrated office system design. One is the need for, and difficulties in, determining the value of this information resource.

Costs of information processing, knowledge worker productivity, and the increasing need for interactive systems, as well as the overlapping of the technologies are used by IRM proponents to argue that information is a valuable commodity. As the investment in information increases, there is more incentive to manage it more effectively. This means that investments in information resources must now undergo the same cost–benefit analysis as do the investments in other resources. In order to conduct this analysis, the benefits or value of the information provided must be determined as well as the costs of providing the information.[53]

To date, methods for determining the value of information as a resource are in their infancy. Assigning a value to information as a resource is a long and complicated procedure. There are psychological as well as practical considerations. Managers and professionals must become accustomed to thinking about the information they use in their decision making as a resource, for example, just as staff members are considered a resource which requires considerable capital and human investment.

Some of the difficulties in the development of the IRM concept center on the subjectivity in placing a value on information (and hence, the viability of regarding information as a separate resource), and the need to think in terms of having access to information as a means for improving effectiveness, not just efficiency. IRM advocates say that for information to be viewed as a valuable commodity competing with other company resources, a prevalent opinion must be overcome—namely, that information is lacking intrinsic value because it is not a physical commodity and is not acquired, stored or consumed, and accounted for like other resources.

A hard dollar cost-justification was appropriate for efficiency-oriented systems, such as operational control systems. However, as the new information sytems evolve, there will be an increasing emphasis and responsibility on the user. If the user is convinced that there is value in information and is willing to be accountable for specifying that value, then there is merit in considering an investment in that information.[53]

Traditionally, the software, hardware, and people costs to provide information were estimated. It was possible to measure the costs of providing information simply by totaling the clerical, computer, and report production costs. Information systems have been viewed as inherently good for improving the efficiency of the organization. The justification of the information system was based on cost displacement savings. However, a cost–benefit analysis based on improved efficiency used for the clerical, computer, and report production costs cannot simply be applied in the same format to justify an integrated office system, where the main objective is to improve productivity. The value added benefits of having access to the right information at the right time and in the right form must be defined. Once defined, hopefully a dollar value can then be assigned to them, although this procedure has not been fully developed.

Another problem faced by IRM advocates is the lack of a comprehensive methodology to implement the IRM concept. Broad methodological outlines have been developed. One has been outlined by Oplinger. The steps are as follows: sensitize the organization to the cost of information; secure commitment to the IRM philosophy; inventory the existing information resources; portray administration activities as communication events; separate information costs from overhead; budget and account for information expenditures; shift the focus on information use; encourage broader information policies; investigate organizational restructuring alternatives, focusing on transition/policy; create a climate of shared responsibility, practical and political sensitivity, and compromise.[54]

A third set of problems relates to the narrowness of IRM. For example, IRM does not really address most information that is important to the organization. Most approaches to IRM deal only with computerized information, which account for a small proportion of the information which is created, stored, processed, and retrieved. Because IRM is an outgrowth of the narrow world of data processing, it lacks, to date, the comprehensiveness required to deal with the total information picture in an organization. A good example is the case of manual records. Paper-based records systems will be with us for a long time to come, and any reasonably complete approach to integrated office system design must include assessment and design techniques for records management.

IRM is also a narrow concept in terms of its definition of a "system." Systems, for computer professionals, consist of hardware and software. But experience has shown that the new systems also consist of new responsibilities, interaction patterns, career paths, job designs, organizational structures, and so on. To ignore this generally means failure.

Some practioners have argued that IRM is not only adequate as a framework for the new technology—it is actually a dangerous roadblock. Some fighting words from Connell:

> IRM theory is full of holes. Its strident advocacy by the sages of information processing lends credence to the belief that IRM is an ill-disguised attempt to provide a sinecure for aging data processing managers. Unfortunately, rather than provide a positive benefit, IRM proponents may do a disservice of extraordinary proportions to business in general and the information processing field in particular.[55]

It is not disputed that information is important. The problem stems from the notion that it can and must be managed. Managing information is akin to managing air or water. We manage the mechanisms to bring us air and water, not the two themselves. Information is very different from people, money, materials, and facilities. Its worth is subjective, not intrinsic. It does not vary in value because of external conditions as capital does. It is not consumed in its use as are materials. It has no physical properties which could lead it to be treated as an asset in the accounting sense. The tools for acquiring, storing, moving, and retrieving information may be physical, but the information itself is intangible. The danger in IRM is that it shifts the emphasis from the management of information processing and communications to the management of the illusive information itself.[55]

For Connell, IRM constitutes a staff function where a line function is required. An IRM function will concern itself with the policies and procedures governing the use of the information "resource"—such as its content, completeness, validity, authenticity, availability, timeliness, and so on. However, what it required is a line function which puts the emphasis on managing people, the machines, and facilities involved in the user of information.[56]

A final category of problems stems from the genesis of IRM. The main problems with the new generation of systems relate to the failure of those from traditional DP and MIS backgrounds to fully and effectively deal with the complex human, organizational, and measurement issues of system design and implementation. If IRM is truly the logical extention DP/MIS as those some in the business purport it to be, this may be cause to exercise caution.

It is difficult to say if IRM may evolve into a viable framework for integrated office system design. The main difficulties centers on the subjectivity involved in placing a value on information, the viability of regarding information as a separate resource, the narrowness of current IRM approaches, and the traditional inability of many from the DP/MIS breeding ground of IRM to understand the nontechnical issues in system design and implementation.

3.4. DECISION SUPPORT SYSTEM APPROACH

A fourth approach to office system design is decision support. Interactive decision support systems (DSS) seek to provide decision makers with powerful tools to aid in accessing and analyzing information. The goal is to apply computer-based technologies to unstructured tasks that require some balance between judgment and analysis.[57] A DSS combines the human skills used in decision making with the power and capabilities of the computer to efficiently manage large volumes of data and a variety of visual display alternatives.[58]

A DSS approach implies that computers have the role of assisting knowledge workers in their decision processes; supporting, rather than replacing, judgment; and improving the effectiveness of decision making rather than its efficiency.[59]

Decision support systems have existed for some time, but tended to be viewed as variants of management information systems. However, during the late 1970s it became clear that the DSS approach was significant enough to merit a distinctive label.[58]

Still some whose purview is traditional DP/MIS systems have attempted to bridge the gap by arguing for the design of interactive access to corporate data bases and labeling the result decision support.[60] While the goal of such endeavors may be admirable, the cavalier equating of MIS with DSS tends to muddy the water.

How is DSS different from MIS?

In general, DSS aims to have a direct impact on the quality of decision made, thereby improving the effectiveness of anyone who makes decisions. MIS impacts specific managerial tasks where the information requirements are predefined with the goal of increasing efficiency by reduced operating costs. Table 3.2 summarizes some distinctive features between DSS and MSS as gleaned from the literature.[59, 61-64]

Simon has classified decisions as structured or unstructured. For an unstructured task the decision maker must rely on personal judgment, especially in identifying the exact nature of the problem. Keen and Scott Morton merged these two taxonomies. In relatively unstructured tasks, the user must initiate and control the problem-solving process and sequence; and his or her judgment, objectives, and interpretations must guide the choice of solutions. This is where DSS can make a significant impact.

A DSS can be a central component in an integrated office system environment. The ability and flexibility to make decisions quickly through the use

Table 3.2. DSS vs. MIS Systems

DSS	MIS
Purposes:	
Supporting decision making	Transaction processing
Supporting decision implementation	Business reporting
Uses:	
By any decision maker	By managers only
Ad hoc analysis of data files	Obtain prespecified aggregations of data in the form of standard reports
Estimate consequences of proposed decisions	
Propose decisions	
Presentation of information in an effective form	
Characteristics:	
Active line, staff, and management activities	Passive clerical activities
Oriented toward overall effectiveness	Oriented toward mechanical efficiency
Focus on the present and future	Focus on the past
Emphasis on flexibility, and ad hoc utilization; evolutionary	Emphasis on consistency; involutionary
Judged in terms of value added	Judged in terms of displaced costs

of an information office network can help the knowledge worker in several ways. It can enable faster analysis and consequently quicker response and a faster metabolism for the organization. It can help cope with environmental changes. A flexible DSS can aid in maintaining control in times of political, economic, or monetary instability. DSS can help an organization cope with the increased complexity of an organization's operations, and enable decision makers to carry out low-risk experiments on the impact of decision alternatives. These systems have been found to provide a logical framework for dealing with subjective judgment and uncertainty, and also to increase the persuasiveness of employees in affecting change. The reduction of "key person" dependence for complex tasks which are carried out by one or a few highly experienced and skilled individuals has also been proved significant.

3.4.1. DSS as a Framework for Office System Design

Although this approach focuses on extremely important activities in the office, it is not adequate as a comprehensive framework for office measurement and office system design. The opportunities addressed by decision support are important, but limited. Not all important decision making involves the access and analysis of numerical information. There are a wide range of important activities related to decision making which the new integrated systems can aid, and which are ignored by DSS to date. Examples are the professional worker deciding on how to construct a chapter of an important report, any office employee attempting to schedule a meeting, a highly skilled clerk waiting for work because of inappropriate manual procedures, a manager spending half her/his time in routine travel, and a researcher unable to formulate an investigation plan because of interruptions.

Moreover, a stand-alone DSS will have limited impact. The true power of DSS is experienced when integrated with other information handling and communication tools. It is only then that the complex of activities, processes, procedures, and functions in the office can be addressed in a comprehensive manner.

We can expect that as the measurement for and implementation of decision support systems continues, DSS researchers and practitioners will be thrust beyond the limited framework as originally conceived.

The problem of measuring DSS needs and DSS effects on knowledge workers and organizations and of cost-justifying decision support systems is complex. Advocates of DS systems have really only begun to address this problem. An excellent beginning is Mason and Swanson's work on measurement for decision support.[65] The dilemma posed in all integrated office system measurement confronts DSS proponents head-on: that is, organizational effectiveness is highly intangible, multidimensional, and of an evasive nature which does not lend itself well to rigorous measurement. As a result, there is a considerable challenge to develop methodologies to aid in the selection of decision support opportunities, in improving the nature of the decision-making process itself, and in evaluating the impact of these new systems.

3.5. QUALITY OF WORK LIFE APPROACHES

From nine to five I have to spend my time at work. My life is very boring, I'm an office clerk. (Martha and the Muffins, from the song "Echo Beach")

One of the newest schools beginning to specifically address the question of integrated office system design and measurement can be called "quality of work life." Quality of work life (QWL) is a term used to embrace three interrelated sets of ideas. First are those dealing with a body of knowledge, concepts, and experiences related to *the nature and meaning of work* and the *structure* of work organizations; second are those dealing with the nature and process of *introducing and managing organizational change*; and third are those dealing with outcomes of results of the *change process.*[66]

QWL is used here as a very broad framework, covering the notions of job design, sociotechnical systems theory, organizational design, job satisfaction, workplace democracy, and social indicators.

The traditional approach to this design dates to Frederick Taylor's 1883 theory of Scientific Management. Variants of this approach have historically been the norm for making organizations effective. Workers were viewed as being lazy, untalented, and unable to learn. As a result, the model work system should have a number of attributes. Work should be broken down into the simplest possible tasks, which are highly specialized and repetitive. Responsibility and decision making at the worker level should be minimized. Training and development should be minimized so that workers can be moved from one job to another without a disruption to production. Planning and administrative functions should be restricted to managers who should also closely and tightly supervise employees.

Work systems built on this approach have a number of characteristics. Jobs are designed by experts who consider the worker as a replaceable part. In the goal of efficiency technology can be used to compensate for people's faults or, better still, eliminate the people where possible. Worker motivation is external, achieved through compensation and rigid policies and practices. Workers are supervised from above, tightly, to ensure conformity to management requirements.

Scientific management has come under sharp attack. Some argue that the deadening, alienating jobs created under this system are not an acceptable price to be paid for corporate profit. But more recently, it has been shown that this approach is simply not working, especially when compared to new methods for building high-performance organizations. Such methods emphasize employee involvement in the design of their jobs so that motivation for work can be internal, and the work itself meaningful, self-fulfilling, and consequently more productive. A number of researchers and practitioners are attempting to apply the tools of their trade to the design of integrated office systems. The QWL framework emphasizes that the greatest gains of these systems are to be found in their impact on the nature of work, the motivation of the worker, and the character of the organization. QWL argues that there is a systematic relationship between the quality of work life and the quality of the product of that work. That is, if work is designed as a meaningful activity for the people involved in its production, then chances are that the product of that work will better suit its users.[67] The advent of advanced office systems provides both a catalyst and a technological tool to redesign individual jobs to enable increased worker effectiveness; increase worker motivation and responsibility; positively change the ways in which individuals work together; and change the ways in which organizations are designed and function.

Johnston et al. describe some salient features of QWL:

> In Quality of Work Life the organization itself is conceived as an "open system" constantly coping with and adapting to its external and internal environments. . . . this contrasts with earlier organizational concepts based on the principles . . . in which structures and functions are carefully delineated and prescribed in clockwork fashion ("closed system"). There is a great deal of evidence that many organizations conceived and designed in the traditional manner are encountering serious difficulty coping with and adapting to today's rapidly changing world.
>
> QWL treats people as the critical constituent of organizations, and change as an inherent characteristic of organizational life. It is primarily concerned with the changing nature, structure and functioning of modern work organizations and the roles of individuals and groups in relationship to one another and to the objectives of the organization. In many organizations the employee is perceived simply as an economic entity whose role is to function as a highly specialized element or cog in some complex production or service apparatus. The traditional value system has its roots in the late 18th and early 19th century, and although it might well be defended in the context of the social values of the time, it is increasingly under attack today.[66]

3.5.1. Sociotechnical Systems Analysis and Design

The most appropriate candidate to link QWL with office system design and measurement is the sociotechnical systems approach to designing high-performance organizations. Beginning with some innovative experiments in the British coal mines and continuing with job design research in the United States, this approach has gained increasing acceptance among researchers and practitioners of organizations.[68, 69]

QWL is a broad term which can be used to describe a conceptual framework for advanced office systems. On the other hand, sociotechnical systems refers to an *intervention strategy* to design, implement, and measure these systems as part of the design and implementation of an overall work system. It contains both a theory and a procedure.[70]

Every work system can be considered to be composed of two parts. One is a *technical system* (or subsystem) composed of the tools, techniques, and methods involved in doing the work. Another is a *social system* of human beings who do the work. This social system operates to join together the disconnected tools, methods, and jobs; to coordinate them and to enable the adaption of the technical system to environmental demands. Sociotechnical work system analysis and design seeks to jointly optimize the requirements of the social subsystem, as well as the technical one, by starting with the *total work system* rather than a piece or pieces of the technical subsystem alone.[67] This is the most intelligent approach to enhancing organizational effectiveness, because the achievement of a desired organizational outcome requires the joint operation of both systems. That is, "it is impossible to optimize for overall performance without seeking to optimize jointly the correlative but independent social and technological systems." [71]

3.5.2. QWL and Integrated Office Systems

Soft evidence derived from experiences with integrated office systems indicates that these systems have the potential to profoundly affect QWL in its broadest sense. To date the focus has been on worker attitudes towards the system.[36, 72-74]

However, it is possible to develop a less subjective and more comprehensive approach to measuring the impact of office systems on QWL and in turn on knowledge worker and organizational effectiveness. Such an approach could be combined with an overall sociotechnical systems strategy for the design and implementation of advanced office systems.

Integrated office systems can effect QWL and in turn knowledge worker and organizational effectiveness in many ways. They can increase worker motivation by enriching the content of knowledge work. Hackman and Oldham examine "what causes people to get turned on to their work." [75] They outline three key factors critical in determining a person's motivation: Knowledge workers must *experience meaningfulness* (individuals must perceive their work as worthwhile or important by some system of values they accept); *experience responsibility* (they must believe that they personally are accountable for the outcomes of their efforts); *have knowledge of results* (they must be able to determine, on some fairly regular basis, whether or not the outcomes of their work activities are satisfactory). Johnston et al. outline other factors.[66] These include the need for a job which offers the worker a challenge; provides the worker an opportunity to expand upon his or her knowledge and range of skills; has variety; enables a sense of belonging; and leads to some kind of desirable future. When these conditions are present a person tends to feel good about him/herself and can perform well. Evidence from early case studies indicates that integrated office systems could impact all of these factors.

In addition to affecting individual worker motivation, office systems can provide both a catalyst and a cause of changes in the working relationships between people and in the entire structure of organizations. Examples shown to date include changing communication patterns to reduce isolation and organizational uncertainty; opening new career paths, especially for women; adding flexibility in work locations and work hours; and changing the organizational span of control, to name just a few.

One of the strongest cases for a QWL approach to office system design and measurement is a negative one. That is, the implementation of an advanced office system involves a massive and far-reaching intervention into the work system of an organization. Unless the designer and implementor are cognizant of the sociotechnical nature of the system and the many "organizational" and "people" issues to be resolved, the system will likely fail.[76]

Another case for the QWL approach derives from a macroeconomic or societal level. That is, the knowledge work sector of the economy is growing rapidly. There are many indications of increasing dissatisfaction among these workers, widespread alienation, and social dislocation. Cherns and Davis point to some reasons for this:

> We are moving rapidly toward the time when dissatisfaction with the nature of their jobs will be as widespread among white collar workers as it has been among blue-collar workers. The reasons are not hard to find. Income differentials (between white and blue collar workers) have become eroded; the greater security of white collar employment is neither so marked as it was in the past, nor so vital since social security benefits ward off the direct effects of unemployment for most. But, above all, factors intrinsic to the jobs themselves have been undergoing change. In the interests of "productivity" and "efficiency" principles derived from "scientific management," work study, systems analysis, operation research, and other techniques have been applied to white collar jobs. More recently [with] the invasion of the computer, systems analysts . . . have designed the jobs of the white collar employees without their experienced counterparts in manufacturing, the industrial engineers, but with similar outcomes. Many offices have undergone "improvements" which have reproduced the atmosphere of the assembly line.[77]

The cost of worker alienation, badly designed jobs, declining job satisfaction, and underutilized skill is difficult to quantify. Thus, on a macro level, the economic implication of quality of work life are not known. Davis and Cherns argue this is because "Western thinking has adhered too firmly to a view of life which separates economic from social consideration. In eastern Europe it has been far easier to adopt policies giving economic weight to any desired objective, although in fact quality of work life does not appear to have been assigned any focal significance." [77]

As a result of the growing awareness of such problems, job design, sociotechnical intervention, and other organizational design programs have been given substantial attention in the last few years. [75, 77, 78, 79]

It is not surprising that persons skilled in QWL are taking a leading role working on the issues of integrated office system design, implementation, and measurement. The breadth of the QWL perspective enables it to deal with the multifaceted complex of question which integrated systems raise.

3.5.3. QWL and Office System Design

QWL approaches to designing integrated office systems focus in building the best fit between the social and technical components of a planned work system. Methods of determining user requirements and evaluating the impact of systems can be drawn from the tool kit of organizational assessment. [80, 81] Such work, however, is in its formative stages.

One of the first and most important efforts was that of Pava. [70] He described the fact that many champions of office automation decomposed office work into elementary activities like text creation, duplication, sorting and dispatch, telephone contact, and dictation. Appropriate technological solutions were then applied to each of these isolated activities. For him a more integrated approach was necessary beginning with an understanding of the overall context that shapes these activities and the potential use of technology.

Pava argued that there is a need to differentiate between routine and nonroutine office work. Routine work is usually conducted by clerical personnel and involves structured problems, characterized by a need for accuracy and detail and usually narrow in scope. Nonroutine work involved less structured problems and is characterized by general information inputs, variable data, extended and unfixed time horizons, discretionary decision making, and so on. Routine office work lends itself well to sociotechnical systems design, which had its origins in production settings with linear, stepwise conversion processes. On the other hand there must be considerable work done to adapt the sociotechnical approach to nonroutine office work, which proceeds through a nonsequential conversion process.

Pava outlines a six-step method to analyzing nonroutine office work:

(1) Mapping The Client System: Techniques such as tracing "sequences of deliberation" are used to derive a map of communication behavior in the client organization.

(2) Structuring Client Capacity For Self-Design: Here a contract is built with the client to maximize the client's activity in the design process.

(3) Initial Scan: This first portion of the analysis is similar to that in traditional sociotechnical analysis. The objective is for the design team to establish a shared image of their organization at a broad ("big picture") level.

(4) Technical Analysis: Here the tools and procedures used to convert input into output are scrutinized. Rather than examining an assessment of variances in this process, as with the case of routine work, this work should focus on an analysis of management deliberations and their defects and opportunities for improvement.

(5) Social Analysis: Here the "role network" for each deliberation is mapped along with the values characteristically championed by each party. Values which appear to diverge, along with those which appear "reciprocally interdependent" or engaged in the same deliberation with divergent values, are identified, along with the "discretionary coalitions" which result.

(6) Design Proposals: A complex procedure is outlined to enable a best fit between social and technical components of the new work system.

This methodology is subjected to ongoing revision as it is applied to various organizations. It is significant in terms of its pioneering character, bringing QWL into the world of integrated office systems.

A somewhat different application of QWL tools was conducted by Whaley.[48] Here the goal was not customizing a system to a user environment, but designing integrated office system *products*. The job diagnostic survey, which measures various aspects of a job that relate to motivation and productivity, was administered along with an office work activity survey to a large sample from 13 different companies. As well, a smaller group was observed in their daily activity. Using sophisticated analytical procedures the researchers were able to derive a profile of the "multifunction worker." From that they then inferred a number of needs of this type of worker and features of the kind of system which would aid these people in their work.

However, there are a number of problems in developing a complete QWL methodology for integrated office system design and evaluation.

There is no coherent theory of QWL, let alone a theory of QWL and office systems. However, sociotechnical systems theory appears to be emerging as a possible beginning. Taylor argues that

> we believe STS design a more suitable approach to improving the quality of work life and productivity than either the individual job design schemes (e.g., job enrichment, work simplification) *or* the more systematic or comprehensive proce-

dures (e.g., operations management, technical engineering), not because it is necessarily better than any of them, but because it demands a broader perspective.[67]

Research into QWL is still very limited, especially at the lower levels of
organizations. As well, there is limited research in certain sectors of the
knowledge work population, especially the public sector.

Many different theoretical frameworks for QWL have resulted in a large
variety of disjointed research methodologies and intervention strategies.

QWL covers the disciplines of economics, psychology, sociology, industrial relations, engineering, systems theory, as well as drawing on insights
into the nature of work and work organizations. Like office systems, the
scope of QWL is very great. This is either an asset or a liability of the QWL
approach, depending on what kind of rush you happen to be in.

The QWL community has considerable work to do to become knowl-
edgeable about the technical side of office systems. It was only in 1981 that
leading individuals in this field started giving serious attention to the advent
of office systems.[82]

Chapter 4

Understanding the Office and Organization

Wittgenstein: *"Whereoft one does not understand, one should not speak."*
(From Tractetuc Logica Silophicus)
Hammer: *"Whereoft one does not understand, one should not automate."*

(Michael Hammer, 1981)

Typically, when studying the user, practitioners shoot in the dark at the illusive products, processes, activities, etc. of the office, without clear understanding of the nature of organizations and a plan for investigation.

4.1. A CONCEPTUAL MODEL OF THE OFFICE

In addition to a conceptual framework regarding the impact of integrated office systems, it is necessary to have a conceptual model of the office and organization as a whole. Such a model enables an organization to develop a coherent strategy for investigating its requirements and evaluating the impact of office system implementations. Organizational models are basically theories of organizational functioning. Different models will emphasize different constructs, relationships among the constructs, and approaches to evaluating the performance of the organization.[1] A comprehensive summary of eight popular models of organizational functioning is contained in Lawler, Nadler, and Cammann.[2]

Too often practitioners separate the *office* from the *organization* or *business unit* as a whole. The result can be changes in the office which are judged to be beneficial, but which are not beneficial to the entire organization. A genuine understanding of the office can only take place within a broader understanding of the organization, its mission, history, and current status. So any office systems model should be applicable not only to a given office but to a more fundamental unit of the organization.

4.1.1. An Office Systems Model

This model conceptualizes what takes place in the office and organization. A hierarchy of constructs is presented, with the overall goal of organizational effectiveness. The relationship of the model to effectiveness is explained in Chapter 5. The model depicts an office or an organization as a unit which takes *inputs* and processes them into *outputs*, within stakeholder requirements. This unit contains a hierarchy of levels:

(1) Mission (Goals). There can be a hierarchy of global objectives which an organization seeks to realize.

(2) Key Result Areas. These critical areas in which the organization has a number of general objectives which logically fall together. The degree to which the organization can realize the desired results in these areas will determine the degree to which it can fulfill its mission. Examples of key result areas are high productivity, organizational growth, organizational stability, and employee satisfaction.

(3) Functions. Every knowledge work organization contains a number of functions or independent operations with predetermined specifiable inputs and outputs. Examples of functions are marketing, research and development, personnel, accounting, and finance. Functions can be broken down into subfunctions. For example the personnel function could include a training subfunction, which in turn could include design, teaching, and evaluation subfunctions.

(4) Processes, Procedures, and Jobs. A number of *processes* are involved in the execution of a function. A process can be defined as a concept which shows the relationship between a series of work activities which are undertaken to perform a given function. Examples of processes are managerial, work flow, supervisory, communications, performance appraisal, information conversion/processing, and decision making.

In addition to processes, functions are executed through a complex of *procedures*. Procedures, like processes, consist of a number of related work activities. Unlike processes, a procedure is not just a concept, but a group of activities performed for a specific and usually specifiable purpose. Depending on the organization and the organizational level examined these procedures may be very structured (as in clerical work) or relatively unstructured and general (as in some professional work).

A third dimension upon which work activities can be aggregated is *jobs*. Activities in the office are assigned to persons with different jobs— secretaries, accountants, presidents, research officers, salespersons, supervisors, clerks, etc. While activities are not assignable exclusively to jobs (everyone in the office undertakes the activity of telephoning, for example), a given job can be described in terms of its constituent activities. More important, a given function can be described in terms of the jobs which enable its execution.

(5) Work Activities. This is the lowest level of the hierarchy. Work activities are undertaken in the performance of office functions. These activities are related to each other as part of a given process. For example, the communications *process* consists of a number of related *activities* such as typing, meeting, filing, traveling, phoning, reading, opening mail, dictation, and scheduling.

This "office systems model" is schematized in Figure 4.1. This "office model" is useful as it enables us to understand what takes place in an office and consequently to sort out the debate over "conceptual frameworks." An appropriate strategy for system design and the measurement of system effects can thereby be developed.

The office is a unit which processes inputs into outputs to be consumed by users. For example, an office which is charged with the accounting/finance function may take *inputs* such as invoices, purchase requisitions, financial resources, expense statements, requests for advances, timesheets, and so on, and process them into *outputs* such as bill payments, expense cheques, payroll cheques, financial reports to management (accounting summaries, status reports, are we meeting our objectives, etc.), and so on.

The processing of the output and the output itself must meet *stakeholder requirements*. Stakeholders are individuals or organizations who have an interest in the output and how it is produced. For example, the head office of a government department may produce outputs such as reports, new legislation, new program proposals, etc., but this must be done within the requirements of stakeholders such as the government employees' union, businesses which will be affected, consumer organizations, and regulatory bodies from other government departments and/or agencies.

The model enables a definition and subsequent measures of effectiveness to be external to the unit. Efficiency, on the contrary, is measured within the unit. If the time and/or costs involved in the production of the output decline as the result of office system technology, the office is functioning more *efficiently*. If, on the other hand, the product's utility to the user increases (better quality, format, support, packaging, or more timely, etc.), there has been an increase in the *effectiveness* of the office unit. Such changes in effectiveness can best be quantified at the point of consumption (by the user) rather than at various points of production (by the office worker).

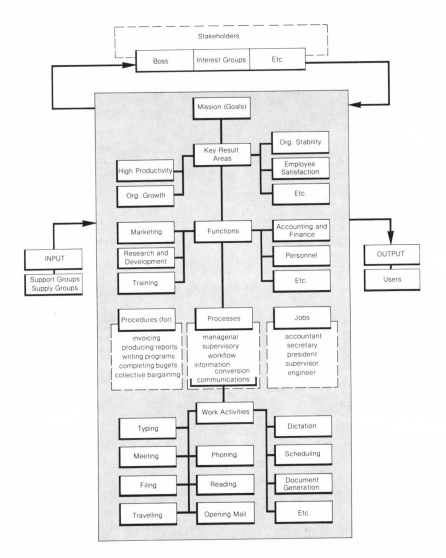

Figure 4.1. Office model.

From a review of the five conceptual approaches outlined in Chapter 3, it is clear that none have the scope, depth, or corresponding methodological sophistication necessary. It is also clear that the development of such an approach and methodology is not on the immediate horizon. However, it is possible to begin to formulate both a new framework and a research methodology.

4.1.2. Towards a New Framework

The five approaches are different in scope.

Figure 4.2 roughly depicts the present scope of the five approaches, in terms of our office system model.

As can be seen from Figure 4.2 the Communication, and Information Resource approaches are restricted to the level of processes. The Functional and Decision Support approaches penetrate through the level of functions to the key result areas of an organization. The QWL approach has the deepest scope as it may involve a change in the objectives of the organization.

An overall comparison of the *main* strength and weakness of each of the five approaches is presented in Table 4.1.

To summarize, each of the five approaches has merits and problems. None provides an adequate or comprehensive framework. But from each we can take useful aspects to synthesize a new framework.

In all fairness to researchers and practitioners from each of the "schools" it should be repeated that the five approaches are really not mutually exclusive. For example, some functional practitioners and researchers hold that QWL methods are applicable to office system design and evaluation. Some from the decision support school argue that job design, organizational change, and quality of work life are essential aspects of a DSS approach. To many QWL practitioners, the considerations of organizational communication fall under the purview of the QWL and sociotechnical framework. For many IRM managers, the development of rationalized procedures

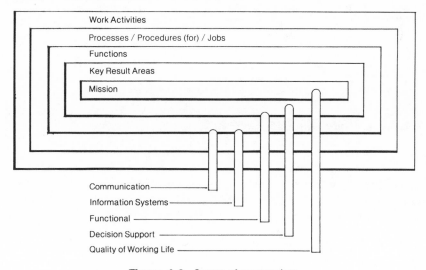

Figure 4.2. Scope of approaches.

Table 4.1. Main Stength and Weakness of Each Approach

Approach	Main strength	Main weakness
Organizational Communication	Communication is the dominant process in offices and the communications approach contains sophisticated measurement methodologies.	Focuses on *means* (processes) rather than *ends* (functions, products) of office work; is therefore relatively superficial and limited.
Functional	Focuses on basic functions, therefore less superficial than most approaches.	There is no methodology to examine the impact of office systems on functions.
Information Resource Management	More comprehensive than traditional DP and MIS approaches. Can provide a subjective basis for cost-justification of office systems.	IRM is a flawed concept. Unlikely at present to provide a convincing basis for cost-justification given current willingness to invest in "soft" benefits.
Decision Support	Focus on critical process (decision making) to provide a comprehensive, flexible, and responsive tool.	Limited in scope. There are no adequate methodologies to measure system impacts on decision making.
Quality of Work Life	Situates system development processes correctly in the context of a total sociotechnical work system and consequently does not overlook critical job design, motivational, etc., factors.	Has not won wide acceptance in North America as a valid approach to knowledge worker effectiveness. Weak on all aspects of office system technology.

and the improvement of office functions should be part of the objectives of any system design.

4.2. Case Study: Modeling an Office

An example will help clarify (see Figure 4.3).

The commercial office may take *inputs* from various support groups and supply groups and process them into *outputs* to be consumed by various users. Inputs could include requests for service, customer inquiries, billing information from the accounting department, telephone number and equipment assignments from the traffic department, equipment records listing present and past equipment in subscriber premises, or scheduling information from district management, just to name a few. These inputs are processed into outputs such as responses to customer inquiries, new equipment records,

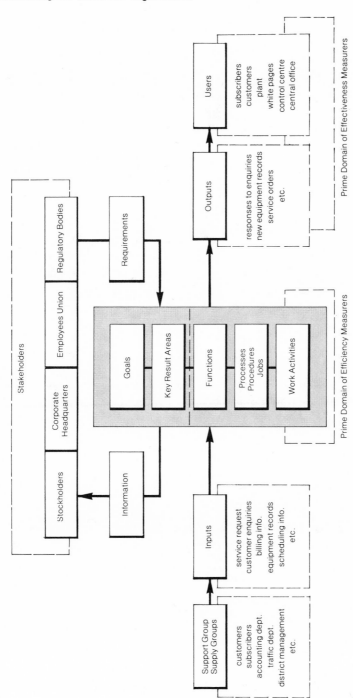

Figure 4.3. The telephone company's commercial office.

and service orders to be consumed by such users as "plant" (installation and repair), "white pages," accounting, central office frame, the control center, etc.

This processing of inputs into outputs must be done within the requirements of various stakeholders who have an interest in how the output is produced. Stakeholders include the corporate headquarters, who are concerned about the efficiency and effectiveness of the commercial office, and about the balance of human and material resources among the corporate departments. The stockholders, who as stakeholders do not consume the output but rather have an interest in what is produced, and how it is done, and the employees' union are concerned about such aspects of the production process as working conditions, wages, hours of work, benefits to employees.

Integrated office systems can affect the *efficiency* of the office by displacing or avoiding the costs involved in processing the inputs into outputs. These systems can also have impact on the *effectiveness* of the office organization by enabling improvements in the products—for example, more accurate new equipment records, better responses to customer inquiries, fewer errors in distribution of service orders, faster throughput of service orders and as a result, better services to the end user—the customer.

Using this example and the generic "office model," we can better understand the debate over alternative conceptual framework for office system design and evaluation.

That is, office systems must be designed and evaluated with regard to their impact on the results or *products* of office work. An adequate conceptual framework must therefore facilitate measurement and understanding of the impact of office systems through the hierarchy of

- Work activities,
- Processes, procedures, and jobs
- Functions, and
- Key result areas,

to the impact on the overall *conversion of inputs into useful outputs.*

This migration path for office systems research and evaluation is depicted in Figure 4.4.

An adequate framework must take important acquisitions from all five approaches.

Probably the most important is the notion of a sociotechnical system developed by the QWL school. A frequency distribution of system autopsies would show that the failure to adequately consider both technical and social components of a system design is the number one killer. We have entered a new "JET" age in which the collective optimization of JOBS, ENVIRONMENT, and TECHNOLOGY hold the key.

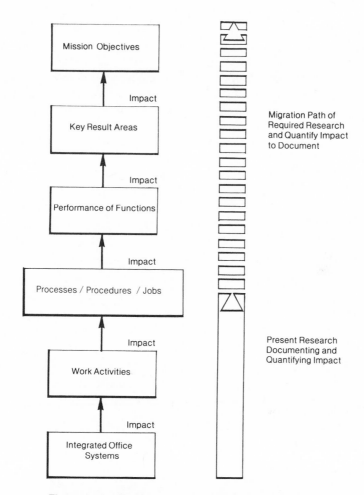

Figure 4.4. Migration path of office systems research.

Another central lesson can be learned from the functional school. Near the top of the killer list has been the failure to focus system design on meeting basic objectives of the organization and improving the execution of its functions. Just as the starting point for office systems should not be "elegant technical solutions in search of a problem," it should also not be preoccupation with lower-level work activities. The rationalization of office procedures and application of the new technologies can result in improvements which are striking even to the office systems zealot.

The Communications, IRM, and Decision Support approaches bring us a focus on three important processes. Most office activities can be viewed as part of the communications process, and the analyst will do well to examine opportunities for improvement here. Information capture, storage, processing, and retrieval are central to the office and the "information" sector of the economy. Improvements here can, as part of broader improvements, be significant. Especially important is the need to build well-planned and managed data bases which the IRM practitioners are pioneering. And the augmenting of human intellect, as Douglas Englebart predicted in the early 1960s, in part can be accomplished by the new generation of decision support systems. Examination of the process of defining assumptions and making decisions can often lead to important opportunities for systems.

No one framework is adequate, but all have important contributions.

Chapter 5

Office Efficiency, Effectiveness, and Productivity

The vendor tells us that we've doubled our productivity because we doubled the number of memos and reports we can generate in a week. Somehow it just doesn't feel right. . .

(Anon)

Integrated office systems can have a positive impact on efficiency, effectiveness, and productivity in the office. However, to determine the desired impact, design the correspondingly appropriate system, and evaluate its effects, it is necessary to have a clear understanding of these concepts. Put briefly, office systems can impact the following:

(1) Efficiency. Systems can (a) reduce inputs into the office such as costs of labor, materials, services, etc., or (b) result in greater output (with the same or less input) such as more sales, contracts negotiated, accounts processed, etc.

(2) Internal Efficiency. Systems can reduce the inputs which are internal to the office. Examples are less time spent scheduling, filing, waiting for work, looking for information, filling out forms, etc.

(3) Effectiveness. Systems can improve the quality of the products of office work. Examples are improved service to customers, better management reports, more effective products, more revenue, etc.

(4) Productivity. Systems can improve the overall ratio between input and output in the office, by improving the quantity or quality of the products of office work using, in general, the same or less input resources.

5.1. EFFICIENCY AND EFFECTIVENESS IN OFFICE WORK

To begin, it is essential to distinguish between efficiency and effectiveness in office work. Efficiency can be described as a measure of the dollars per unit of output. Effectiveness refers to the production of the right output. Whether a product is "right" can be judged along a number of *dimensions of utility* such as timeliness, format, correspondence to market demands, packaging, costs, delivery, support services, etc.

Table 5.1 charts some distinctions which are useful to make between efficiency and effectiveness. To clarify these distinctions, it is useful to briefly discuss the notion of productivity. Recently, researchers in the office systems area have concerned themselves with measuring the impact of these systems on office workers or organizational productivity.[1-7] While the goal of many of these individuals is similar to that of the present author, we must caution that the term "productivity," undefined, can be confusing and misleading.

> Figures of *production* tell how much is produced, while *productivity* tells how well the resources have been used in producing it.[8]

The industrial economist thus defines productivity in terms of efficiency—that is, the efficient use of resources. If production is labor-intensive, the main ingredient is speed.[9]

Productivity can then be seen as the mathematical inverse of efficiency. That is,

efficiency = number of units of work or resource to produce a unit of output

productivity = number of units of output per unit of work or resource

Table 5.1. Useful Distinctions between Efficiency and Effectiveness

Efficiency	Effectiveness
Dollars per unit of output	Production of the right output
Performance of a given task as well as possible in relation to some predefined performance criterion	Identification of what should be done
Doing things right (Drucker)	Doing the right things (Drucker)
Can be measured in terms of cost and time	Requires a detailed understanding of the variables that affect performance to be measured
Can be a key concern in stable environments	Key concern in unstable environments
Can be defined, described, and measured internally to the organization	Is best defined, described, and measured in terms of its external impacts

or put another way,

$$\text{efficiency} = \frac{\text{input}}{\text{output}}$$
$$\text{productivity} = \frac{\text{output}}{\text{input}}$$

From a traditional industrial approach, the objects of measurement and the metrics are the same for both efficiency and effectiveness. From this perspective, *effectiveness* differs from both efficiency and productivity, in that it introduces (1) the quality of the product; (2) its utility to the user; and (3) the desirability of measures external to the organizational unit involved.

However, when measuring how the new computer and telecommunications technologies can aid in office work, the focus must be on effectiveness, not efficiency. Targeting efficiency, as is often done in industrial production interactions, would provide a misplaced emphasis in the office. This is true for a number of reasons.

Office work is, in the main, much more complex and unstructured than work on a production line. The typical approach to productivity in industry cannot be applied to offices.

Areas where the industrial productivity model *can* be applied, such as typing, account for a small proportion of overall office costs. For example, it is possible to increase typing efficiency or productivity through the use of word-processing technology. But typing costs amount to approximately 2% of overall office labor costs.[1]

Efficiency and effectiveness in office work are not necessarily positively correlated. A person or unit or organization can be working very efficiently, yet completely ineffectively at the same time. A few examples are instructive:

Centralized word-processing systems can increase typing efficiency in an office. But often centralized systems cause knowledge workers to spend more of their time getting material in and out—the typing operation. This can lead to a reduction in research time, planning time, and other activities which have a direct bearing on the quality of the knowledge worker's output. Consequently such systems can *increase* typing *efficiency*, but *decrease* overall organizational *effectiveness*.

Or consider an efficient MIS, in which an organization's computer center is said to be highly efficient. It generates more output (management reports) than almost any other center in the country. The computer downtime is low and the machine is fully utilized. Inputs are quickly processed and outputs are delivered promptly. Unfortunately, however, the reports are not seen as useful by those who receive them. The formatting makes them difficult to read; there are too many data and not enough netted-out information.

The system is very *efficient* but completely *ineffective*. The cost per unit of output is low, but so is the utility.[10]

Or, finally, suppose the manager of an applications programming team seeks to increase programmer efficiency. "Interruptions" to efficient coding are reduced by cutting back on team meetings, ending coders' design responsibilities, and discouraging interaction by the programmers. The number of lines of code per programmer per day increases. But the quality of the output is reduced by factors such as redundancy, lack of programmer synergism, and a decline in worker motivation which inhibits creativity, care, and so on. Efficiency has increased while effectiveness and the utility of the output have decreased.[11]

The centrality of effectiveness rather than efficiency in office work, and the soft evidence that office systems can improve effectiveness dramatically, point to the need for valid and reliable effectiveness measures.

Corresponding to the notions of efficiency and effectiveness in office systems measurement are the notions of *cost displacement* improvements and *value added* improvements.

Improvements in efficiency result in the displacements of costs in a given organization. Improvements in effectiveness result in added value to the organization. One supporter of this view is Kujawa, who argues as follows:

> Increased effectiveness occurs when the outputs that receivers and managers want are judged to be "right," produced through activities performed more efficiently. Office automation contributes to effectiveness because it generates the capacity within which tasks can be performed to a higher degree of acceptance. It may provide capacity for tasks not being performed now to be done.[12]

This relationship is depicted in Figure 5.1.

However, a pragmatic approach to office systems design and measurement cannot *exclude* efficiency as a desirable goal to be pursued. With a proper system design implementation, improvements in efficiency can be translated into improvements in effectiveness. For example, by spending less of the day looking for people, time is freed up which can result in better work being performed and better quality outputs being produced. This relationship is depicted in Figure 5.2.

5.2. MEASURING OFFICE PRODUCTIVITY

It is prudent to go beyond the approach taken by traditional industrial economists who view productivity as simply a relationship between the quantity of input and the quantity of output within a given production unit. The products of office work can be improved, both in terms of their quantity (efficiency) and quality (effectiveness). This overall relationship between effi-

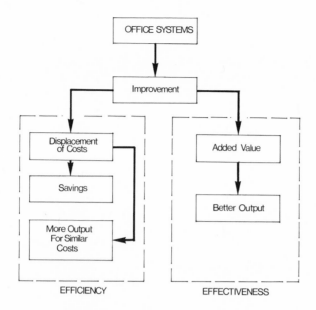

Figure 5.1. Efficiency and effectiveness.

ciency, effectiveness, internal efficiency, and productivity is depicted in Figure 5.3.

The products of office work, then, have dimension relating to both effectiveness and efficiency. That is,

$$\text{Office productivity} = \frac{\text{Output (quantity and quality)}}{\text{Input (quantity)}}$$

Unfortunately, nearly all office "productivity" measures are invalid. These measures fall into several categories.

Subjective Measures. Measures such as asking "how much has your productivity increased?" cannot be considered actual measures of productivity.

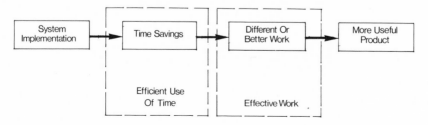

Figure 5.2. From efficient to effective work.

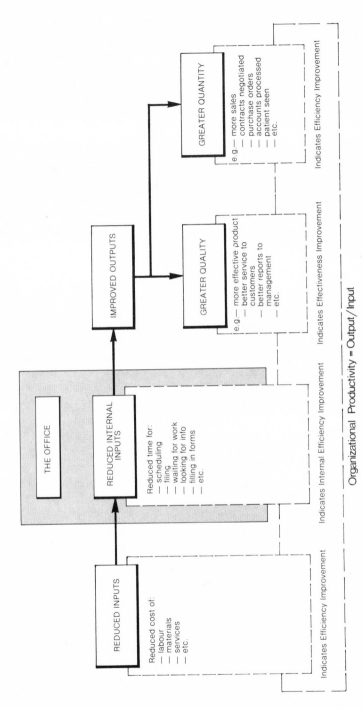

Organizational Productivity = Output/Input

Figure 5.3. Office efficiency, effectiveness, and productivity.

In some cases, respondents have been given a piece of paper describing an integrated office system and then asked to indicate how much such a system would increase their productivity. While the answers to this question were of considerable interest, it was wrong for the researchers to conclude that office systems increase productivity by, say, 15%.

Internal Efficiency Measures. For example a measure of "time saved" cannot be equated to a productivity measure. Saving a professional one hour per day does not mean that this person will produce an equivalent amount of output, or output of better quality. It simply means that you have created an *opportunity* for a productivity increase.

Qualitative Measures. It is possible to show how office systems improve communications, employee motivation, and so on. Measures like this, while useful, are not *productivity* measures. Improvements such as these can *result in* productivity improvements, but these qualitative measures are not valid productivity measures.

Misleading Output Measures. Strict application of the industrial production model to the office often results in "productivity" measures such as the "number of memos" or "number of purchase orders produced." Such measures ignore the *purpose* of such output. Increasing the number of memos or the number of reports generated may or may not be desirable. To simply measure the output, with no reference to its utility, may be misleading.

To show a productivity increase, it would be necessary to show how a group of employees using an office system improved their output (products), or decreased their input (costs), as a result of using the system. The main problems in doing this are in developing valid ways to measure the output of office work, and controlling for all the nonsystem variables which could also affect productivity.

This dilemma poses a serious problem. Without valid productivity measures, it is not possible to anticipate how various system designs will affect productivity. As a result, it is difficult to formulate appropriate system designs, and even more difficult to cost-justify them. Some have argued that the focus should be on global measures of *organizational performance*, rather than looking at efficiency and productivity at the level of the individual, or even office.

Gale outlines an approach to evaluating the wisdom of capital investments, such as in automation.[13] He develops the term "value added," which represents the amount that purchased raw materials and components increase in value when they have been converted into the products of a business. Put another way, value added equals sales minus purchase, or labor plus capital plus pretax income. Value added divided by the number of employees gives a measure of labor output that is comparable across businesses. He notes, as did Karl Marx over a hundred years ago, that investment in automation can increase productivity but will likely reduce the rate of profit. There are many examples of capital-intensive, low-profit businesses such as commodity paper, chemical, and steel products to name a few. Management, he says, thus faces a dilemma, of often needing to automate in order to keep competitive and maintain market share, while at the same time lowering the return of investment (ROI):

> Those projects that indicate a negative net prospect for percentage ROI often promise a favourable one for dollar results because the lower percentage is applied to a larger investment base. In such cases, it seems that management faces a difficult decision; it must choose between increased sales and dollar profits on the one hand and a decreased rate of profitability on the other.

To avoid this "investment intensity trap" where the substitution of capital for labor results in unprofitable productivity, Gale argues that the main measure should be *operating* effectiveness. This is a measure of the actual value added per employee divided by the par value added per employee (where par is the average for businesses of this investment intensity).

A related approach has been developed by Dahl and Morgan for the Upjohn Company.[14] They argue that traditional approaches to measuring organizational performance have focused on the return of capital investment. For them, even more important is the rate of return on investments in the human resource. Because office automation can provide tools to make people work more effectively, it can improve the ROI in human resources. According to an Upjohn study the total career investment in an individual is about 160 times their initial starting salary. As a result it is important to get an optimal and measurable return on this investement. This requires some special measurement and analysis activities, however, as most companies income, balance sheet, and cash flow statements do not separate the major resource investments. Expenses are combined under the traditional categories such as marketing research and development, administration and finances, operations and so on. Like Gale they argue that the measure of "value added" helps an organization measure its performance. Return on investment can be seen as having two components: net value added divided by adjusted assets (assets less depreciation) and net value added divided by total employee expenses. These two can be compared graphically along with a third axis—return on investment. The optimal position is to have high value added for both people and capital as well as high return on net assets. By understanding the impact of one on the other, the optimal position can be sought.

Two strategies can be employed to deal with the general problem described above—that is a lack of well-accepted productivity measures on the one hand, and the lack of knowledge regarding what is the actual impact of integrated office systems on performance.

First, measures should be taken *both* of internal office activities and of overall global performance measures.

It is possible to quantify and therefore anticipate the effects of office systems on the lower-level work *activities* and *processes and procedures* indicated in the office model. By identifying time saving in activities and improvements in processes (such as the communications process) and procedures we can, through successive investigations, migrate up through higher levels of the model. As the measurement methods become more sophisticated and the normative data more complete, it will be possible to control for lower-order variables and to measure the impact of systems on the higher-level functions and outputs of office work.

At the same time it is necessary to develop whatever primitive measures of *outputs* (products) and global *organizational performance* that can be attempted at this time.

It appears from initial applications that a cost–benefit analysis, based on detailed and carefully validated information of this type, provides an adequate business case for the "chooser"to act.

Second, a customization strategy which focuses on the implementation and evaluation of *pilot* systems is used. Through initial experimentation with pilot office systems, the effects of the system on (a) internal processes and procedures and (b) office products and organizational performance can be measured. Using posttest and system-monitoring data, it is possible to anticipate with some confidence what the effects of an extension of the pilot system to a full operational system will be.

User Driven Design

An organization can be viewed as a system of people, within an organizational structure, using technology to do tasks. A change in any one of these elements will ripple throughout the system, impacting in some way each of the other three.

(Peter Keen, 1979)

6.1. ASSESSING THE ORGANIZATION

At the heart of a User-Driven Design approach to office systems is an investigation strategy. The measurement or assessment of the organization is required to identify appropriate persons to be included in the system; determine system requirements for the user group(s); provide data for a cost–benefit analysis; and secure base-line measurement for downstream evaluations.

However, assessment for User-Driven Design, is, in many ways, different from other approaches to measuring organizations.

6.1.1. Multidisciplinary Assessment

Investigation of the user organization should draw on the strengths of a number of research disciplines. These include traditional systems analysis, organizational assessments, field research and evaluation, action research, the study of records management, quality of work life diagnosis, and operational research. This is depicted in Figure 6.1. Although these disciplines are not, in all cases, mutually exclusive, it is useful to describe them separately to explain their various contributions.

(1) Systems Analysis. A variety of investigatory procedures have been

81

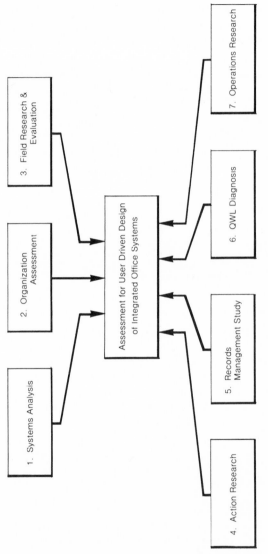

Figure 6.1. Assessment disciplines in User-Driven Design.

developed to facilitate the design of traditional data processing, MIS (management information system), and other systems. The objectives are to identify problems in information processing within an organization and to recommend computer or other system solutions. Typical methods include interviews and observational techniques to chart the flow and processing of information, to inventory current system facilities, to examine inefficiencies, bottlenecks, and redundancies. The sytems analyst usually acts as a liaison between the end users and the programmers who translate his/her algorithms into computer programs. Most categories of data collected for traditional systems analysis are often necessary in the assessment of requirements for office systems, but the latter is much broader in scope.

(2) Organizational Assessment. Recently there has been a growing interest in assessing the performance of complex organizations. A number of major projects and recent works have attempted to grapple with the diagnosis and change of behavior and structure of overall organizations, work groups, and individual jobs.[1-3] Organizational assessment researchers and practitioners have stressed the development of scientifically valid and practical approaches to assess organizational performance and effectiveness in relationship to the environments in which organizations function. The school has grown from the perceived need by many management scientists and behaviorists to adapt organizations to meet changing social aspirations by workers and new economic constraints. The discipline uses a broad range of tools, procedures, models, and techniques with the goal of providing comprehensive assessments and organizational change programs.

(3) Field Research and Evaluation. Industrial psychology, applied to the office, has been concerned with the measurement of work and the assessment of organizational efficiency and effectiveness. Various kinds of field research have been conducted by academics interested in developing and testing hypotheses and theories, and also by corporate specialists seeking to diagnose organizational problems or measure the extent to which a given action, activity, or program has achieved its objectives. More than with other disciplines, investigators have placed importance on obtaining valid and reliable measures.

(4) Action Research. As French and Bell define it,

> action research is the process of systematically collecting research data about an ongoing system relative to some objective goal, or need of that system: feeding these data back into the system; taking action by altering selected variables within the system based on both data and on hypotheses; and evaluating the results of actions by collecting more data.[4]

Action research advocates downplay the importance of rigorous objective quantification in favor of the full *involvement* of the various persons being studied and acted upon. Because of its special relevance to User-Driven Design, the topic of action research is discussed at greater length later in this chapter.

(5) Records Management Study. According to Maedke et al., records management is

> the application of systematic and scientific control . . . exercised over the creation, distribution, utilization, retention, storage, retrieval, protection, preservation and final disposition of all types of records within an organization.[5]

Fairly well-structured methodologies for assessing the records management needs of organizations have been developed. These include "walk-through surveys" to assess existing records and records-handling practices, detailed records inventories, and techniques for auditing and analyzing the content and use of records and the effectiveness of records management programs. Many of these methods are directly applicable to assessment for User-Driven Design.

(6) Quality of Work Life Diagnosis. Overlapping with organizational assessment are diagnostic methodologies for job design and the quality of work life (QWL). The objective of these, in general, is to identify problems in the content of jobs, the nature of work in a given organization, the relationships between people, the reward systems and motivation of employees, and current levels of job satisfaction, with the view of implementing QWL programs. A number of instruments have been developed, many with reliability and validity indices with extensive normative data from previous use. Because an integrated office system is a sociotechnical system, there are many important tools and concepts from the QWL school which should be applied to User-Driven Design.

(7) Operations Research. Operations Research (OR) is

> the study of complex systems of (humans), machines, money, materials, and the systems are studied by deriving a mathematical or analogical model which expresses the performance of the system in question.[6]

OR models can be very complex, but underlying each is a relatively simple structure. That is, OR models take the form of an equation in which a measure of the system's overall performance (P) is equated to some relationship (f) between a set of controlled aspects of the system (C) and a set of uncontrolled aspects (U). This is expressed symbolically as

$$P = f(Cj, Uj)$$

That is, performance is a function of controlled and uncontrolled aspects of a system. Because OR strives to use a scientific method, a systems orientation, and an interdisciplinary approach, it appears well suited to contribute to assessment and evaluation of office systems. However, OR has yet to become comfortable with office system technology and to be extended fully to knowledge work functions.

Assessment for User-Driven Design includes aspects of all of these disciplines but in the long run is broader than all of them. Because the goal is to build integrated systems that eventually will touch all aspects of office work and organizational functioning, the assessment methodology must touch the content area of all these disciplines, as well as draw on the methods which have developed.

6.1.2. Assessment as a Process of Change

It is wise to view the process of "implementation" of an office system as extending throughout the gamut of the systems development process, beginning with the very first exposure of the potential user to the assessment team. The "respondents" in the office systems study will become the users, whose first impression of the process will be formed as part of the study.

Because of this, assessment is very much a process of change. This is not just in the traditional sense that the data will be used for "real world purposes." Nor in the sense that the goal of assessment is "not just prediction, but making things happen." Rather, the investigation itself has a dual function of acquiring the complete information necessary, and at the same time, beginning the process of attitudinal and organizational change. For example, it has been found that often half of the time spent in the first interviews is spent by the interviewer having to carefully explain his/her presence, the rationale for questions, likely opportunities for systems, and likely effects. Another example is that the introduction of the study is a critical juncture, in the success of any systems project. Respondents' attitudes towards the assessment will effect both the validity and reliability of the data and also the likelihood of a successful implementation.

6.1.3. Participative Assessment

In assessment for User-Driven Design, the subject acts as a coresearcher (See Figure 6.2). The typical approach to organizational investigations is that the investigator defines the problem and the methods to be used, "conducts" the research, analyzes the data, interprets and presents the results with recommendations for an appropriate system solution. Invariably, this approach fails or causes serious problems for the implementation team. It fails to take into account that unless the users are partners in the assessment the data will be questionable, the design inappropriate, and the user acceptance and user

Figure 6.2. Role of the designer.

education levels inadequate. Lawler and Drexler debunk five incorrect assumptions about field research.

A first is the notion that "the researcher has most or all the information and knowledge needed to carry out a well-designed research project." [7] This is mistaken because every environment is unique, requiring specialized knowledge of what is important, and what particular facets should be investigated.

Another is that "any instrument the researcher designs or selects will be accepted by the organization's members." This is incorrect because instruments must be adapted to each environment.

A third assumption is that "client does not need to know the researcher's orientation or the purpose of the research." In reality, without client knowledge of project objectives, fundamental errors in research recommendations are likely.

A fourth is that "client commitment to participating in research can be obtained in the interests of science." This has proven to be false.

Finally, there is the notion that "adoption and implementation will follow assessment, diagnosis and solution identification." This is less likely if clients have not been taken through the same discovery process as the investigators. Far-reaching recommendations which appear "out of the blue" often lack success, independently of the validity or utility of the recommendation.

Participatory assessment results in better data, better designs, and better user acceptance of the system.

(1) Better Data. Many measures which should be taken are highly dependent on respondents cooperation. For example, time use diaries can provide either very useful or completely useless data, depending on the degree of respondent cooperation. The more the respondents know about integrated office systems and how they will improve the quality of their work life, the more they will be likely to take the time and effort to provide valid data.

There is no such thing as a "generic" office system measurement instrument which is applicable to all organizations. Organizations differ in structure, goals, composition, culture, and so on. As a result the measurement instruments and assessments program must be "customized" for the same reasons that a "custom" system solution will be required.

(2) Better Designs. It goes without saying that better data should result in better system designs. Yet today organizations are plagued by so-called "experts" who assess organizations from on high and propose inappropriate or inadequate system designs.

The statement "the end users know best what they need" is only partially true. Members of an organization will have a number of critical insights about their problems and opportunities for improvement. But because of the newness and complexity of the new office systems they will, especially at the beginning, have a limited understanding of their needs or even how to identify their needs. Both sides of this problem can be addressed by a collaborative and consultative relationship between the office system experts and the users. Participative design is iterative design. The client and users themselves should receive few surprises. Rather, through an ongoing collaborative process of study, discussion, and collective evaluation of results "coproduced" solutions emerge.

(3) Better User Acceptance and Understanding. Through participative assessments users can acquire the sense of "system ownership" which is necessary for a successful implementation. Acceptance of a system, commitment to make it work, and a willingness to change and integrate the new tools into one's job, are best established through active involvement by the users in determining the design. In Havelock's review of the literature on the acceptance of research results, it was found that proposed innovations were more likely to occur if collaborative and reciprocal relationships were established between the investigator and user systems.[8] When the innovation is as far-reaching as an integrated office system, the point should be well taken.

Moreover, commitment to a system does not simply entail positive attitudes. It also requires a complete *understanding* of the system and the problems it addresses. Consequently, the assessment process should also be an educative process, where the potential users acquire the knowledge necessary to become committed and effective users.

6.1.4. Role of the Investigator

In User-Driven Design the researcher and the practitioner are the same person. The consultant conducting the investigation has the responsibility of acquiring the required data. But his/her role is also one of a systems designer, educator, and change agent. The investigator will interface with the highly skilled technical design and organizational design specialists if they are, in fact, different persons. At each step of the investigation, it is the ultimate design and evaluation considerations which shape the assessment. The investigation should "unfreeze the situation" and create a positive climate for change. It should, through a user-study team, begin to cement the feedback relationships between the user community and the system architects and implementors. Finally, it should contribute to the process of educating users and "choosers" alike in the opportunities for improvement in their organization and in the potential of the new systems in general.

6.1.5. Assessment Mutually Acceptable Ethically

This is not a simple issue. Participative design is an issue of methodology. That is, it makes sense from the viewpoint of sound design methodology for the respondents and future users to participate fully. However, it is also an ethical issue. It is important that those who will be affected by change have an adequate degree of control over their destinies. Hult argues that a minimal ethical requirement for the investigator is to state clearly the value premises of his or her work.[9] Beyond that, there is a general case (both tactical and ethical) that the office sytem should not be injurious to the users, but rather, should improve their quality of work life. Across the board, there is no reason why this should not be the case. It is obvious that the probability of a successful implementation will be very different for a system that will benefit the users as opposed to a system that will harm them. However, on the broader ethical level, there is a case for the investigation, design, and implementation of the system to take place within a clearly understood and mutually agreeable ethical framework. The potential users should understand the objectives of the designer along with the likely effects of the system. If either of these runs contrary to the interests of the potential users, there is little ethical basis to solicit their support.

6.2. APPLICATIONS DEVELOPMENT WITHOUT PROGRAMMERS?

The notion of *programming by end users* or its flip side called *application development without programmers* has become very popular in traditional data processing circles.[10]

What is the relationship between this notion and the User-Driven Design approach outlined in this book? First, a review of applications development without programmers.

By the early 1980s IBM had won fairly wide acceptance for its "Information Centers." Here, users could go for assistance in constructing small customized applications for themselves. The concept really became a hit with the publication of James Martin's book *Applications Development Without Programmers.*[11] He and others from a data-processing background had noted that traditional application development methodologies were neither succeeding nor appropriate in a world where users are increasingly interfacing directly with computers. The development time was too slow, given the mushrooming requests for customized applications, and as a result, huge applications backlogs had grown in many organizations.

Also, a trend away from the traditional languages (COBOL, FORTRAN, etc.) toward more powerful languages (APL, PL1, MARK IV, etc.) began to make programming a much less detailed and time-consuming activity. This was an important precondition to end users constructing simple applications themselves. By the beginning of the 1970s there were a number of data base management systems (DBMS) such as IMS, TOTAL, System 2,000, ADABAS, IDS, and Codasyl-type DBMS which provided powerful ways to access data. However, these were not yet appropriate for end users, because they required knowledge about the structure of files and access routines. In the 1970s we saw the advent of data management systems (DMS). These systems provide tools for input format design, interactive queries, report generation, and data dictionaries. By the beginning of the 1980s and the office system explosion, English-like languages were being added to data management systems. These began to permit users to specify what is to be done, rather than how it is to be performed. Extensions of these systems, called decision support systems, enable users to easily construct numerical data bases, models, graphics, and do interactive queries or statistical routines on the information. Examples are the interactive financial planning system (IFIPS), Empire, and very simple system such as VISICALC. End user programming caused considerable flack in DP circles. However, this seemingly novel concept really dates back to 1962 when Douglas Englebart wrote the classic paper "Augmenting Human Intellect: A Conceptual Framework." [12] In it, he argued for the notion of knowledge workers directly developing and accessing their own information tools and data bases. So "end user programming" is, in many ways, simply a buzzword by-product of the migration of data processing towards integrated office systems used directly by generalist office workers.

6.2.1. End User Programming and User-Driven Design

What is the relationship between "applications development without programmers" and the User-Driven Design methodology outlined in this book?

This relationship is depicted in Figure 6.3. The former refers to the use of an integrated office system to develop simple application, models, statistical analyses, etc., and to interactively query larger data bases, generate reports, produce graphical output, and format material for the screen or for paper.

User-Driven Design encompasses this. It is the entire process of specialist facilitators working with users to determine the character, size, location, and overall implementation strategy for a sociotechnical office system.

Once an office system is implemented, users will, of course, develop many of their own "applications" as they have been doing for some years. Many examples of this can be given. Users have been working with decision support tools to build budgets and financial models for some years. Another example is the use of interactive information retrieval tools to construct customized data bases, such as client files, bibliographic references, financial information, etc. Standard routines are available for generating graphics such

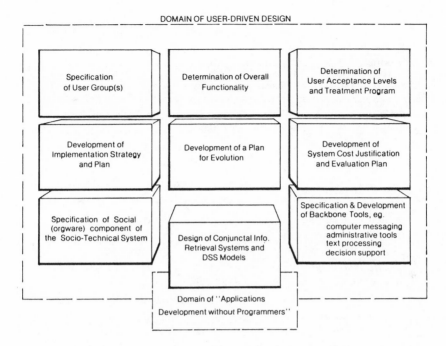

Figure 6.3. End user programming and User-Driven Design.

as histograms, bar charts, graphs, and scattergrams. Videotex page and data base creation tools for elegant graphic and textual output are now becoming commonplace. Users have also directly worked with administrative tools for creation of calendars, scheduling, administrative lists, etc. Other examples are the use of computer-based messaging systems for creation and search of textual message data bases: interactive statistical packages for extensive analysis of data: and interactive query facilities for retrieval and formating of information from larger corporate bases.

6.3. A CUSTOMIZATION STRATEGY

A User-Driven Design methodology contains a strategy for determining system solutions which are customized, that is, based on the requirements of the organization and its people.

The strategy centers on the implementation and extension of manageable pilot office systems. Lacking hard data about the likely impacts of systems, few organizations are willing to make a substantial "blind" investment in a full operational office system. Most choosers want to get their feet wet; to learn how a system will affect their organization; to have an initial low-risk exposure to the problems of managing organizational change; to acquire data on how users learn, use, and benefit from office systems and apply these data to subsequent cost–benefit analyses. Meyer and Lodahl put it well:

> A high leverage office-automation pilot is the first step in a strategy to incrementally build towards the automated office. It provides a safe testbed for automation concepts while training the implementors, building their visibility and credibility, and readying the users for change.[13]

There can be many different types of pilot systems:

(1) The Small Pilot Group. A group of approximately 20–50 employees are given electronic work stations. The functionality could be a subset of the functionality of the future operational office system. Or it could be a superset, from which employees will "naturally select" the most appropriate system features to be used. With the use of control and comparison groups the effects of the pilot can be evaluated and the user group expanded.

(2) The Incremental Pilot. Some hardware (for example additional terminals) and software (for example a messaging package) are added to the existing DP/MIS system. Costs can often be minimized, although the functionality may also be too small for success.

(3) The Single-Application Pilot. For example, a decision support system is implemented to a small group of managers. After evaluation of system effects on error rate, quality of decision, output of the group, etc., the system may be extended in number of users and/or functionality.

(4) The Operational Data Pilot. In this case a pilot system is based on one operational data base. Critical on-line information is at the core of the pilot functionality, (e.g., sales information from regional offices) and additional capabilities are added around the main data base (e.g., text editor and electronic mail).

(5) Other Pilots. Various combinations of the above are possible. As pilot systems continue to proliferate there will undoubtedly be many other types.

Pilot systems can be different from operational systems in a number of ways. These are outlined in Table 6.1.

One simple conclusion for both the analyst and designer is that operational systems require a more extensive user investigation and design effort.

6.3.1. Office System vs. MIS/DP System Design

Because the customization strategy is based on a pilot implementation which evolves into an operational system, the electronic office system design process must be more elaborate than with traditional DP or MIS systems. The various stages are contrasted in Figure 6.4, along with example corresponding outputs and chooser decision points.

Table 6.1. Differences between Pilot Systems and Operational Systems

Pilot office system	Operational office system
Usually separate from existing DP/MIS systems	More hooks into existing systems
Experimental, tentative, have manual systems to fall back on	Committal
Discrete parameters, constraints limits its expansion	Constantly evolving, expanding
Usually relatively small system resources required	Substantial system requirements
Limited compatibility issues	Often difficult and numerous compatibility requirements
Ownership, control, and responsibilities easy to define	Cross-functional responsibilities
Usually limited security issues	Often far-reaching and complex security issues
Unlikely to have convincing, immediate cost-justification	Solid business case possible
Implementation relatively straightforward	Implementation complex

6.4. DESIGN PHASES

The design process can be organized in a number of ways, depending on the requirements of a given organization. This book outlines one approach to designing a pilot integrated office system. This approach, which has proven to be successful for a number of organizations, has three phases leading to the implementation of a full operational system. The approach, and various activities and reports, are outlined here in detail to provide a framework for the reader to build a design approach for your organization.

The three phases are the *prepilot phase,* the *pilot phase*, and the *operational system phase*. At each phase data are taken from the user and user environment to propel the design process. This approach is schematized in Figure 6.5.

6.4.1. The Prepilot System Phase

During the prepilot phase, a series of investigations and measurements are taken with the objective of identifying and specifying a low-risk, high-profile pilot system. Measurement activities, decision points, and outputs are schematized in Figure 6.6.

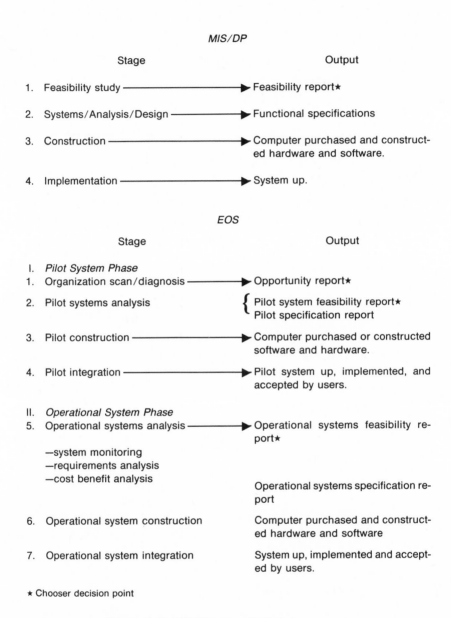

MIS/DP

Stage	Output
1. Feasibility study ⟶	Feasibility report★
2. Systems/Analysis/Design ⟶	Functional specifications
3. Construction ⟶	Computer purchased and constructed hardware and software.
4. Implementation ⟶	System up.

EOS

Stage	Output
I. *Pilot System Phase*	
1. Organization scan/diagnosis ⟶	Opportunity report★
2. Pilot systems analysis	{ Pilot system feasibility report★ Pilot specification report
3. Pilot construction ⟶	Computer purchased or constructed software and hardware.
4. Pilot integration ⟶	Pilot system up, implemented, and accepted by users.
II. *Operational System Phase*	
5. Operational systems analysis ⟶	Operational systems feasibility report★
—system monitoring —requirements analysis —cost benefit analysis	Operational systems specification report
6. Operational system construction	Computer purchased and constructed hardware and software
7. Operational system integration	System up, implemented and accepted by users.

★ Chooser decision point

Figure 6.4. MIS/DP versus EOS design process.

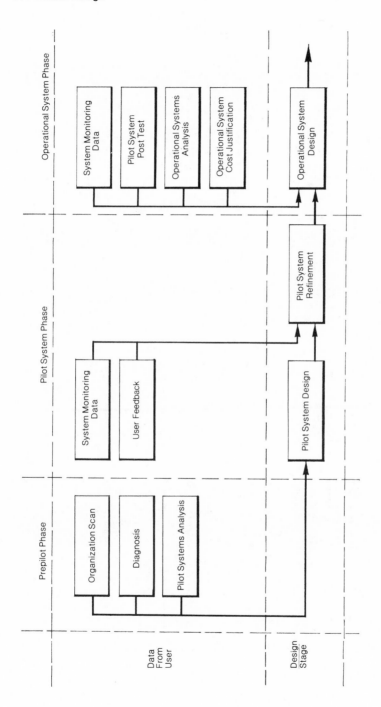

USER DRIVEN DESIGN

Figure 6.5. User-Driven Design.

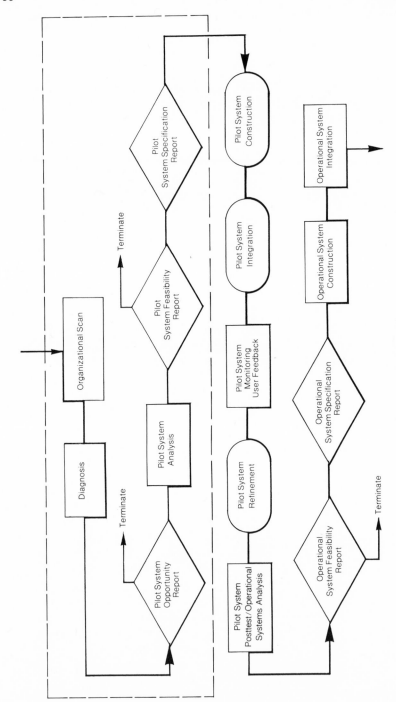

Figure 6.6. Design project flow: prepilot phase.

There are three measurement stages during the prepilot phase.

6.4.1.1. The Organizational Scan

The organization is scanned to acquire the basic information necessary to enable the consultant to discuss with the client the advisability of investigating the opportunities for office systems; formulate an investigation plan; and adopt an agreement with the client regarding work plan, deliverables, and costs.

Typically the organizational scan consists of three types of measurements:

Discussion with appropriate top management are held to obtain a first cut picture of the organization: objectives, current systems, current system plans, organizational history. As well, managers are briefed on key aspects of the topic of office systems and methodology of the consultant team.

Structured interviews are conducted to investigate opportunities relating to communications, information management, administration, decision making, and quality of work life. These interviews are conducted with a sample of all office employees.

Secondary sources, such as organizational charts, planning documents, and corporate objective statements, are obtained to provide objective data and give the consulting team a better overview of the organization.

Information from the organizational scan is used to customize the instruments for the *diagnosis*.

6.4.1.2. The Diagnosis

During this stage it is useful to administer a questionnaire to a sample of key employees. Depending on the organization, this questionnaire has a combination of functions.

One is to help employees define an "improvement" in effectiveness in their organization. Improvement areas are determined through the organizational scan. Typical improvement areas are: communications, human resource utilization, administrative support, information management, time use, employee motivation, and decision making. The questionnaire can also help quantify opportunities for office systems identified in the organizational scan. For example, questions can ask for quantifications of perceived time use in various activities. Such an instrument can also provide attitudinal and demographic data for an initial investigation of levels of user acceptance of EOS; provide base-line preimplementation information to enable pretest–posttest evaluation of the effects of the system; and provide information to enable the customization of the pilot systems analysis instruments.

The output from the organizational scan and diagnosis is contained in some form of *opportunity report*. A typical opportunity report has four sections:

(1) Introduction to Electronic Office Systems: A brief overview of Electronic Office Systems is made.

(2) Opportunities within the Client Organization: Results of the initial investigations within the client organization are presented, summarizing client objectives, opportunities for improvements within problem areas, and user acceptance levels.

(3) Possible Pilot Alternatives: Various high-profile, low-risk, pilot alternatives are outlined and discussed.

(4) What's Next? A plan to identify the most appropriate pilot application is presented, if it is recommended that the investigation proceed. This includes a description of the pilot systems analysis, costs of the next phase of study, and deliverables.

6.4.1.3. The Pilot Systems Analysis

A number of measurement techniques, including questionnaires, logs, and observation, can be used together with appropriate analytical procedures to provide user data for the pilot design and provide presystem base-line data for the pretest–posttest evaluation of the impact of the system.

A *pilot system feasibility report* can be produced and presented for modification and adoption by the client. An example of the outline of a pilot system feasibility report is contained in Figure 6.7.

Once the client has reviewed the feasibility report, a *pilot system specification report* can be drafted. The recipients of this report are the system designer, programmer, and implementor. The purpose of this report is to provide an adequately detailed functional specification to enable purchase of the appropriate hardware and software and the construction of the overall system. As well, the report sets the stage for the "intergration" of the system into the user environment by the implementation team. There will be variation regarding who constructs the system, depending on the arrangement made. Alternatives include in-house systems personnel, the vendor, internal office system consultants, or consultants from a different company. The client has the option of terminating the project at this point. An example of the topics covered by this report is shown in Figure 6.8.

6.4.2. The Pilot System Phase

The pilot system specification report enables the designers and program-

The pilot system feasibility report
1) Summary of opportunities for improvement
2) Summary of pilot alternatives
3) Pilot proposal
   - Configuration
   - functions of the system
   - Size of pilot group
4) Functional description of the pilot
5) Proposed hardware and software description
6) Description of approximate costs and anticipated benefits
   (Costs and anticipated benefits specified in the Pilot System Feasibility Report are estimates only.)
7) What's Next?
   (Outline of the specific steps leading to the pilot system specification report.)
   - Executive briefing and demonstration for some key sub-groups within the proposed pilot group.
   - Final determination of the pilot group must be made at this time.
   - Prepare a draft report covering the system specification. This should include:
   Organization design considerations, Technical specifications, Cost, acquisition plans, and, Possible patterns for future growth of the system.

Figure 6.7. Outline of the pilot system feasibility report.

mers to construct the pilot system. System monitoring data are collected from the outset of the system integration into the user environment. As well, user feedback is obtained through structured interviews, observation of training sessions, and unobtrusive observation of system use. These data are used to refine the system. Refinement ranges from fine tuning to addition, modification, or deletion of applications.

The pilot phase is depicted in Figure 6.9.

6.4.3. The Operational Office System Phase

Once the pilot system has been successfully implemented and has been used for the period stated in the pilot system specification report (usually 6–12 months), various user measures will be taken. Data from these measures form the basis for the extension of the pilot into an operation system, if appropriate.

Four categories of user investigation lead to the operational system design. The output from these is an operational system feasibility report. If the recommendations in this report are adopted the analysts and designers draft and operational system specification report.

(1) System Monitoring Ongoing system accounting data are summarized to give a picture of system use. This includes overall utilization of the system,

1. System Architecture
   1) Technical
      - System components
      - System interfaces
      - Overview of hardware/software
      - Context—relationship to existing systems
   2) Social
      - Procedures
      - Job design
      - Environment
2. Hardware components
   - Configuration/detailed equipment specification
   - System site plan—physical environment for system resources
   - Specification of any hardware construction
3. Software
   - Appropriate packages
   - Detailed specification of software to be written (applications, user interface, interconnections, etc.)
4. Organization Design
   - Workflow, etc., procedures
   - System responsibilities
   - Job design
   - Physical environment (lighting, workstations, etc.)
5. Implementation plan
   - Implementation steps
   - Organization and responsibilities during implementation (user committees, role of consultant, etc.)
   - Management of change (unfreezing, change, consolidation, refreezing)
6. Training
   - Training responsibilities (vendor, client, consultant, individual users)
   - Outline of training program
   - Evaluation plan for training program
7. Evaluation
   - System monitoring, accounting plans
   - Procedure for refining, extending pilot system
   - Posttest evaluation plan

Figure 6.8. Outline of the pilot system specification report.

identification of learning curves, use of various applications, description of the communications network on the system, resource utilization, and other topics.

(2) Pilot System Posttest. The instruments from the original pilot systems analysis are readministered to both the pilot group and any other control or comparison groups which were used. This enables an evaluation of the impact of the system and a comparison between the anticipated system effects and the actual system effects.

(3) Operational Systems Analysis. In addition to data from the pilot

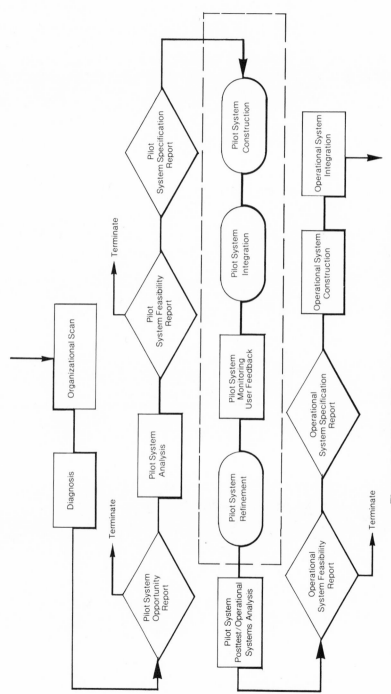

Figure 6.9. Roles in the design process pilot system phase.

system posttest, other investigations are undertaken to enable identification of the proposed operational system and, if adopted, its detailed specification.

(4) Operational System Cost Justification. Data from the system monitoring and posttest showing the actual impact of the system are combined with data from the operational systems analysis to develop cost–benefit equations for the operational system. Because it is to measure system effects within the specified environment, it is also possible to estimate the effects of the operational system with some confidence.

The operational system phase is schematized in Figure 6.10.

6.5. TWO MEASUREMENT THRUSTS

The measures taken have two principal applications—systems analysis and evaluation.

The measures produce data which are used to assess opportunities and requirements for electronic office systems. As explained earlier, the output of these measures are the opportunity report, the pilot feasibility report, and the pilot system specification report. As well, measures are taken, prior to design of the operational system, to determine new requirements and opportunities.

The measures also serve an evaluative function. Measures taken during the prepilot phase are used as pretest measures, to be followed by posttest measures once the pilot has been working for some time. As well, there are a variety of ongoing system monitoring measures to enable evaluation of the system and its use. These measures provided input to the system refinement process.

Any given measure conducted before the pilot design may have either a system analysis or evaluative function, or both.

6.6. ROLES IN THE DESIGN PROCESS

The traditional roles of the systems analyst and programmer are summarized by Tsichritzis in *Datamation*, September 1980. Roles in office systems design are somewhat different because of the additional responsibilities and tasks which must be undertaken.

One is the *office systems architect.* Tsichritzis develops the notion of the "Architect of Systems Design." [14] To him the role of the architect is to oversee the entire design process:

> Architects are expected to understand human needs and develop functional solutions. They are master builders, using parts and tools they understand but seldom produce themselves. . . . Determining what users want is a real art. Defining user

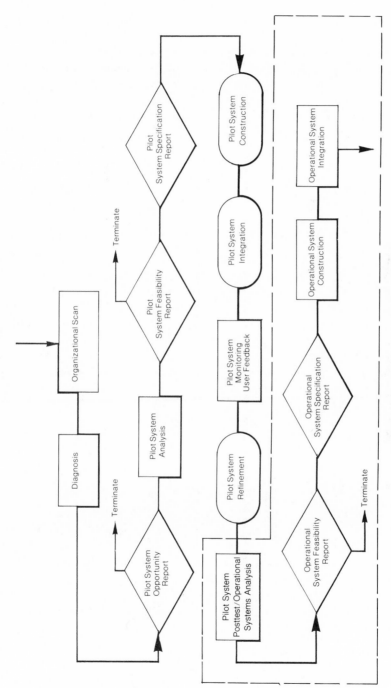

Figure 6.10. Operational system phase.

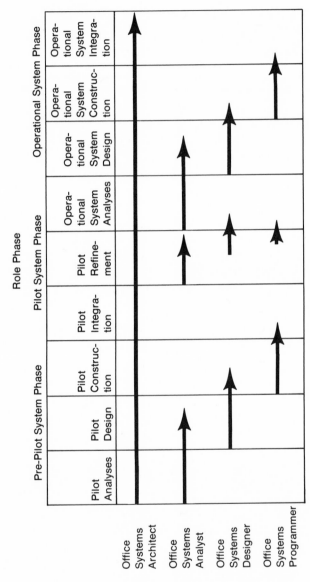

Figure 6.11. Roles in the design process

requirements is important for both large and small systems. In fact, the primary job of the architect of a large system is finding out what the user wants, just as the principal job of the architect of large buildings is to understand people's requirements and come up with a good abstraction of the building.

The notion of the office sytems architect is similar. The tools and experience of User-Driven Design are taken and applied to a given environment to ensure the development of an appropriate and beneficial system. The architect does not actually construct the system, but rather oversees the process of its definition and implementation.

The office system analyst is a measurement expert and change agent. Responsibilities include discussing the methodology with the client; customizing measurement tools to the user environment; conducting the studies, and managing division of labor; education of users as part of the interview process; analyzing and interpreting data; working with the office systems designer in producing the office systems feasibility and specification reports; and planning and conducting ongoing evaluation and posttest follow-up.

The office systems designer works with the analyst and users to develop the functional description and functional specification of the system. On the other hand the designer works with the programmer in ensuring that the system is constructed to specification. The designer also provides the technical expertise to work with the vendor(s) in defining commitments and ensuring that they are met. One of the responsibilities of the designer may be to oversee an ongoing evaluation of current vendor offerings.

The office systems programmer has the usual programmer's role with a difference. As the programmer writes code, perhaps to build an interface between the office system and a corporate data base, there will be a need to interact directly with users as well as the designers. The programmer can present simulations to the user and ask questions such as "How *do* you like this" rather than "How *would* you like this?"

The roles of the various team members at various junctures of the design process are depicted in Figure 6.11.

Chapter 7

Assessing the Organization: Research Design

The great tragedy of science: the slaying of a beautiful hypothesis by an ugly fact.

(Thomas Huxley)

Measurement has two functions. One is the acquisition of initial data to enable an assessment of user requirements and propel the system design. A second is the acquisition of data once a system has been implemented for purposes of evaluation, refinement of the system and its extension, and cost justification.

To do the latter, it is important that the system implementation is situated in the context of a controlled "research design." It is not always possible to do this. In small organizations it may be unfeasible to introduce experimental controls into the evaluation program. In "technology trials" where there is informal experimentation with new technologies, a controlled research design is also usually inappropriate. In some organizations it may be impossible to select a "comparison" or "control" group which is similar to the group which receives the office system.

However, in cases where resources are available and there is a need for an evaluation regarding the impact of a system implementation, it is generally prudent to be as scientific about the matter as possible.

There are a number of types of research designs currently being used to study the impact of integrated office systems.

7.1. RESEARCH DESIGN

The overall research design which is chosen will depend on a number of factors, including the conceptual approach taken, the funds available, characteristics of the population available for study, and so on.

Unfortunately, another factor is the degree of research expertise of those conducting the study. That is, because most studies to date have been conducted by people lacking expertise in research methodology, most "designs" used do not meet the basic requirements for valid research.

The central goal of office automation research can be seen as the measure of how the introduction and use of an advanced office system (independent variables) result in changes in knowledge worker effectiveness, communication, interaction, quality of work life, time use, output, etc. (dependent variables). To do this, a valid causal relationship between an independent and dependent variable must be shown.

There are three necessary conditions to show that a relationship between two variables is causal and that the direction of causation is from A to B.[1] The first is temporal antecedence—a cause must precede an effect in time. A second is that the treatment or treatments must covary with the effect, for if the potential cause and effect are not related the one could not have been the cause of the other. Statistics used for testing covariation and arbitrary criteria have been established for deciding whether there is or is not real covariation in the data (e.g., $p < .05$). A third necessary condition is that there must be no plausible alternative explanations of B other than A. For example, an office system could be introduced into an office and six months later an increase in worker job satisfaction is measured. However, it is possible that the change in job satisfaction was due to a change in management style which occurred coincidently with the introduction of the system. Consequently a measured relationship between the system and QWL would have been spurious.

It is useful to isolate four kinds of validity which can be applied to office system research:

Statistical conclusion validity refers to the validity of conclusions we draw on the basis of statistical evidence about whether a presumed cause and effect covary.

Internal validity refers to the validity of any conclusions we draw about whether a demonstrated statistical relationship implies cause. That is, it is valid to assume that the experimental treatment made a difference in this specific experimental instance.

Construct validity refers to the validity with which cause and effect operations are labeled in theory-relevant or generalizable terms. A measurement has construct validity if it in fact measures the attribute, relationship, or construct being measured.

External validity refers to the validity with which cause and effect relationships can be generalized across persons, settings, and times.[1]

There are a number of design types which could be used for office system research, each having different implications for the validity of the conclusions which can be drawn.

7.1.1. Laboratory Experiments

Subjects are randomly assigned to experimental and control groups in a setting where the researcher can schedule "treatments" and measurements for optimal statistical efficiency and control. Random assignment enables the researcher to achieve maximum preexperimental equivalence of groups. This is called a "true experiment."

Laboratory experiments on office systems conducted to date have had either an ergonometric or social-psychological focus. An example of social-psychological laboratory experiment is Reference 2.[2] As part of an ongoing research project Hiltz, Johnson and Turoff explored the impact of computer conferencing on group problem solving and decision making. The design is shown in Figure 7.1.

Subjects in the different groups were given a problem to solve. Hiltz, Johnson and Turoff examined dependent variables such as the quality of the solution, time to solution, amount of participation by subjects with the discussion, and interaction content (using Bales Interaction Analysis).

The main independent variable was the *communication mode* (face-to-face versus computer conference). The main covariate was how good the group decision had been in earlier trials. The data have not been fully analyzed, but some initial results are reported here to illustrate data from an office automation laboratory experiment. The authors found that the face-to-face groups reached 100% consensus where the computer conference groups reached closer to 90% agreement. Demographic data indicated an explanation—that is, in face-to-face problem solving the women gave in to the men. In another finding, the computer conference groups scored higher on the scale: "the issues involved are completely clear." In yet another finding, the

	Face to Face (FTF)	Computer Conference (CC)
Scientific Problem	4 groups	4 groups
Human Relations Problems	4 groups	4 groups

Figure 7.1. Group problem solving.

face-to-face groups did not differ from the experienced computer conference groups in how satisfied they were with their ability to "exchange opinions."

Laboratory experiments, in general, provide data which can be more easily interpreted than other research designs. In fact all true experiments (in which subjects are randomly assigned to treatment groups) tend to have greater internal validity than other designs. In true experiments the researcher has more control over extraneous variables having to do with characteristics of the groups being measured. Other factors jeopardizing internal validity can also be minimized. In addition, because inferential statistics were developed largely with true experiments in mind, there are more powerful and appropriate statistical tests available for them.

In fact, Hiltz and Turoff note that laboratory experiments using computer conferencing have advantages over face-to-face laboratory studies in problem solving:

> One problem in experimental studies of problem solving groups is the impossibility of completely standardizing "treatments" of groups and conditions for each of many separate trials when the experiments are conducted and administered face-to-face. When used to administer all problems, instructions, etc. automatically, computerized conferencing allows experimenters complete control of certain categories of exogenous factors that have always acted as potentially confounding sources of variation in face-to-face group experiments, such as
>
> a) Variability among several experimenters in their behavior, or even for the same experimenter from, day to day (e.g. how much experimenters smile when delivering instructions to the group or how loudly they talk);
>
> b) Variability in the appearance and behavior of the subjects as it affects the reactions and motivations of other group members. Examples are facial and other nonverbal expressions (smiling, frowing, fidgeting while instructions are being given), appearance (attractive versus unattractive), and verbal mannerisms (stuttering, accent, etc.).
>
> Since the subjects do not see each other and instructions can be delivered over the terminals exactly the same way for each trial, more complete control over all factors other than those that are purposefully being manipulated is possible.[3]

Laboratory experiments, however, have severe limitations for investigation into the effects of office systems, especially at this early stage of research.

A first problem is their *limited scope*. Laboratory experiments cannot probe important aspects of the day-to-day, real-life use of office systems. The laboratory cannot recreate important conditions of a knowledge worker's job. How do these systems improve project tracking? What happens to relationships between supervisors and employees? These are two of myriad questions that require a "live" environment for investigation. Hiltz and Turoff also note that laboratory experiments cannot gain insights into the use of office systems in areas of work such as at home, applications to the disadvantaged, mass media impacts, new employment offerings, and transportation–communication tradeoff.[3]

Lab experiments also have *limited external validity*. The activities, functions and processes of knowledge work in an office are very complex. Laboratory experiments which attempt to select or sample these run a risk of superficially measuring isolated events. The artificial elimination of potentially important covariates can result in the researcher making invalid generalizations of his/her findings to the real world of knowledge work.

A third problem is *the early stage of hypothesis formulation*. While there are a number of possible conceptual approaches to office system measurement, there clearly is no adequate theory of how these systems impact knowledge workers. As a result, it is possible only to formulate very primitive hypotheses to be tested. Laboratory experiments can best be used to test specific and limited factor hypotheses about the interrelationship of variables that form subsets of much more complex sets of variables that determine the actual impacts of these systems. But lacking theoretical foundations, such hypothesis formulation is a risky business. Hiltz and Turoff argue that the conventional wisdom repeated by Shinn, that an investigator should move "from laboratory to the field," does not apply to computer communications systems.[3] That is, rather than developing a theory from controlled laboratory experiments and then seeing if the theory holds in the real world, it is more appropriate to monitor actual system applications in order to generate a theory.

Another problem has to do with *the subjects/respondents*. It is difficult to obtain representative samples of knowledge workers. Few professional or technical workers will spend their time in a laboratory as subjects. Most subjects in psychological and sociological laboratory experiments have been students who can more easily be induced to cooperate with a researcher.

A final problem is posed by *the learning curve*. Clearly one of the most important variables in the impact of office systems is the amount of user experience with the system. It is not possible to bring subjects into the laboratory, turn on their terminals, and measure their communications etc. It takes time to become comfortable with a system, learn it, and get over the learning curve of (self-reported) clumsy and unproductive use. The limited research that has been done shows a threshold of productive use appearing up to 6–8 months after introduction of the system.

7.1.2. True Experiments in Office (Field) Settings

Like true experiments in a laboratory, true experiments in which there is random assignment of respondents to groups can be conducted in a field setting—an office. These "field experiments" have many of the advantages of laboratory experiments and are missing some of the disadvantages. Unfortunately, true experiments in field settings have limited applicability in measuring the impact of advanced office systems.

The major advantage of field experiments designs is that, like laboratory experiments, they can have very high internal validity. That is, in these designs the researcher can be relatively confident that it was the experimental treatment that made a difference, not some other variable. Campbell and Stanley outline eight threats to internal validity.[4]

History refers to the specific events occuring between the first and second measurement in addition to the experimental variable. *Maturation* refers to processes within the respondents operating as a function of the passage of time per se (not specific to the particular events), including growing older, growing more tired, and the like. *Testing* refers the effects of taking a test upon the scores of a second testing. *Instrumentation* refers to changes in the calibration of the measurement instruments. Changes in the observers or scorers may also produce changes in the obtained measurements. *Statistical regression* occurs when groups have been selected on the basis of their extreme scores. *Biases* can result from differential selection of respondents from the comparison groups. Finally, *selection–maturation interaction* effects can be confounded with (i.e., might be mistaken for) the effect of the experimental variable.[4]

In good field experiments these effects can be minimized or eliminated.

As well, some of the problems of laboratory experiments in office system research mentioned earlier do not exist in field experiments:

(1) Scope. Because they can be conducted in real life situations their scope is not as limited. Hiltz and Turoff suggest that the "lab" can be brought to wherever there is a telephone—an economist's office or a slum storefront.[3]

(2) External Validity. The generalizability of the findings of office system research would tend to be greater for research conducted in a live field setting.

(3) Hypothesis Formulation. The importance of specific hypotheses is not as great since the researcher can more easily conduct exploratory research in a field setting.

(4) Subject/Respondents. Once access is gained to the field, the problem of samples which are unrepresentative of classes of knowledge workers can begin to be dealt with.

(5) Learning Curve. An office system can be installed in a field environment for a long enough period of time to enable the respondent to pass required thresholds of use.

However, there are major problems conducting True Experiments in field settings to examine the impact of office systems:

(1) Random Assignment Violates System Utility. The purpose of an office system, regardless of one's conceptual approach, involves the improvement of communications, information access, and the performance of knowledge work or office functions. However, random assignment of persons to participate in an integrated office system, *a priori* ensures that the system will be of minimal utility and value. For example, it is next to useless to randomly select a group of people who have no need to communicate with each other and place them on a office communication system. The primary concern of the researcher is in measuring how these systems meet *genuine needs*, in this case for effective communications. An office communication system which does not include the actual or desired nodes of a communication network will not be used to meet communication needs. Another example: the information retrieval system will be of limited use if it does not incorporate data from functionally related input sources. Incomplete and unrelated budget information, for example, is of little utility.

(2) Random Assignment of Units Violates Trueness of Experiment. In an attempt to avoid the above problem, some researchers may try to randomly assign *organizational units* of related persons to different groups. This is not objectional from a research point of view, as long as the researcher realizes that s/he is likely no longer conducting a true experiment. That is, unless the number of units assigned to each group is very high, it is likely that equivalence of groups has not been achieved. Because of the high costs of office systems it is unlikely that the researcher will be able to sample a large enough number of organizational units to assume equivalence of groups. As a result, the research design will likely have to include a pretest to measure variation between (or among) the treatment groups.

A hypothetical example of a true experiment in an office setting is a pretest–posttest control group design with random selection of organizational units from a large organization. The design could be configured as follow:

$$R \qquad O \qquad X \qquad O$$
$$R \qquad O \qquad \qquad O$$

where R is a random assignment, O is an observation, and X is the treatment.

Forty units are randomly selected from a large organization and then randomly assigned to two groups—control and experimental. The workers in units in the experimental group are each given electronic work stations. Both groups are measured in various ways before the system has been introduced and after it has been used for several months.

Even with this design there are a number of problems, which will become clear in the next section, on quasi-experiments.

7.1.3. Quasi-experiments in Office (Field) Settings

Quasi-experimental designs are useful when it is not feasible to randomly assign subjects to groups. Because of the difficulties in achieving equivalent experimental groups through randomization in office system research, quasiexperiments often provide the most appropriate research designs.

An example of a quasi-experimental design is the OICS Pilot Research conducted at Bell-Northern Research, Toronto.[5] The design was a variant of Design No. 10, outlined in Campbell and Stanley.[4] It is configured as follows:

$$O \qquad X \qquad O$$
$$O \qquad\qquad\quad O$$

where O is an observation and X is the treatment.

Some problems discussed by Cook and Campbell in conducting true experiments in field settings can be adapted to both experimental and quasi-experimental research in office settings:

(1) The Treatment in the No-Treatment Control Group. Numerous unintentional "treatments" can be inadvertently introduced into the control group. For example, just the knowledge that, unlike the experimental group, members of the control group have been denied electronic work stations could become a "resentment treatment." Changes in coworker attitudes, management styles, company policies, content of work, etc. which have come about as a result of the introduction of an office system could become new treatments changing important attributes of the control group.

(2) Treatment Contamination. When persons in the various groups can communicate with each other they may react differently because they know they are being treated differently. For example, in a single treatment-control group design, the treatment group may consider themselves "special" or "privileged" workers because they have been given an office system. Conversely the respondents in the control group may consider themselves "second class citizens." This could affect a range of variables from performance through job satisfaction to attitudes towards technology.

(3) (Treatment) System-Related Refusals to Participate in the Experiment. Persons who have been selected to be part of the office system group may refuse to participate. This could be because of their attitudes towards technology, towards the researchers, and other factors related to the introduction of the system. As a result the experimental group may, through a process of selection, evolve into a unique group with different attributes from the control group(s). One way around this problem is to restrict the population to those who agree *before assignment* to be in any group to which they are assigned.

(4) (Treatment) System-Related Attrition from the Experiment. Previous office system research has indicated that being an "augmented knowledge worker" can be an important factor in someone deciding not to leave their job. Conversely, some people have found it alienating and impossible to use an office system to do their job and have resigned (if the system is poorly designed and introduced, users improperly trained, etc.). Because experimental treatments differ in their attractiveness to office workers the number and nature of persons remaining in the experiment or quasi-experiment may differ between conditions if the experiment last very long.

(5) Respondent Knowledge of Hypotheses. It must be explained to subjects in the experimental group how the system can help them in their jobs. The "treatment" is not just a piece of hardware, but an elaborate training program on how to use the system to do one's job more effectively. Because of this, respondents cannot help but become aware of the kinds of hypotheses which are being examined. This problem also applies to the control group(s) if the researchers attempt to motivate control respondents (to carefully complete questionnaires or logs) by explaining the importance or significance of the research project.[1]

7.1.4. Non-experimental Designs

Most research conducted to date on the impact of office systems falls into a category which can be described as a *nonexperimental design*. While such designs may be useful in exploratory research to aid in hypothesis formulation, they usually are not adequate to permit testing of hypotheses.

(1) The Treatment Group Posttest Only Design. This is the most frequently used design in office system research. It is sometimes called the "case study" or "user survey." This design involves making observations on persons who have used or are using some form of office system. There are no pretest observations of persons before they come on the system and there is no control group of persons who do not receive access to the system. Because of this, none of the factors jeopardizing internal validity can be eliminated. The design can be eliminated. The design can be diagramed as follows:

$$X \qquad\qquad O$$

where O is an observation and X is the treatment.

Examples of this design in office system research are Bair,[6] Conrath and Bair,[7] and Bair's[8] evaluation of the Augmented Workshop, Edward's[8] survery of users of the NLS system, and Vallee et al.'s[9] examination of use of the FORUM system.

(2) The One Group Pretest–Posttest Design. This design is frequently used in organizational research. The pretest observations of a single group

are recorded. They can receive an experimental treatment, after which post-test observations are made. This design can be diagrammed as follows:

$$O \qquad X \qquad O$$

where O is an observation and X is the treatment.

A key threat to the internal validity of studies using this design is *history*. That is, any posttest changes in knowledge worker effectiveness, job satisfaction, etc. could be the result of events occurring between the pre and posttest in addition to the introduction and use of the system. Because of this problem, the main value of such design is to aid in formulating hypotheses.

(3) Posttest Only Design. Sometimes office system research will be *ex post facto*. That is, the system is implemented before the researcher knows about it, or can prepare for it. Because no pretest has been conducted, any posttest differences between the groups can be attributed either to the treatment effect or to *selection* differences between the nonequivalent groups. This design can be diagramed as follows:

$$X \qquad O$$
$$O$$

where O is an observation and X is the treatment.

Like other nonexperimental designs, this design is useful in hypothesis formulation. Modifications to the design can render some of the data interpretable.[1]

7.2. ACTION RESEARCH

Action research (AR) goes back to the 1940s and Kurt Lewin's writing on understanding minority problems.[11] Papanek discusses the genesis of Lewin's thinking on the matter.[12] One landmark was the Connecticut inter-group relations workshop of 1946 in which Lewin invited the participants to join research staff in the evening feedback sessions. The successful innovation convinced Lewin that "we should consider action, research and training as a triangle that should be kept together for the sake of any of its corners."[10] Lewin held the view that in order to gain insight into a process it is best to generate a change and then observe its variable effects.

Contemporary action research is primarily a methodology for diagnosing requirements for, effecting, and evaluating organizational change. The goal is to have action-oriented "hardhats" who are interested in solutions to specific problems, working along with, or as, research-oriented "eggheads" who are concerned with findings of theoretical relevance. Together they can

create new understandings, unavailable to either one—as Brown calls them—
"hard-boiled eggs." [13]

Typically AR is part of an organizational development (OD) program.
Organizational Development has become a popular approach to solving a
myriad of problems besetting organizations. These programs begin with a
diagnosis and continue with the ongoing collection and analysis of data. Such
diagnostic activities have two functions: to understand the current state of
things and to know the effects of consequences of actions. [14] Consequently
action research may seem ideally suited for determining needs for and implementing and evaluating integrated office systems. While action research does
have a number of contributions to make, it also has limitations as a comprehensive approach to office system assessment.

Action research has a number of underlying themes which are directly
applicable. It seeks to *involve* individuals in defining problems, identifying
needs, solving problems, laying out plans, and implementing decisions. It
views the consultant as a *facilitator* for organizational diagnosis and change,
rather than a solitary architect. The goal is not simply *research*, but organizational planning and the execution of change. It emphasizes the *evaluation* of
change programs. Its approach to understanding organizations is to create
and then evaluate a change, rather than to simply study an organization at
one point in time.

Its principal components are an action research group composed of
members of the organization and an action researcher or consultant skilled in
directing group decision making and subsequent action. [15]

Figure 7.2 outlines one view of the AR process. For other approaches see
French and Bell [16] and Cunningham [15]

In the first step a key individual in the client organization identifies a
problem(s) which requires some kind of change or action. Examples are high
employee turnover, lack of team cooperation, unresponsiveness of the organization, etc. Sometimes awareness of the need for change comes from a consultant or other interested person, in which case full commitment from top
management must be secured in order to proceed. A second step can occur in
which the client discusses the problem with a consultant skilled in AR. The
two become aware of each other's expectations, objectives, responsibilities,
resources, etc., and agree on a plan to proceed.

Next an action research group is established. Ideally membership in the
group would include all those in the client organization who are in a posistion
to initiate action. [15] Usually this is not feasible. Membership in the group
should be voluntary so initial discussions are held with likely candidates to
involve them and explain the concept. The goals of the AR group are established collectively by the members.

The preassessment activities of Step 4 can include such activities as

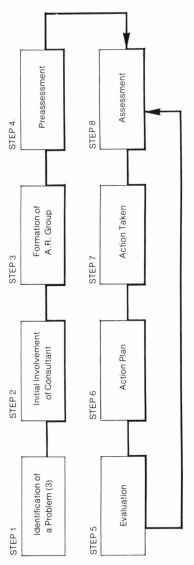

Figure 7.2. The action research process.

detailed problem and objective definition, construction of measurement tools, and formulation of a detailed work plan.

The next step involves data gathering using techniques such as questionnaires, interviews, observation, and examination of secondary source data. The focus is not on rigorous scientific measurement, but more simply on getting a good picture of the organization and a better diagnosis of the problem. The data are analyzed and jointly interpreted by the consultant and other members of the AR group.

An action plan is then collectively formulated by the AR group and presented to other stakeholders for approval (i.e., top management, unions, other affected employees, etc.)

The action plan may be first implemented in a pilot or trial form. Action may be procedural changes, an improvement in employee compensation and benefits, individual or group training, policy changes, etc. Refinements to the plan, resulting from the experience of a trial action, can be made before the entire plan is implemented.

The final step of the first AR cycle is to evaluate the efficacy of the action to determine the validity of the original problem definition, hypotheses, and action plan. The results of this evaluation feed into new problem identification and the development of new research tools to assess the organization, define new plans, which in turn are reevaluated, and so on. This cycle of rediagnosis, plan formulation, action, and evaluation continues and becomes an ongoing part of the organization's developmental process.

There have been many diverse and varied applications of action research. Lind has discussed its application to community planning.[17] Moore explains how AR can be applied to improving teamwork.[18] One of the most common uses is the diagnosis of training and development needs.[19] Kirkhart and Gardner have presented the results of a symposium on OD in public administration where AR was used to diagnose and treat a variety of problems.[20] Action research has been used widely to identify and solve intergroup social problems.[21] One of the most common applications is the diagnosis of job satisfaction and the prediction of the impact of OD programs on the quality of work life.[22] Cunningham describes an AR approach to decision making, where the goal is to enable decision makers to use AR in their organizational planning.[25] Action research has been used for applications as diverse as the improvement of safety, job satisfaction, and performance of coal miners.[23]

7.2.1. Limitations of AR for Office System Design

Action research obviously is limited as a comprehensive approach to measurement for integrated office systems. It may be useful for diagnosing problems within organizations and creating a climate for organizational change, but it lacks both the scope and specificity for the design of complex office systems. Tools and methods from the other assessment disciplines identified in Figure 7.1, along with new approaches germane to office systems in particular are required to complete the picture.

Beyond this there is an additional category of problems. Cunningham writes that

> the underlying assumption of action research is that organizational members are better able, than anyone else, to define their problems and propose solutions for them because they are more acquainted with their own situations.[15]

This may be true in the general sense, but it is only partially true when speaking of office systems. Most individuals in organizations have limited insight into how the new generation of office systems can help them. As a result, any measurement methodology must probe beneath the subjective views and opinions of the potential users and objectively assess the office, its activities, processes, etc., with the goal of identifying complex opportunities for improvement. To do this, there is a need for detailed measures which are as objective as possible, using a scientific measurement methodology.

There has been some discussion as to the scientific merits of action research. In the most comprehensive defense of AR, Susman and Evered argue that the criteria of positivist science are inapproapriate to judge the scientific merit of AR. They argue that there is a crisis in the field of organizational science. The main symptom of this is that as research methods become more sophisticated they have also become increasingly less useful for solving the practical problems that members of organizations face. Although action research is found to be deficient when judged against the criteria of positive science, it is found to be superior in terms of its ability to generate the knowledge required for understanding and managing the affairs of organizations:

> ...in action research, the ultimate sanction is in the preceived functionality of chosen actions to produce desirable consequences for an organization. Action research constitutes a kind of science with a different epistemology that produces a different kind of knowledge, a knowledge which is contingent on the particular situation, and which develops the capacity of members of the organization to solve their own problems.[24]

A nice thought. Unfortunately, in order to design an integrated office system, data are required which go beyond the methodological bounds of action research. Objective and detailed information is needed regarding how people spend their time; what the human communication network looks like; what the flow of information is; how current technologies are being used, etc. These data are needed for purposes of detailed technical design, cost–benefit analyses, posttest evaluation of the system, identification and prediction of user acceptance levels, and generalization to broader populations, to name a few. While it is important to involve users in every way, as encouraged in AR, it is also necessary to draw on the important acquisitions in behavioral and social sciences, to provide valid and reliable data.

Detractors of the AR approach have noted that many studies labeled "action research" do not even correspond to Lewin's original conception since they involve very little actual measurement:

> They seem to have opted for the label action research to be scientifically respectable despite the fact that they are 95 percent action and 5 percent measurement. . . . Although assessment measures require some additional work, there is every reason to believe that they will be worth the effort, for they can make the evaluation of change a quantitative-data-based art. All too often in "action research" the evaluation is based on casually gathered unquantitative data and the research reports end up as nothing more than case studies in change.[25]

Chapter 8

Assessing the Organization: Measurement

Skinner's Constant: That quantity which, when multiplied by, divided to, added to, or subtracted from the answer you get, gives you the answer you should have gotten.

One of the most important tasks in investigating the organization and user requirements is to develop useful, valid, and reliable measures. On the one hand it is important that the organization does not become bogged down in a costly quagmire of overdetailed and unnecessary measures. On the other hand, without adequate attention to the issue of measurement, it is simply not possible to drive an appropriate design, implement, evaluate, and extend a system effectively. The failure literature points inescapably to this conclusion. There are few known cases of "overmeasurement," where implementors concluded that they had erred on the side of too carefully investigating their needs and evaluating system impacts. The tragedies have fallen on the other side, where systems did not correspond to user needs, could not be cost justified, did not adequately take into account the user and organizational climate, and were not refined when required, etc.

8.1. OBJECTIVES OF MEASUREMENT

Bair outlines four levels of measurement[1]:

Assessment of the *equipment level* includes measures such as response time, error rate, costs per operations or unit time, reliability, and keystrokes per operation. Measures taken at the *user level* include time use, learning rate, lines of text per unit time, user fatigue, user error rate, individual attitudes towards the system, number of messages created, and output per user hour.

Example measures at the *organizational level* are end-product turnaround, end-product completion rate, human communication network, time use (aggregated), objective attainment, procedure streamlining, error rate, organizational climate, operating costs, and decision turnaround time.

Relevant measures at the *level of the economy* include the unemployment rate, global productivity, social indicators, investment climate, interest rates, and measures indicating the state of various markets.

It is important to be cognizant of these different levels when constructing a measurement methodology. All of them are relevant to office systems, although in any given implementation not all may be examined.

The two measurement thrusts in any system implementation—needs analysis and evaluation—can be broken down into more detailed measurement objectives which should always be addressed. Table 8.1 shows the objectives of measurement activity at prepilot, pilot, and postpilot phases.

The process of User-Driven Design, outlined in Chapter 6, contains a number of *types or categories* of measurement instruments. These include tools for conducting an organizational scan, a diagnosis, and a systems analysis, along with tools for system monitoring, cost–benefit analysis, and office systems research. These categories of instruments are not mutually exclusive but overlap. Measurement with a given instrument may provide data for several different measurement functions. For example, data from a diary on

Table 8.1. Objectives of Measurement

Prepilot phase (before implementation)	Pilot phase (after implementation)	Operational phase (postpilot evolution and extension)
Identification of pilot (and comparison) Group(s)	Monitoring system use	Identification of users for expansion to operational system
		Evolution of system impact
Prediction of user acceptance	Assessment of user acceptance	Assessment of user acceptance
Determination of user requirements and pilot system attributes	Determination of required system enhancements, refinement, and additional training needs	Determination of user requirements and operational system attributes
Contribute to user education and climate for change		Contribute to user education and climate for change

time use may be useful for cost-justifying a system, determining user needs for an extended system, and adding to the normative data base for office systems research. The relationship of these categories of tools is shown in Figure 8.1.

Another way of looking at the question of measurement is to compare the objectives of measurement for *system customization* to a given user environment, versus *product design* activities conducted by the vendors of office system hardware and software. Measurement has an important role to play for both. Office system *products* can have a User-Driven Design as well as office system customization for users in a specific organizational setting. This is illustrated in Figure 8.2.

8.2. MEASUREMENT INSTRUMENTS

There are a variety of measurement instruments which can be developed and used. These can be grouped into ten categories.

(1) Survey Questionnaire. The main application of survey research is to assess respondent attitudes along appropriate variables. It is also useful in soliciting demographic and other self-reported data. Questionnaires can be administered through interviews, or self-administered by the respondent. Sophisticated scaling procedures and other statistical techniques are available to analyze questionnaire data and help assess their reliability and validity. Questionnaire data are useful, for example, when attitudinal data are desired; or to supplement behavioral data; or when no behavioral measures are possible.

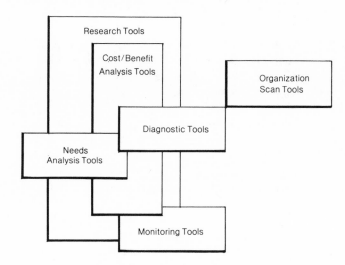

Figure 8.1. Measurement tools.

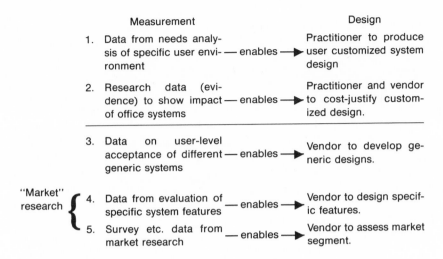

Figure 8.2. Measurement, system customization, and product design.

Different types of survey techniques can be employed.

Interviews can be structured or unstructured. Structured interviews can use a questionnaire to guide the interviewer. Prompt cards can be shown to the interviewee. This technique is particularly useful when direct contact with the respondent is desired but when there is adequate a priori knowledge about the situation to be able to structure an interview. Interactive dialogue between researcher and respondent may uncover a greater richness of data than with a self-completed questionnaire. Unstructured interviews can be used similarly and, through dialogue, contribute to setting a climate for change. Aggregation and analysis of data is very difficult using this technique. Both kinds of interviews are useful in situations like the initial organizational scan or during evaluation of a system when little is known about the respondent's views and in-depth probing is required. However, interviewing is a time-consuming and costly activity.

Self-completed questionnaires can contain closed- or open-ended questions. Typical closed-ended questions use response categories, Likert scales, and semantic differentials. Open-ended question are usually used to solicit additional information in a somewhat unknown situation, but where interviewing is inappropriate (perhaps for reasons of costs).

(2) Diary or Log. The respondent is provided with an instrument to aid in logging some behavior or event. Typical examples are communications logs (to record all communications involving the respondent) and time-use diaries (to keep track of how the respondent spends his or her time). While such instruments can be more useful than questionnaires in providing data of

this kind ("how much of your time do you spend doing such and such?"), they also pose problems. They are very dependent on respondent cooperation. It is often difficult to select mutually exclusive and/or meaningful categories. They are of little help in understanding new dimensions. The validity of log responses can be examined by comparing them to behavioral data, such as those derived from system accounting or observation.

(3) Activity Sampling. Subject activity is observed at random intervals by the researcher. This technique enables a fairly objective measure of behavior. It also puts the investigator in the middle of the user organization for a period of time, during which a fuller understanding of, and better relationship with, the user is likely to be acquired. However, the kinds of activities and their corresponding functions which can be sampled by an observer are somewhat limited. The technique also requires considerable resources.

(4) Network Analysis. This category includes a series of techniques to capture the interaction and relationships between people and groups in the office. Various relationships can be identified, including nodes, links, networks, stars, clusters, liaisons, bridges, and cliques. Output measures include intensity of a relationship, reciprocity, transactional content, size, connectedness, reachability, interrank membership, and visibility. There are different types of network analyses, including positional analysis, decisional analysis, and interactional analysis.[2]

One of the most useful for office systems assessment is the interactional analysis technique. Usually the respondent is asked to indicate with whom they communicate in a "typical" specified time period. Other data regarding such typical communications can also be recorded. The technique developed under the auspices of the International Communication Association can be linked to very sophisticated analytical techniques. With these techniques it is possible to measure, weigh, and graph the communication network in a given organization or organizational unit. The technique is, however, subjective, although similar analyses can be performed using diary or log data.

(5) Content Analysis. This is a broad category to include a variety of instruments and techniques which seek to quantify the content of given material, communications, etc. Interaction techniques such as Bales' Interaction Process Analysis attempt to describe the process of face-to-face interaction.[3] Numerous classification schemes exist to examine the content of written work. An example application of this technique occurs when dictation and text production tools increase the amount of text produced per user. Content analysis can be used to ascertain if the increase in material produced is due to the capture of previously uncaptured work, or due to the generation of unuseful (i.e., garbage) text.

(6) Observation. Various techniques can be used to observe the behavior of subjects. Some of these overlap with other measurement techniques. *Un-*

structured observation can be used to study the most complex and least understood aspects of a knowledge worker's job and behavior. However, because it is nonsystematic and highly dependent on the subjectivity of the observer it is likely to produce unreliable data. *Structured* observation helps avoid some of these problems. *Unobtrusive* observation is used when it is important that the subjects are unaware that they are being observed. *Participant* observation can be used to enable the researcher to get a better understanding of the factors involved in a highly complex situation. In this case there is a danger that the participant observer may contaminate existing behaviors and attitudes.

(7) Critical Incidents. This technique requires the respondents to indicate and somehow quantify incidents which are judged "critical" according to some given criteria. The technique is useful in studying, in some depth, aspects of a given environment, job, behavior, etc. The results are highly descriptive and can best be used to supplement "harder" data or to aid in postulating hypotheses, etc.

(8) Secondary Sources. These can be extremely useful as they can often be more objective than other data sources. Examples of secondary sources in the office milieu are: archives, budget information, organizational histories, and personnel information. End-product quantification or description can be used to evaluate the products of office work. The problems in proving that a system implementation has caused a change in an end-product are immense.

(9) Tests. These can be administered to subjects to measure constructs such as proficiency, competence, and speed of learning. Tests can be used to enable grouping of respondents and to measure degree of knowledge of the system, etc. Caution must be exercised to prevent the testing itself from becoming an uncontrolled variable.

In one interesting use of tests, users who had been generating very little traffic on an electronic messaging system were given a proficiency text. It was found that most of them did not know how to use the "send mail" command. Once they had been taught this command, usage increased quite dramatically!

(10) System Accounting/Monitoring. This is one of the most objective and potentially fruitful measurement techniques. It enables the researcher to measure, with complete objectivity, respondent behavior on the system. Among other things, the respondent's actual behavior on the system can be compared to his/her perceived behavior (as measured by other instruments) to validate more subjective instruments.

Typical measures generated from the accounting tools of an integrated office system include log-in time, number of commands used, amount of text generated, number of messages sent, amount of disk space used, preferred applications, and communications patterns. Telephone call detail recording

(CDR) can be used to collect presystem data regarding telephone use, and pretest–posttest data regarding the impact of a system on telephone activities and time use in general.

There are, however, a number of important ethical and privacy issues raised by this technique. It is possible to monitor very closely someone's activities using system accounting tools. To avoid invading privacy and creating possible user hostility, it is important to have a contract with the user regarding exactly what will and will not be monitored.

The ten categories of instruments, their uses, advantages, disadvantages, and major applications are summarized in Figure 8.3.

8.3. WHAT IS A GOOD MEASUREMENT INSTRUMENT?

Volumes have been written about the characteristics of good measurement. Some of these, as directly applicable to office system measurement are as follows:

(1) Validity. In general, a measurement instrument or item has validity if it successfully measures what you are trying to measure. A negative example is self-estimate, time-use studies. Respondents are asked what percentage of their time they spend in various activities. Usually the investigator is attempting to measure how people spend their time, but the instrument used is not valid. Rather than giving valid information regarding time use it more likely gives information regarding how the respondent perceives their time *should* be spent, or what the short- to medium-term *recall* capacities of the respondent are.

There are many different kinds of validity over which there has been a raging debate for some time. The different types relate largely to different validation methods. Some of these are relevant to office system measurement.

Construct validity refers to the ability of an instrument to measure some underlying attribute or construct which is not operationally defined.[4] QWL is a such a construct. On a test of the construct "computer literacy," system analysts should perform better than insurance brokers if the instrument had construct validity. Or on a scale that purports to measure user acceptance of office systems, a group of high-use workers should score higher than a group of workers who do not use the same system.

Convergent validity, is the degree to which different measurement instruments designed to measure the same construct produce similar results when used in the same situation.[4] Valid observation techniques and activities diaries should produce correlated results when applied to the same group of office workers.

Discriminate validity is the extent to which measurement instruments

	Can Measure	Major Advantages	Major Disadvantages	Example Useful Applications
1. Survey Questionnaire	—Attitudes —Demographic data —Other self-reported data	—Easy to administer, efficient —Quick —Sophisticated analyses possible	—Subjectivity of data	—When behavioral measures not possible —To supplement behavioral measures
2. Diary Log	—Communications —Time use —Attitudes	—Can provide detailed and valid data	—Dependent on respondent cooperation —Time consuming to complete —Costly to analyze	—When cooperation is assured and detailed data required
3. Activity Sampling	—Activities of office	—Measures behavior —Not subjective	—Difficult to map against function of activity	—When resources permit
4. Network Analysis	—Communication network	—Easy to administer —Quick —Can provide very useful data	—Complex analyses required	—When communications approach taken
5. Content Analyses	—Content of material interactions, etc.	—Can provide objective data	—Time consuming analysis	—Group dynamics —Content of increased output

6. Observation	—Behavior	—Can probe new dimensions of situations, jobs, etc.	—Subjective, dependent on observer —Danger of unreliability, invalidity	—In complex, unknown situation —For least understood aspects of office
7. Critical Incidents	—In depth aspects of jobs, activities, functions	—Enables deep investigation	—Limited in scope —Requires full commitment	—Content of jobs —Group Dynamics
8. Secondary Sources	—Financial, Admin., organizational, personnel info, etc.	—Can be very objective —Necessary supplement to behavioral and attitudinal data	—Data frequently unavilable, incomplete or inadequate	—Archives, budget info., organizational histories
9. Tests	—Constructs such as proficiency, competence, speed of learning	—Useful to pre/post measures	—Danger of respondent alienation	—Study acquisition of system proficiency
10. System Accounting	—Use of system	—Can be unobtrusive —Very objective, valid and reliable data	—Accounting software —Cooperation/ethical issues	—Learning curve, communication networks, info. retrieval time use

Figure 8.3. Types of measurement instruments.

designed to measure different constructs produce different results in situations which are judged to be different.[5]

Face validity refers to whether a measure has the appearance of measuring what it purports to measure. Questionnaire items examining communications relationships should appear to be measuring these, not something else like "loyalty to the boss." Measures with face validity may or may not actually be valid.

Internal validity, external validity, and statistical conclusion validity were discussed in Chapter 7.

(2) Reliability. This refers to the consistency, stability, and dependency with which the measurement instrument collects similar information under similar conditions. Measures designed to determine quality of work life, for example, should correlate with each other, correlate upon repeated testings in the same situations, and correlate with the same measures taken in a similar situation.

(3) Usefulness. All fancy methodological footwork aside, the measurement instruments should provide data which can be usefully applied to the problem at hand. The practical utility of an instrument in achieving the basic and applied organizational objectives is sometimes called *extrinsic validity.*[6] The key to this is a well-planned measurement strategy based on a clear conceptual framework and measurement objectives. The measures should address salient domains and collect data which are interpretable.

(4) Sensitivity. The instrument should produce variability when used in a range of different situations. If it is designed to detect problems in the decision-making process, it should register high scores in situations where there are problems and lower scores in situations where there are not.

(5) Friendliness. As the precursors of an office system implementation, measurement instruments should be "friendly." They should have variety and be interesting to complete. They should be as unobtrusive as possible, not excessively time consuming or disruptive. Often, long questionnaires or time-use diaries appear unfriendly to the respondents, although it may be necessary to use them. The instruments should individually and in their totality be as nonthreatening as possible. They should avoid being provocative or unnecessarily raising sensitive issues. It is usually important to collect information regarding, for example, superior–subordinate relationships, the political environment, and employee compensation, but care must be exercised in how this is done. Computerese jargon should be avoided. Hopefully the office system implemented will have a plain English (or other human language) interface. The same should be expected from the measurement battery.

(6) Customizability. As instruments will likely be reused in different organizational contexts they should be customizable. The flexibility of the

investigator and his/her instruments will determine the validity of the data. Instruments will also be used over time, and should be modified as conditions warrant. At the same time, efforts should be made to preserve as many common data elements as is feasible to enable pre–post analysis, comparisons between different organizational groupings, and the construction of a normative data base.

(7) Controlled Reactivity. This is the extent to which the use of an instrument changes what it is trying to measure.[2] Usually in the social sciences this is an undesired effect which should be eliminated in the interests of "science." However, in office systems investigation, one of the goals of the measurement exercise is precisely to change the respondent's attitudes and behavior and to create the climate and organizational preconditions for change. Therefore controlled reactivity should be built into the measurement instruments. For example, one of the most important by-products of a good interview is respondent support and enthusiasm for the office system program. On the other hand, it is important to identify such "contaminating" variables when conducting pre–post evaluations of a system. For example, "to what degree were changes in productivity due to artifacts of the measurement process, or more broadly to the Hawthorne effect, (i.e., when the act of measurement itself changes the behavior or attitudes of subjects) and to what degree were they due to the provision of powerful office system tools?"

(8) Analyzability. A common problem in office system measurement is the collection of reams of data which do not easily lend themselves to aggregation, synthesization, and analysis. This is particularly true of interview or questionnaire data from open-ended questions, or the massive amounts of data which can be generated in observation, diaries, or system accounting and monitoring. An analysis strategy should be formulated as the instruments are constructed rather than after administration.

(9) Cost-benefit Measures. The amount of effort expended in the measurement undertaking should be considered as part of the "cost" side of any cost–benefit equation for the system as a whole. Doing this helps ensure that the resources used in measurement will not be extravagantly inappropriate. Some techniques are more costly and more difficult to administer than others. Professional data collection activities, such as interviewing, observation, critical incident group sessions, etc., are expensive and should be used only when necessary.

8.3.1. Work Needed in Developing New Measures

The synthesis of measurement tools from traditional systems analysis, organizational assessment, field research, action research, records management, QWL diagnosis, and operations research, and their application to office system design is in its formative stages. Work is needed in a number of areas. The first which requires improvement is the development of conceptual frameworks for office system measurement. The frameworks outlined in Chapter 3 are a first step in defining approaches to what should be measured to enable user-driven office design. However, the formulation of an acceptable framework is an ongoing process which will evolve as systems and organizations themselves evolve.

A second area is new instrument development. Traditional measurement tools do not suffice, and major work remains to be done developing, testing, and refining tools. This involves the adaption of existing tools from the batteries of the seven assessment disciplines listed above. It also involves the ongoing generation of new tools. This will occur as individual organizations develop measurement methods for themselves and also as researchers and consultants build generic tools that can be customized to individual situations.

The capacity to translate measurement data into *design conclusions* must be strengthened. There is still a considerable gap between the measurement and assessment professionals who have expertise in understanding organizations and the system designers who have expertise in the technical design of systems. To bridge this gap, each must broaden their horizons and skill set. This book is intended to contribute to that process.

Existing and new tools must be made more available. Lawler, Nadler, and Camman make this point regarding organizational assessment in general.[5] Tools must be disseminated both beyond the scientific community and also between user organizations. Designers and implementors have a lot to learn from each other's experience. Unfortunately many researchers and practitioners are protective of their tools in a way that undermines all of us.

There is considerable work to be done improving analytical techniques. To date there has been strikingly primitive analysis of data from office system research. This, in and of itself, is not a problem as most data collected to date are of such questionable reliability and validity that extensive analysis would be both unwarranted and, likely, misleading. However, it is possible to apply analytical procedures currently used in the behavioral sciences to office system data. Work is required to improve the sophistication of these techniques as they apply to the office systems domain.

8.4. ANALYTICAL PROCEDURES FOR DATA

Powerful analytical tools can transform reams of assessment data into *information* which can enable an effective systems design. Within any large organization there are likely to be individuals with expertise in the analysis of data. These people should have a role to play in the design and implementation of the new office systems. An example of this was the work done in the early 1980s at Bell Northern Research. A variety of statistical procedures were used to help the investigators assess user requirements and evaluate the impact of an integrated office system on clerical, professional, and managerial personnel. These included descriptive statistics such as frequency distributions, measures of central tendency (e.g., mean, median, mode), measures of dispersion (e.g., variance, standard error), etc. Univariate inferential statistics such as chi-square, t-test, analysis of variance, correlation, analysis of covariance, etc., were also used. In addition, work was done using multivariate inferential statistics such as multiple regression, multivariate analysis of variance, discriminate analysis, canonical correlation, and factor analysis along with scaling procedures such as Likert and Guttman scales.

There are a number of computer programs and statistical "packages" currently available to aid in analyzing data of this character. One of the most popular and easy to use in SPSS (Statistical Package for the Social Sciences). This is the most widely used package for analyzing data in the behavioral sciences and has been used extensively for office systems investigation. It is useful for a number of statistical applications.[7] Others include SAS, the Interactive Statistics Package (which runs on the UNIX operating system), and OSIRIS. As well, there are specialized programs that have been developed to analyze data from specific instruments used in assessment. One important example is network analysis programs, which are used for analyzing communications data. Such programs have been developed by the International Communications Association, the University of Waterloo, Simon Fraser University, and Bell-Northern Research.[8–10] As well there are end user programming languages which can be used to easily construct analytical packages. A good example is the well-known language APL. Using matrix algebra and APL a number of simple procedures or sensitive multivariate analyses can be performed.

Chapter 9

Assessing the Organization: System Design

Definition of traditional office systems design: elegant (or sometimes not-so-elegant) solutions in search of a problem.

What kinds of measures can be taken to collect the data necessary to have a *user-driven* rather than a *technology-driven* office systems design?

This chapter outlines some guidelines on how to assess system requirements over the three phases outlined in Chapter 6: Organizational Scan, Diagnosis, and Pilot Systems Analysis.

There is no "best way" of determining user requirements for all organizations. Just as the office system will be customized to the user organization, there will be changes made to any design methodology to ensure the collection of data that are pertinent and useful. Upon entering the organization to be investigated, the initial objective of the team are to formulate a conceptual framework, measurement objectives, research design, and measurement strategy. This is done through initial discussions with the client and the intitial scanning of the organization.

Based on an appropriate assessment approach, it should be possible to fulfill the other objectives of the process. These are, first, selection of the optimal pilot group, along with an appropriate comparison group. Second is determination of the system, including the technical components (hardware, software), the social components (job design, procedures, organizational change), and any changes to the environment. Third is development of an implementation strategy that takes into account user acceptance levels, training needs, the political climate, and so on.

The following is not intended to provide a "cookbook." Rather, some lessons regarding application of office data to systems design are presented.

9.1. THE ORGANIZATIONAL SCAN

As explained in Chapter 6, the office investigation begins with an organizational scan, designed to obtain client agreement and involvement in a plan to further assess the organization. An appropriate measurement strategy is built during this stage and should contain all the components discussed in previous chapters. Initial discussions with the client should enable the construction of a structured interview questionnaire. A sampling of individuals at all levels of the organization should be taken, making sure that all important stakeholder groups have representative interviews. Examples are managers, professionals, secretaries, clerical employees, unions, employee associations, and persons in key functions such as data processing, personnel, finance, and marketing. The content of this instrument will vary from situation to situation, and in general, a number of areas of concern should be covered.

Respondents' views of the objectives of the organization, their group, and their own personal objectives must be identified. This includes the organizational structure as it is relevant to their area of activity, along with where the various work groups are physically located.

What are the indicators of group performance? How does the respondent know when she/he or his/her group is doing well? How is this related to the reward system? What are the key products of the group/organization? What does the respondent produce? What are the *procedures* which are undertaken to produce these products? Who are the key individuals working on these products?

The communications process should be given an initial scan. It is important to get a picture of telephone use, the amount of time spent in meetings, etc. With whom does the respondent communicate? Where are these people located? What perceived communications problems are there? What are the respondent's attitudes towards the communications process?

Information handling should be probed. The goal here is to identify general areas for further investigation regarding the capture, storage, processing, and access of information. Does the respondent receive the information she/he requires? What about accuracy, timeliness, completeness, and format?

An organizational scan can also review decision making. What are the important decisions which the respondent makes during a typical week? Are the tools and information available to exercise good judgment?

Administrative support in the office is another topic for scanning. An initial picture is required. Areas to cover include typing, photocopying, filing, and administrative form completion. Are professionals and managers spending time in appropriate administrative activities?

An overview of jobs and the physical environment is useful. Quality of Work Life (QWL) is a sensitive issue and may be best handled informally. What are employee attitudes towards the organization, each other, and their jobs? Attitudes towards the office environment can be solicited and linked to simple observation of the office.

It is also useful to solicit opinions regarding who should be on the study team. The team should include key opinion leaders, those with expertise in organizational assessment, those with a special interest in the area of office systems, and those from key stakeholder groups. Finally, information and opinions should be solicited from various stakeholder functions and groups. For example, individual from the computer facility should be queried regarding current computer facilities, as should those from the communications department or from administrative services. Representatives from the union should be questioned regarding the labor-relations atmosphere and the union's current view of office system technology. It is important to get a feeling for the degree of commitment from top management to proceed with office systems.

From these interviews, combined with information from secondary sources such as organizational charts, company brochures, etc., it should be possible to identify some general problem or "opportunity" areas which can be further investigated. A study team is selected. A measurement strategy is formulated which includes an initial view of the salient domains for assessment. A work plan is presented to the client for agreement. The next stage of the measurement—the Diagnosis—can also be prepared.

9.2. DIAGNOSIS

With top management support, a workplan, and a study team in place, it is possible to customize a diagnostic instrument. It is usually in the form of a self-completed questionnaire that can be completed by a wider sample of employees. The objectives of this phase are to enable employees to define what would constitute "an improvement" in their organization; to identify candidate groups for a pilot system implementation, along with a pilot group recommendation; to further involve client individuals in the process of assessing their needs; to provide base-line data for posttest evaluation once the system has been implemented and running for long enough to take effect; and to provide additional information regarding the organizational climate and the strategy for the next measurement phase.

A Network Analysis has also proven to be a key diagnosis instrument. It gives a picture of the organizational communication relationships and indicates likely candidates for a pilot communication system. Other instruments can be used as appropriate.

The output from the Pilot Systems Analysis is the Opportunity Report, described earlier. Among other things, this report outlines the pilot system alternatives and makes a recommendation. The selection of the most appropriate pilot is a critical decision in the design process. The most important variable is the opportunity addressed. That is, the key requirement for a pilot system is that it be located where there is a real need. This need can be identified using the methodology described herein.

However, there are other requirements to be considered.

There must be adequate levels of *user acceptance*. The degree of support, commitment, and enthusiasm in selecting a pilot group should be heavily weighted. *Costs* should be relatively low for the pilot, as a hard dollar cost justification is not possible at this stage. To maximize the impact of the pilot experience the group should have *high visibility*. A stunning success which is buried somewhere in the enclaves of the organization is of little value. Another requirement is that the pilot group be *important* to the organization. The pilot group should be "nonmarginal." A success in an area which is not central to the work of the organization will be judged to be less significant, and possibly discounted as a nonrepresentative aberration.

The pilot group must also have adequate *size*. Most pilots will contain some communications tools such as text and voice messaging. For these to succeed there must be a large enough number of people in the pilot group for a "critical mass." Without an adequate mass which has a genuine need to communicate with each other, the communications tools may not be used enough to warrant their continuation. This critical number does not necessarily have to be *in* the pilot group as the proliferation of private and public messaging systems may cut across the pilot group.

Another requirement is *measurability*. A central objective of the implementation is to derive improvements which are measurable, in order to provide the data necessary to extend the system to a fully operational system. The measurability of the activities, outputs, and overall performance of some groups is much greater than for others.

The pilot group selected should be one where an implementation will have *minimal disruption*. It is usually advisable to avoid a major organizational change at the time of the pilot implementation. This may well come during the transition to an operational system; however, the emphasis for the initial pilot is to get a quick success that appears relatively painless and has a high payoff.

The pilot should also be *extendable* to an operational system. Some pilots do not easily lend themselves to be extended. Single-application pilots, such as a stand-alone decision support system, are an example. A key goal of a pilot implementation is to position the organization to enable evolution into a major systems implementation, which can have a profound impact.

An important consideration is the *political advisability* of various pilot alternatives. There will be numerous political considerations to be taken into account. The pilot should be located in the organization where it can facilitate the political motion towards office systems. It may be wise to start with the MIS/DP group, giving them exposure to these new systems and to begin the process of reorientation from traditional system approaches. Alternatively, location in the department of one of the other political stakeholders to win their commitment and support to the overall program is also advised. It is important that it be placed in a group where the management has a vested interest in seeing it succeed.

Ease of implementation is another requirement. Once the pilot systems analysis has been conducted it is important to implement the system quickly as the climate for change may dissipate or become negative. Some pilot alternatives may be judged to be easier to implement than others. Considerable applications development work and in particular, systems programming should be avoided in most cases. Pilots with many geographical locations are more difficult to implement than pilots in a few locations. Pilots also tend to be easier to implement when some of the users have some degree of exposure to office systems.

Finally, *good timing* is required. Some alternatives will be judged to be impractical within the time frames specified. This could be due to factors such as a peak-period work load, political problems, complex systems issues, user acceptance problems, changing work content, staff attrition and recruitment, etc.

A useful technique to facilitate selection of a pilot group is a "decision analysis." Here the various criteria are described and weights attached to each. Then each of the pilot alternatives is scored in terms of how well it meets the weighted criteria. The products of the weights and scores are added, giving a "bottom line" for each pilot alternative.

The main purpose of the "decision analysis" is to provide some structure for the process of examining the various criteria and systems alternatives rather than to simply arrive at a numerical "winner." Arriving at a common view of the relative importance of such criteria can be difficult. A decision analysis process can help the choosers achieve homogeneity regarding their assumptions and what they think the overall objectives of the pilot implementation should be.

An example of a decision analysis for selecting a pilot group is shown in Table 9.1.

9.2.1. Case Study Diagnosis

It is useful to describe the results from one part of a diagnostic questionnaire. The questionnaire had been customized to the client organization based on information from the organizational scan. It was distributed to a sample of about 100 employees out of a total office population of about 200. The sample was stratified, that is chosen deliberately to have adequate representation from various important "strata" in the organization.

The instrument was called an "Organizational Effectiveness Questionnaire."[1] It solicited opinions as to what would constitute an "improvement" in the organization's internal functioning. The possible improvements indicated on the questionnaire all could be addressed by integrated office systems. The organization's perception of where improvements were needed helped in the design of the pilot systems analysis tools. Where possible the improvements were specified in a measurable way. For example, rather than indicating "time savings" as a desired improvement, the questionnaire indicated "re-

Table 9.1. Example Decision Analysis for Selecting a Pilot Group

	Weight	Pilot I Rating (R) Score (S)		Pilot II Rating (R) Score (S)		Pilot III Rating (R) Score (S)	
	(W) (1–5)	(R) (1–5)	(S) (W×R)	(R) (1–5)	(S) (W×R)	(R) (1–5)	(S) (W×R)
High user need/political payoff	3	3	9	1	3	5	15
High user acceptance	3	4	12	2	8	5	15
Low costs	3	5	15	3	9	4	12
High visibility	1	3	3	3	3	4	4
Non-marginal group	1	4	4	3	3	4	4
Size (critical mass)	2	4	8	4	8	4	8
Measurable	2	4	8	3	6	5	10
Minimal disrution	1	3	3	3	3	2	2
Extendible to operational system	1	3	3	3	3	3	3
Facilitative politically	2	3	6	2	4	4	8
In line with corporate objectives	2	4	8	4	8	4	8
Ease of implementation	1	3	3	2	2	4	4
Practical within time frame	2	3	6	1	2	5	10
Total scores			88		62		103

ported time savings," which were quantifiable using, for example, a time-use diary.

The desired improvements were grouped in five categories: time use improvements, project control improvements, communication improvements, information improvements, and improvements in job design and QWL. The desired improvements are listed below, and the specific improvements for each category are listed in descending order of importance.

(1) Time-Use Improvements. Desired changes included a decrease in the composition of one's day spent in ineffective activities and an increase spent in effective activities.

Specifically, the "improvements" which scored the highest on the questionnaire were an increase in management time spent planning, a decrease in routine administrative tasks, a decrease in time spent on redundant tasks, an increase in delegation of professional time to subordinates, and a decrease in management time spent in routine meetings.

(2) Project Control Improvements. A need was expressed by employees to have better control over their projects. Specifically, the desired "improvements" which scored the highest on the questionnaire were better estimations of project budgets and personnel requirements, and increase in communicating critical information to managers, such as project slippage and overspending, better ability to forecast project financial status, and project financial information being available on demand.

(3) Communication Improvements. Employees expressed a desire for improved communications as measured by a variety of attitudinal and interaction variables. The desired "improvements" which scored highest in this area on the questionnaire were improved visibility and accessibility of executive management; better quality and better distributed meeting minutes; increased vertical communication more information regarding the decisions made at meetings; more communication between managers and executive management; and more communication between managers and technical staff.

(4) Information Improvements. A desire to decrease the disparity between "information needed" and "information received" was expressed. Specifically, the desired "improvements" which scored the highest on the questionnaire were better integration of the internal company data bases; more immediate access to relevant precedent-setting decisions; direct accessibility to internal information by managers; more immediate access to skills inventory information; and the capability to content-search reports.

(5) Improvements in Job Design and Quality of Work Life. Improvements in a number of areas of QWL were indicated. The desired "improvements" which scored highest on the questionnaire were decreased staff turnover; decreased waiting time by staff for future assignments; increased staff moti-

vation and morale; decreased work fluctuations; and better assignment of personnel to appropriate projects.

The summary results for all employees were also broken down by various subgroups to identify variances in opinions of key constituents. Coupled with other information from the diagnosis questionnaire and the organizational scan, it was possible to prepare the prepilot system opportunity report. The report outlined two possible pilot system alternatives and recommended one of them as first choice. This was an integrated office system for a group of managers, professionals, and administrative support persons where each would have an electronic workstation and access to electronic mail, text processing, project control, and data base tools. Upon management acceptance of the recommendation it was possible to conduct the detailed pilot systems analysis to pin down the actual functionality, features, and components of the system; to determine the implementation plan; and to acquire the base-line pretest measures for latter posttest evaluation of the system.

9.3. PILOT SYSTEMS ANALYSIS

To derive a functional description of the pilot system as well as pretest data, it is necessary to conduct further investigations in a number of areas. Information is needed regarding communications, information handling, decision support, document production, administrative support, and data processing requirements and opportunities. Data are required to enable rationalization of procedures, and both job and environmental design. Data are needed to customize an implementation strategy. Also, there must be complete information regarding current technology in the organization and an up-to-date evaluation of current and anticipated vendor offerings. This is illustrated in Figure 9.1 and serves as a guideline for the rest of the chapter.

Sounds like a lot of work, you say? The actual effort involved will vary between organizations. The number of instruments used, and the depth of the investigation, will depend on variables such as the degree of importance placed on designing the best and most cost-beneficial system; time available to conduct measurements; degree of respondent cooperation; funds available; stage of office system implementation in the organization; size of the organization; management objectives; need for detailed measures; nature of the business case to be made for the system; peculiarities of the organization; and anticipated system applications.

There is a degree of science and of art involved in the selection and customization of these tools to a given user enviroment. This comes with experience.

The measurement instruments selected for these additional investiga-

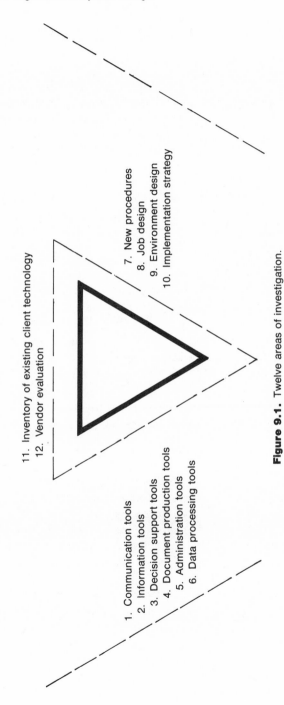

Figure 9.1. Twelve areas of investigation.

7. New procedures
8. Job design
9. Environment design
10. Implementation strategy

11. Inventory of existing client technology
12. Vendor evaluation

1. Communication tools
2. Information tools
3. Decision support tools
4. Document production tools
5. Administration tools
6. Data processing tools

tions will fall in one of the ten categories from Chapter 8. One of the key decisions is which areas or domains of the office are judged to be salient for further probing. Based on the organizational scan and diagnosis, critical opportunity areas will have been identified. For example, it may be determined that "this organization has a real communications problem," or a major problem in terms of its procedures, job design, or administrative support system. Using this knowledge, appropriate areas for focused assessment can be determined and corresponding measurement instruments selected or developed.

Another consideration is how the pre–post evaluation will be conducted. The measures taken during the pilot systems analysis will be repeated downstream to measure the impact of the system and provide data for the major expenditures which will be required to extend the pilot to a fully operational system.

In this light, work done developing measurement instruments for the pilot systems analysis will be useful for later on. The same or similar tools can be used to conduct an operational systems analysis after the pilot has been implemented and has been running smoothly for a period of time.

By listing the following 12 areas of investigation, there is no implication intended that individual office system tools which correspond should be designed. It goes without saying that the system design must *integrate* various systems tools in such a fashion that they collectively address the key "opportunity area" identified.

9.3.1. Determining Communications Opportunities

If opportunities for communications improvements have been identified during the organizational scan and diagnosis, additional measures can be taken to define the communication tools for the new system. There are a variety of measurement instruments and approaches which have been developed to assess organizational communications, some of which were discussed in Chapter 3. Using these and other specifically constructed analyses, opportunities can be identified to integrate communications tools such as electronic messaging (text and voice), computer conferencing, and teleconferencing into a broader pilot system.

There are a number of opportunity areas related to communications: use of time, organizational communications relationships, substituting for paper communications, requirements for a written record of communications, reducing undesirable travel, and reducing current communications costs.

If valid and adequately detailed measures are taken, volume requirements for the new system, and a strong financial case, can be made.

(1) Time Use. The goal here is to identify problems in the communica-

tions process which result in inefficient and ineffective use of time. Useful techniques are communications diaries or logs and observation. Self-reported time use is notoriously invalid, but may still be used under some circumstances—for example, when subjective estimates of time use are required. Problems in the communications process which can be identified include the following:

Shadow Functions. The unplanned activities such as telephoning busy numbers or playing telephone tag consume up to 20% of a professional's day. Voice and text messaging can dramatically reduce these.[1]

Interruptions. Telephone use logs and other diaries can help quantify the undesirable interruptions in one's day which make concentrated work and good time management difficult. By designing asynchronous tools into the system, the number of interruptions can be reduced.[2]

Meetings. Often too much time is spent in face-to-face communications. Transferring some of this to electronic messaging, teleconferencing, or computer conferencing may be appropriate. These technologies can actually improve the quality of face-to-face communications as well.[2]

Media Transformations. These can be identified through questionnaires, interviews, end-product tracking, and observation. There have been many cases of severely counterproductive media transformations. One example is the company where managers received textual information from the field office; compiled this information using handwriting and sent this to a secretary to type on a typewriter. The typed copy was then sent to the word-processing center (which would not accept handwritten material); the copy was then sent to the manager, who made corrections by hand and returned it to the word-processing center for correction. The final report was then sent back out to the field, using the post office mail system. The media transformations in this example not only waste the time of authors, secretaries, and word-processing operators; they result in slow turnaround of vital information and a slow organizational metabolism and responsiveness. This entire process could have been done using one or two media—an electronic document production and communication system, perhaps combined with dictation.

(2) Organizational Communication Relationships. Superior–subordinate relationships, cliques, isolates, lack of peer collaboration are examples of opportunity areas for office systems. Integrated into a broader system, the new communications tools can improve many aspects of such relationships. Among the techniques which can be used for diagnosing problems are network analyses (which give a picture of the human communication network) and questionnaires (which can measure attitudes towards the communications process within the office).

(3) Delays. Opportunities for moving information at the speed of light rather than through slower paperbased communications systems can be iden-

tified through most of the measurement techniques discussed in Chapter 8. This can be linked to procedure analysis, end-product tracking, assessment of contingencies in decision making, information processing analyses, etc.

(4) Need for Recorded Information. Text-based electronic communications systems can fulfill a common need for a permanent searchable record of many communications. Critical incidents analysis can point to past problems in this regard which were important to the organization.

(5) Undesirable Travel. Secondary sources (travel budgets, trip information, etc.) can be combined with interviews (to identify the purpose of travel) and time measurement techniques (to quantify the amount of time spent in various forms of travel) to produce a strong business case for teleconferencing and computer conferencing.

(6) Current Communications Costs. Telephone bills, especially long distance costs, can provide an important component of a cost justification for an office system containing electronic messaging tools. Because messaging can use a packet-switched network and because it avoids many of the time consuming and unnecessary personal salutations in messaging ("How's the husband, kids, and dog?"), it can enable considerable cost savings on long distance telephone bills.

One of the most important products of a thorough communications analysis, can be a list of names of the person to be included in the pilot group. An office system containing communications tools must have a "critical mass" of people who have a genuine need to communicate with each other. Lacking this, the communications tools will not be used in such a way as to justify their existence. A network analysis, or well-analyzed diary or log data can give a clear picture of who has a need to communicate with whom and help identify a "high probability of success" pilot group. This can also be useful later on, when planning to extend the pilot to an operational system.

9.3.2. Determining Information Requirements

Traditional systems analysis techniques can be used to identify design requirements for the "information systems" component of the office system. Unfortunately, many are inadequate for office systems design as they are not oriented to the concept of directly supporting knowledge workers with information handling tools. There is no need to review these approaches here.

There has been important work in the area of defining and planning data bases which is important to review.[35] As well, a number of authors have been giving attention to the relationship of data base systems to office systems. As full operational office systems spread deeper into the organization, they encompass traditional data base management systems (DBMS). Lowenthal argues that data bases should play a more important role in office atuomation. Office systems designers need to analyze the volume of information to be involved on the system, as many systems are justified on the basis of the tonnage of paper they will reduce. Once a system is installed, there is a tendency for it to search up more information, and thereby require DBMS techniques. Also, there is a case, he argues, that information should be controlled in a shared resource environment. In general it is not efficient to have large personal files stored at each work station. Rather, these could be stored using DBMS, saving storage costs and improving the ability for others to access these data, if appropriate.[5]

It is generally agreed that the majority of data bases designed during the 1970s were failures. Consequently, there is a big challenge before designers to construct data bases which will succeed in being stable and durable. Various approaches have been developed to do this. The best known is IBM's Business Systems Planning (BSP) methodology, which looks, in a very coarse way, at the general information needs of an organization. Martin outlines an approach to building data bases which goes beyond BSP.[4] More detailed levels of investigation include *Subject* data bases (such as for products, customers, parts, vendors, orders, accounts, personnel, documents); *entities* (such as plant, warehouse, etc.), which are anything about which data is stored; and finally *activities.*

There are other techniques for identifying opportunities for information systems. For example the International Communications Association "communications audit" use a unique set of questionnaire items to identify gaps between the information which is "needed" and "received."[6] Respondents indicate how much information they receive and need to receive across a variety of source, topic, and channel variables. Using this it is possible to locate deficiencies and also infer likely systems solutions. For example if the deficiencies relate to the source "peer," topic "research information," and channel "telephone," then a computer conference may be able to help. If the gaps relate to the source "subordinates," topic "budget information," and channel "written" then a financial planning or project control system may be appropriate. If the deficiencies related to source "outside information providers," topic "stock quotations," and channel "publications" then a videotex information system may be an important component of a system.

9.3.3. Determining Decision Support Requirements

The widespread adoption of the financial planning tool "Visicalc" in the early 1980s pointed out to many designers the importance of decision support systems (DSS). Not only can such tools be extremely useful, but they are often the vehicles whereby a professional or manager will begin to use a computer terminal. Initial positive experiences building a budget or other financial model often lead to exploration of other office system tools.

Opportunities for DSS must be identified during the organizational scan and diagnosis. To do this, key decisions can be identified and their impact on the organization evaluated. The context in which these decisions are made should also be studied.

Decision support systems have been found to be useful in management of investment portfolios, where decisions are made regarding what to buy, what to sell, what mix of investments to maintain, etc. Another good area is financial planning, where decisions are made such as whether to make an acquisition, what amount of capital to spend, how to raise capital, etc. Product planning applications have also become popular. Decisions which can be supported include whether to make a particular change to a product, when to make the change, what inventory levels to maintain, etc. A final example is market planning, including such decisions as what price to charge, how much to spend on advertising, what advertising mix to use, how to utilize the sales force, etc.

Graham was one of the first to develop a method for evaluating user requirements for DSS.[7] He noted that there may be opportunities for decision support where the decisions made have a high impact; the environment is changing rapidly; the decisions made require both human judgment and quantitative analysis; and where there is a need for more analyses and/or a need for analyses to be done more quickly.

During the organizational scan and diagnosis a simple checklist can be constructed to evaluate the viability of a DSS. If the client feels that decision support may be a worthwhile approach to any of these opportunities, they should be studied more fully to determine if a DSS would be useful.

In the pilot systems analysis, a questionnaire or interview format can be constructed to determine what decisions are made; the purpose of each decision; the importance of each decision and the reason for its level of importance (economic, strategic, etc.); what corporate operations are affected by each decision and the nature of the effect; whether each decision is routine or nonroutine; the urgency of each decision (i.e., how quickly it must be made); how each decision is made (i.e., what analyses are done and what judgment is applied to make the decision); and what each decision is based upon.

The constraints on the decision processes of the client should be identified since the purpose of a DSS is not to automate the existing operation but to help improve decision making. As well as lack of information, these limitations could include shortages of time, money, people, or computer power. Further, the analyst should determine what additional decisions the client would like to make if these constraints were eliminated.

Any critical incidents which may impact the decisions should also be considered. A set of criteria which gauges whether a particular incident is critical to an organization should be developed. These criteria must consider both the probability of the incident occurring and the magnitude of its impact. The decision makers should be surveyed to determine what critical incidents may affect the organization. With today's rapidly changing environment, decision makers must plan with these contingencies in mind and decision support systems should be able to cope with identifiable potential critical incidents.

There are a number of off-the-shelf decision support tools which can be selected. Examples of tools for building decision support systems are Visicalc, IFPS (the Interactive Finanacial Planning System), and Empire. If the need for integration of the DSS with other tools is not great, or if the necessary integration software can be written, it may be wise to select a prepackaged system. If it is necessary to design a DSS, a functional description can be drafted using the information collected from the decision support analysis. Additional information will be required to draft a system specification. This includes how the user interface is to be structured to make the system easy to use; what information is required to support each decision; how this information is to be presented; and what data are needed to meet the information requirements and what the sources of these data are. Also to be included is how these data will be managed; what analyses need to be done on the data to produce the required information; what characteristics the hardware and software must have; what level of performance the system must have; and what the constraints on development of the system are.

9.3.4. Determining Document Production Requirements

Henderson makes a useful distinction between "word processing" and "document production." [8] The former refers generally to the secretarial activity of typing and revision of text. The latter refers to the provision of advanced text-processing tools as components of an integrated office system to be used by all office workers, including secretaries. From this, there are two approaches to determining user needs for such text-processing tools. One is to study word-processing needs in a vacuum, and from this derive some kind of stand-alone or shared-logic word-processing system. A more appropriate approach is to investigate text-processing and document production requirements as part of an overall user-driven design. She argues that if one approaches a document production problem from the traditional word-processing framework, the results will be a system that (if you are lucky) will improve efficiency only. Very rarely has a traditional WP approach made quantitative effectiveness improvements for knowledge workers. The reason is quite simple. The document production process is inextricably connected to the capture, storage, retrieval, and communication of information. If one simply automates the presentation of that information, one affects only a small portion of the process:

> Is the information necessary for the document readily accessible? Is the presentation and storage of the document consistent with retrieval requirements? And is the document communicated in the most effective manner? These issues and more cannot be addressed in a traditional WP methodology.[8]

Sensitized paper is the best technique to examine current typing activities in the office, where there are no text-processing tools. This involves having those who type place a piece of sensitized paper behind each sheet they type, either original or to make corrections. Estimations of time use and logs have been found to often provide invalid information.

However, it is also important to look at the overall production of documents as part of a procedure analysis. The first stage of the document production process begins with the creation/input of text. This stage is followed by revision, proof/edit, and print/duplication phases, which may be repeated several times before the document is ready in its final form. The document may then go on to the stages of distribute/communicate, store (for future retrieval), and finally delivery to its destination. The process is cyclical and may be repeated since the original document may be input for future documents.

This process can be understood using observation, interview, and questionnaire techniques along with secondary sources and flow charting methods. As an example, a questionnaire can be devised to investigate the seven phases of the document production process.

(1) Creation/Input. Questions on creation and input deal with sources of information for documents, methods of information capture, information replication, and the general processes involved in text input/creation.

(2) Revision. Questions about the revision stage can provide detailed information on the percentage of total document production spent on revisions, methods used to make them, and where gaps lie in the revision process, and prioritization.

(3) Proof/Edit. Questions on the proof/edit phase of document production should focus in on who is involved in the process, total time spent, and whether the process is a hindrance to the speed of document turnaround.

(4) Print/Duplicate. The print/duplication phase questions provide detailed information on the supply issues surrounding document production, equipment availability, and time spent on the phase.

(5) Distribute/Communicate. The questions asked regarding the distribute/communicate stage delve into such matters as choosing the most effective media to distribute/communicate information and the criteria used to arrive at the choice.

(6) Store/Retrieve. To acquire information on the store/retrieve stage, questions regarding the number of documents currently stored and time effectiveness of the current store/retrieve process are posed.

(7) Destination. Questions regarding the destination phase of the document production process provide information regarding the length of time needed for a document to reach its recipient, whether the document was still timely when it arrived, and if the information contained in the document was in a usable form.

All of the above stages of document production must also be evaluated to determine the time involved from creation to destination.[8]

The document production system will be part of the overall sociotechnical system. As such, data must be collected to aid in the design of a number of system components. The process for the production of text must be specified, in terms of the stages involved, tasks to be performed, procedures, and responsibilities. More and more professionals have direct access to text handling tools to augment their thinking processes and aid in the translation of ideas into text. Given this, the old notion of secretaries and "principals" is breaking down. The new relationships and responsibilities must be defined. The client must determine the objectives of the system (e.g. high quality, fast turnaround) so that performance criteria can be defined. The hardware and software aspects of the system must be specified, ensuring that the system configuration meets requirements as identified. These include needs for the identified capacity, speed and reliability, security, volume, location of printers, system features, user interface, and so on. There will likely be some job redesign as responsibilities and opportunities change. New career paths for typists and secretaries can be defined. Links between the document production system and the overall corporate or organizational data bases must be specified and a plan presented for their construction. Finally, as part of an overall integrated system there must be evaluation techniques, an implementation strategy, a training program, and a support system.[8]

9.3.5. Determining Administrative Support Requirements

What kinds of measures can be taken to identify opportunities for administrative support tools? This category includes tools such as on-line calendars, to-do lists, scheduling tools, and administrative lists. In a more general sense it could include tools associated with information handling (lists, online access to manual records), decision support (project control systems, budgetary tools), traditional data-processing tools (accounting, payroll, etc.), and tools related to the improvement of office procedures. These are discussed elsewhere in this chapter.

Office systems can significantly reduce routine or unnecessary administrative activities, or provide the opportunity for their delegation. Thus the main focus of measures is to identify such unnecessary or inappropriate activities. Such measures are easily integrated in an overall measurement package.

For example, time measurement instruments like logs, diaries, and observation can help record the amount of time spent by knowledge workers in various administrative tasks. Typically it is found that a group of professionals and managers spend inordinate percentages of the day scheduling meetings, manually aggregating budget information, photocopying, looking for administrative information, or filing. Each of these examples can be addressed by a subset of tools in an integrated office system. Also time savings as a result of office systems being used by secretarial and administrative personnel can create the slack necessary to enable delegation of administrative activities.

Interviews are also useful in identifying administrative problems. Typically businesses are pound foolish and penny wise when it comes to administrative activities. Keeping a "trim" administrative staff has direct implications for the bottom line all right, but not necessarily in the way intended. While overhead costs may be kept low, there may also be downward pressure on the revenue line, due to ineffective use of the time of the most highly paid members of the organization. Implementations of an office system can be an ideal opportunity to examine the distribution of administrative activities across an organization. Structured questions in the interview, coupled with adequate open-ended opportunities to elaborate on office administration, can help get the data needed. Items can be developed to measure specific aspects of the administrative process. For example, the appropriate people to place on a meeting scheduling system can be determined using a network analysis. Output from these programs can show the clusters of individuals who tend to meet together frequently.

Often the main administrative problems can be identified through an overall workflow analysis. If managers are spending 40 minutes a day photocopying (as has been found), this is likely a symptom of a larger problem in the document production process rather than a problem itself.

9.3.6. Determining Data Processing Requirements

Likely, some data-processing applications can be integrated into the system. Others are likely to be so outmoded or inappropriate that the original problem they addressed should be reexamined as part of the investigation. There are various types of traditional DP systems. *Payment systems* include systems for payroll, accounts payable, and accounts receivable. *Financial control data systems* center on the general ledger. *Personnel ad-*

ministration data systems can keep track of personnel status, fringe benefits, skills inventories, etc. *Operations data systems* can automate procedures such as order entry, order processing, shipping, receiving, purchase orders completion, production control, material requirements planning (MRP), and price quotation.

A thorough investigation for office systems should identify requirements in these areas from several points of view. Bottlenecks in the information flow process may be due to problems within the purview of traditional data processing. Inadequate, inaccurate, untimely, inappropriate, inaccessible, or inappropriately formatted information points to problems in the decision support apparatus and can be identified through a decision support analysis. An analysis of office procedures, or end-product tracking can also surface problems/opportunities in the structured data-processing activities in the organization. Instruments measuring aspects of organizational communications such as a communications diary can point to inefficient use of time due to inappropriate data processing. Instruments measuring the quality of work life or diagnosing the design of jobs often uncover opportunities to help victims of the previous days of computer systems. Or they may uncover people doing deadening jobs which can be eliminated through creative data-processing solutions, thus freeing human resources for more useful and rewarding work.

Rather than reconstructing various DP systems, an assessment may indicate that tools should be built to interface with selected corporate or organizational data bases. This kind of work usually is done incrementally. One of the tasks of the assessment is to identify key data bases. These are data bases with some combination of the following attributes: those accessed most frequently; those providing the aggregate information which is judged to be most critical; those where there is the greatest disparity between the information "needed" and the information "needed to receive."

Another measurement undertaking is to assess the sequencing and timing for various data bases to be integrated into the office system. Usually this does not occur until the pilot systems phase is complete and the operational system is being designed. However, in cases such as the "operational data pilot" mentioned earlier it may be appropriate to ground the pilot system on a foundation of key operational data.

9.3.7. Determining New Procedures

Regardless of whether a functional model is adopted, there will be new procedures to be designed as part of an office system implementation.

In the functional case, the entire design process will center on the integration of office technology with new procedures. Such approaches to determining user requirements are in their early stages. However, it is possible to outline a few directions.

Data from instruments designed to measure time use, tasks, information flow, etc., can be analyzed to derive a picture of office procedures. The degree of formality in charting procedures can vary. At one end of the continuum this can be a very informal description of activities at various stages in a procedure (for example time use , elapsed time, information input used, and information outputs produced). At the other end, the procedures can be rigorously detailed, along with measures of the amount of output produced as well as key linkages between the two, especially those which could be modified favorably through office systems technology.[9]

A good example of the more formal approach is the Information Control Net. A simple case is illustrated in Figure 9.2. Work flows (dark arrows)

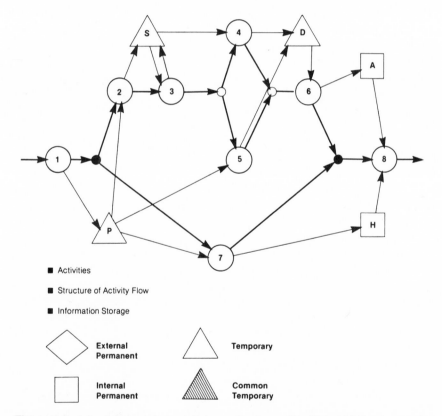

Figure 9.2. Information control net diagram. Courtesy of the Diebold Office Automation Program. Source: Cook, Carolyn. *Office Modeling.* Presentation to the Diebold Working Session, New York (February, 1980).

from one activity (circle) to the next. Information flows (light arrows) to and from information machines or stores (triangles). A highly complex chart can be designed using observation, interview, questionnaires, and various tracking and logging mechanisms. Using the diagram, the workflow and information flow can be streamlined through application of appropriate technologies and procedure changes. This process can be done manually, or as in the case of the ICN, mathematical models and formulas can be applied to enable exploration of various combinations of technology and procedural reorganization

Sirbu, Schoichet, Kunin, and Hammer[10] outline an office analysis methodology (OAM) which centers on the identification and reorganization of procedures. Steps in the process include the following:

(1) Meeting with the Office Manager. This is done to identify the organizational context, mission and objectives, reporting relationships, functions, office resources, key personnel, and procedures.

(2) Data Collection to Produce Initial Procedure Descriptions. Interviews are conducted with individual staff members who perform various procedures. For each step in a procedure the analyst attempts to identify the events precipitating what is done; what terminates the step; timing constraints; inputs and outputs; sources and destinations; data bases; and special equipment utilized. From all of this a detailed procedure description can be formulated.

(3) Development and Analysis of a Draft Procedure Description. Each draft procedure is analyzed for its completeness and consistency. Ambiguities are then clarified. As well, a list of possible exceptions to the procedure are formulated using "what if" questions. Common exceptions are lost documents, missing personnel needed for a decision, information not received, noncompliance with procedures, reversal of earlier decisions, and so on.

(4) Iteration of Procedure Interviews. Respondents receive a copy of the draft procedures for review and are reinterviewed to resolve conflicts and ambiguities in the description; to investigate procedures for handling exceptions; and to look for unplanned, ad hoc decision making which should be brought under more formal procedure guidelines. Also during this round of interviews, more quantitative data are taken. These data help determine where time and effort are being spent and to help in determining the system design and the cost–benefit analysis for the system.

(5) Review of the Procedure Analysis with the Manager. The office manager is then reinterviewed to validate the description. Interview data are also collected regarding the intentions behind the various elements of a procedure; practices for handling of exceptions; and interfaces with other offices. From this a final office description can be structured.

Using this description, the office systems analyst has a detailed understanding of the office (from the perspective of the procedure-oriented functionalist). This can be used to rationalize and streamline procedures, and integrate office system technology where it can improve the process.[10]

In offices where such an approach is inappropriate, it will still be necessary to evaluate current procedures and design new ones. For example, document production tools, as part of an integrated system, will dramatically alter the document production process. The relationship between managers and secretaries will change as managers key at least some of their own text into the system—using the system as a thinking tool. The editing and proofreading procedures will change with online text, automatic spelling checks, and the like. In addition to such procedural change, new procedures are required to govern use of the new system itself. Procedures for the use of messaging distribution lists can help the users avoid spending all day in front of a screen reading inappropriate messages. Procedures are also required for changing the system, disposing of personal system files, security, acquiring new equipment, and conflict resolution between users and other stakeholders. Information from various parts of the requirements analysis can facilitate this work, including data regarding curent conflicts, procedures for manual systems, user attitudes towards systems, the organizational culture, and critical incidents with previous procedures.

9.3.8. Job Design

In any system design, especially an operational system, the design of jobs is probably the most overlooked aspect. Job design is critical for a couple of reasons. For success it is necessary to jointly optimize the social and technical components of the work system. A bad fit will result in idle or misused technology as well as people. On the other hand, unless the system implementation is part of an improvement in jobs of the users and their quality of work life, there is a risk of non–acceptance of the technology. Numerous word-processing systems have failed because the system was detrimental to the lives of the users in the office. The danger with much more complex and far-reaching integrated office systems is qualitatively greater.

As a result, any User-Driven Design methodology must contain tools for assessing current jobs and redesigning them. This goes beyond the problem of simply redesigning procedures. It is true that procedures will change. Redundant or unnecessary steps may be eliminated. Some procedures will be completely redesigned. There is also a need for procedures regarding the system itself and how it is used, managed, changed, etc. But in many ways this is just the tip of the iceberg.

Entire jobs within the office are disappearing and being replaced by new ones. The secretarial position is the first that comes to mind, but there are others (discussed later). The power provided by systems to not only do old things faster and better, but to do things, is also creating the need for new job designs.

Job design is a component of overall organizational design. Organizational assessment can be conducted on a number of levels. *Macro-organizational design* deals mainly with the configuration of organizational structures, span of control for managers, division of labor, and the distribution of power and authority among decision makers. *Organizational unit design* investigates issues such as unit objectives and specialization, personnel composition, unit standardization of procedures and rules, unit decision making, and unit performance standards and control mechanisms. *The design of relations between units* focuses on interunit communications, information flow, influencing, and conflict resolution. *Job design* is concerned with the definition of tasks performed, job expertise required, job description and standardization, job incentives and motivation, and supervision.

Trist summarizes properties of good jobs. *Extrinsic* properties include fair and adequate pay, job security, benefits, safety, health, and due process. *Intrinsic* properties include variety and challenge, continuous learning, discretion and autonomy, recognition and support, meaningful social contribution, and a desirable future.[11] While such properties are too general to serve as principles of work design, such principles have been constructed. Trist notes that the degree of agreement on these is exceptional in so new a field and this has placed work design on a firmer foundation than is usually thought.[16]

The best-known instrument for evaluating jobs is the Job Diagnostic Survey (JDS) developed by Hackman and Oldham.[12] This is a well-respected and highly recommended tool to complement the office systems analyst's tool kit.[13] It measures five dimensions of jobs. A first is *skill variety*—the degree to which the job requires a variety of activities in carrying out the job. *Task identity* is the degree to which the job requires completion of a whole and identifiable piece of work. *Task significance* is the extent to which the job impacts other people, whether inside or outside the organization. *Autonomy* is the degree of provision of freedom, independence, and discretion in scheduling the work and determining the process to complete it. *Feedback* is the degree to which information is obtained about effectiveness of performance.

Using this instrument the investigator can diagnose current jobs and even compare the results to a large normative data base. The results of the survey can then be used to help redesign jobs as part of the redesign of the total sociotechnical work system. These data can also be used as pretest data for evaluation of the impact of the system on jobs and the quality of work life in general.

As those from the sociotechnical school become more involved in integrated office system implementations there are many new approaches to applying job design methodologies.[14] Trist accurately describes the challenge before those in the discipline:

> The designers of the new technologies dependent on computers and telecommunications belong to engineering disciplines far removed from socio-technical considerations. Unless educated otherwise, they will follow the technological imperative and mortgage a good deal of the future.[11]

9.3.9. Environmental Design

Another of the most overlooked components of a good systems design is the physical environment. Often resistance to computer systems, once diagnosed, was not really resistance to computer technology itself but to badly designed jobs and physical environments. This is especially relevant in the case of the full operational system. Because of the somewhat tentative nature of an office system pilot, enviromental issues may be less pressing.

Most of these issues can be examined from the perspective of workstation design. Hopefully many of these have been dealt with by the furniture vendor. In this regard, they serve as guidelines for evaluating vendors.

Anthropometric measures refer to body dimensions and the physical capabilities of the workstation user, such as standing heights, reach, arm angles in keying and eye viewing angles, source document surfaces, etc. The objective here is to maximize comfort and economy of effort.

Sensory measures can be taken to assess requirements for light, sound, temperature, and humidity. There are detailed industry standards regarding various requirements in these domains. However, many of these have not fully taken into account the introduction of personal computer systems in the office. Systems have failed because of noisy workstation printer, glare on the screen from overhead lights or windows, or an intolerable level of background noise due to lack of sound absorbant materials.

Privacy requirements refer to needs for confidentiality, to avoid interruptions, and in general to maintain control over the form of interpersonal interactions. These may vary greatly depending on the job diagnosed. Voice messaging, for example, may introduce new privacy requirements.

Psychological factors are also important in workstation design. These include aesthetics, status of the work-station design, individuality, requirements for face-to-face communications, and a sense of belonging.

Arrangement of work stations can be critical to the workflow and communications process, and to minimizing movement and sound distractions. There has been a convergence between space planning and office systems design as individuals from the two fields understand the importance of the other. This is especially true in the case of new buildings, where multidisciplinary task forces grapple with how the office and office work is changing and what that means for the design of offices.

As part of the assessment program, measures can be taken to determine requirements in these areas. It is prudent to draw upon the resources of space planners and environmental designers for determining user needs in these areas.

9.3.10. Determining an Implementation Strategy

Like technical aspects of the design, the strategy for introducing and implementing the system can be user-driven. The typical mentality of systems implementors is reflected in the term "installation." The system is viewed simply as technology which must be installed, albeit with a little training for the "operators."

Implementation is better viewed as managing change—attitudinal, organizational, physical, and technical. It is the process of managing a smooth transition to a new sociotechnical system. It is also a process which can be planned, using data from the user. Many of the measures taken during the scanning, diagnostic, and pilot systems analysis phases will collect data useful for preparing an implementation strategy.

During the intial organizational scan interviews, candidates for the study/implementation team can be identified. These should include key opinion leaders and representatives from various stakeholder functions, (MIS, finance, etc.), groups (unions, associations, etc.), job types (secretaries, clerks, professionals, managers, etc.), attitudinal groups (positive and skeptical towards office systems), employee types (men and women, minorities, various ages, levels of experience, seniority, etc.). Naturally not all of these can be included, but the goal should be to identify key individuals from as many representative areas as possible.

Presystem measures can be taken to assess the degree of potential user acceptance of an office system implementation. This is useful in a number of ways. It helps the analyst select high probability of success for individuals and groups phasing in the system implementation. It makes sense to start with people who are likely to take to the system in a positive manner. A successful first wave will create some enthusiasm and momentum for other prospective users.

It is also easier to develop an effective treatment program, with valid measures of the variables affecting user acceptance. People have resistance to office system technology for a myriad of reasons. These include fear of the unknown, fear of failure, psycholgical habit, loss of control, previous negative experiences, vested interests, fear of technology, lack of identification with the proposed change, anxiety about possible disruptions to social relationships, and lack of evidence as to the likely business benefits from the change. These fears may be rational or irrational depending on the system. Each of these areas of concern has a different "treatment" or intervention strategy which is appropriate. Given that the strategy adopted will likely effect whether or not the system is successful, it is astonishing to note that most implementors do not carefully investigate which variables are critical in a given situation.

The topic of user acceptance of electronic office systems is receiving more and more attention by researchers, vendors, "choosers" in user organizations, and implementors. Researchers are interested in learning more about "technophobia" in general and resistance to electronic office systems in particular. Vendors are interested in the topic from the perspectives of marketing and product development. Choosers and implementors need to know more about what factors best predict user acceptance, how to identify low-risk applications, and what intervention strategies are appropriate to maximize the probability of a successful implementation in a given office situation.

Most approaches to the topic have used *attitudes* towards office system technology as equivalent to user acceptance. For example, it is typically stated that "people with characteristics X, Y, and Z have positive attitudes towards office automation; therefore people with these characteristics will accept and use an office automation system." While it is important to measure attitudes, these should not be equated with user acceptance.

With a quasi-experimental research design it is possible to go beyond the one-shot attitudinal survey and quantify the attributes which predict(ed) actual behavioral user acceptance or rejection of the system. Dependent variables such as "log-in time," "number of messages sent," "number of commands used," and so on can be used to approximate the construct of user acceptance. Using independent variables (e.g., attitudes, previous exposure to computers, along with demographic variables and measures of time use, communications, etc.,) multiple regression equations can be constructed which enable prediction of the user acceptance variables. These equations can then be cross-validated in subsequent implementations.[15]

Presystem measures can collect the data necessary to customize a *training strategy* as well. Training someone to use an integrated office system is quite a different matter from training someone how to use a telephone or even a word processor. Depending on the system, training can take months or in some cases it is an ongoing process over the years, as the user gets to the deeper levels of a powerful system.

Training programs have to be customized to take into account differences in systems, differences in organizations, and individual differences between groups and users. Data from the user are key to this because it has been found that the best training approach is not to simply teach someone how to use a machine. Rather, users should be taught how to do their (perhaps new) job better, work better with others, and get more enjoyable and productive use of their time through using a system. Teaching someone how to do their job better with the new tools requires a detailed understanding of that job, the individual, and his/her relationship with others. This knowledge, aggregated, can enable the development of an effective training strategy.

Components of a training strategy which require data from the user to plan are as follows:

Composition of training sessions. Depending on the size of the user group, interpersonal relations, the business context, composition of the group, projected user acceptance, etc., the composition of the training sessions will vary radically. Skeptical users, for example, should be trained one-on-one or in a small group with more positive individuals. Senior executives who have been found to be concerned with status or uneasy about loss of control due to the system may be trained indvidually. More than one training session has broken down when an executive, in danger of appearing foolish in front of subordinates, turned the session into a lecture. Lebolt's law, while not quite completely validated, is worth considering: "One's ability to learn and acquire use of an integrated office system is inversely proportional to one's status on the organizational chart." The working relationships between users may also affect the composition of the training session. There may, for example, be a case to enhance the secretary–principal relationship through small training session where the two can interact together on how they will use the system. Or, if there is a need to use the system to improve peer collaboration, training sessions which include peers from across organizational boundaries may make sense.

Length of the training sessions will vary according to the environment. In well-organized offices where there is planning and purposeful activity, longer planning sessions have been found to work. In offices where users cannot plan to attend longer classes, short modularized classes of say 60 minutes can be scheduled.[16]

Course content will vary according to user acceptance levels, previous exposure to computer systems, aptitude of the users, and difficulty of the system. For example where there is low user acceptance, the courses must be rich with motivating techniques, such as examples of other implementations, humor, audio visual aids, and pedagogy aimed at the source of the user concerns.

Other training variables which should be customized from user data are location of the training sessions (in house or off site); overall strategy for user motivation (intrinsic and extrinsic rewards); materials and documentation supplied to the users; and user feedback plan to refine training and enable an ongoing training program in tune with user needs.

9.3.11. Categorizing Current In-House Technologies

A detailed understanding of present computer, communications, and office technologies resident in the organization must be acquired. More than technical data is required. It is important to understand present use of these technologies, both in terms of utilization rate and also in terms of the *purposes or functions* to which they are being applied.

A "technical inventory" can help provide answers to both. A form should be constructed containing various categories for technical and descriptive data. For each piece of equipment, information should be collected regarding variables such as type, make, purpose, configuration, capacity, date acquired, status (rented, leased, or purchased), utilization rate, and user attitudes towards it. In the initial organizational scan, a general picture will suffice. As the process moves into the detailed design, more specific data are required. Some examples from the three main categories of office technologies are given below (recognizing that these technologies overlap and are converging):

(1) Communications Technologies
- number of employees with telephones
- number of telephones not associated with employees
- secretarial or multiline sets
- outside central office trunks
- WATS trunks
- PBX, model, capacity, utilization, etc.
- FX trunks
- Tie trunks
- Telex, TWX
- FAX
- current long distance costs
- local computer networks (LCNs)
- teleconferencing tools
- facilities for wide area networking
- value added communications tools like voice messaging, videotex, access tools for public data bases.

(2) Computer Technologies
- mainframes, minis, and micro computers
- storage technologies (tape drives, disc drives, video disk, computer output and input microform)
- output devices (line printers, letter quality printers, graphics printers, laser printers)

- terminals (VDT's, portable terminals, graphics terminals, integrated voice-data terminals)

(3) Office Technologies
- typewriters (intelligent and otherwise)
- word processors (stand-alone with partial and full display, shared logic, time sharing
- printers, storage and communications capabilities of word processors
- copiers
- microform technologies
- filing and other information handling tools
- dictation tools.

9.3.12. Vendor Evaluation—The Technology Gatekeeper

Using the approaches outlined above the study team can select a pilot group and specify the required functionality of the system. Hopefully pressures to prematurely decide on a vendor, while the analysis is in its early stages, can be resisted. Such pressures come from the vendors themselves, resident technocrats, and the deeply internalized anticipation we all feel to know which selection of shining hardware and software will actually be acquired. On the other hand, when the "moment of truth" has finally arrived, it is important to be able to act quickly, drawing upon comprehensive understanding of the various vendors to come up with the product or products which meet the requirements specified.

For this reason it is necessary to have an ongoing evaluation of the vendors and what they have to offer. The rate at which new office systems products appear on the market is staggering. One way of coping is to throw your lot in with one vendor and hope for the best. More and more this is unfeasible, as no vendor has a comprehensive product line, let alone a superior product line. Moreover, the dangers of being led down the garden circuit become greater when married to a single vendor. The alternative is to assign the resources to keep track of these rapid developments.

Vendor evaluation should be ongoing, both with pilot and operational system implementations and also with overall planning. Because office system acquisitions are aimed at a moving target, they should be rooted in a sound foundation of experience and product evaluation and at the same time position the organization to evolve, in a planned fashion, down the road.

A "technology gatekeeper" project should be formally established to monitor vendor developments. This does not mean that original research should be conducted on each vendor offering. Evaluation services are publicly available from a variety of different publishers and consulting organizations. However, these are not adequate, nor can they ever be. This is because there is no one "best system" independent of context and user need. What is best for one situation may be completely inappropriate for another. The appropriateness of a system will depend on user requirements, funds available, and current in-house technological base.

There are other problems in relying completely on such vendor evaluation services. They are no substitutes for primary investigations, especially hands-on experience. They are not comprehensive in terms of the areas of office systems evaluation. They tend to examine current products, rather than products which are scheduled to appear. It is worth the effort to do some vendor snooping to get a picture of what is on the immediate and medium-term horizon? Most important, a technical comparison of product features conducted in a vacuum is inadequate. Evaluations can take place on several levels:

(1) Integrated Systems. These include the product lines of those vendors attempting to provide system solutions for the gamut of office workers.

(2) Specific Tools. Detailed evaluations can be conducted of individual office tools, such as electronic messaging systems, text editors, PBXs, portable terminals, graphics systems, copiers, and teleconferencing systems.

(3) Local Area Networks (LANs). While an evaluation of various LANs may be linked to the product lines of the corresponding vendors, this topic is large, complex, and important enough to warrant an ongoing investigation.

(4) Data Base Management Systems (DBMSs) These electronic librarians provide users with the information they request from a data base.[17] All the major computer vendors have DBMSs compatable with their hardware. As more and more systems use the efficient relational data base systems, as the number of different systems becomes larger, and as various DBMSs are compatible with a number of different vendor products, it becomes more important to assess them in an ongoing structured fashion.

Macfarlane has outlined a framework for evaluating integrated office systems.[18] It breaks systems down into (a) functional areas; (b) system features; and (c) ancillary features. Six functional areas are chosen to group capabilities of systems. Systems are described, using both a textual data base and also a rating scheme, in terms of their capabilities within each area. Systems are judged, not just in terms of their abstract technical merits, but also concretely in terms of the user organization. An outline of a textual file or report describing the six functional areas within the context of the general needs identified by an organization is illustrated in Figure 9.3.

Under the second topic of "System Features" the following topics should be covered: user interface, network and communications configurations, protocols, and peripherals, operating systems, models, system accounting and self-monitoring tools, and security.

Under the third topic of "Ancillary Parameters" information regarding

1. Communications
   1) Text Messaging
      - Capabilities (scope, filing system, complexity)
      - Identification of the users
      - Integration (with other tools, with central file structure)
      - Additional comments
   2) Voice messaging
      - Capabilities
      - Identification of the users
      - The editor
      - Integration (with other tools, with central file structure, with text)
   3) Synchronous text capabilities
   4) Computer conferencing
      - Capabilities (windowed screens, integration with voice)
      - Additional comments
2. Information handling tools
   1) Local data base
      - Type
      - Data, text
      - Capacity
      - Maintenance and update
      - Editing
      - Integration with other capabilities
      - User interface
      - Additional information
   2) Remote data base
      - what
      - how
   3) Forms handling
3. Decision support systems
   1) Capabilities
   2) Desk calculator
   3) Special function (forecasting, modeling, statistics)
4. Administrative support
   1) Calendar scheduling
      - Multiple person meeting scheduling
      - Searchable record
      - Hard copy
   2) Scratch pad
   3) To do list
5. Document Production
   1) Editor (screen, line, interface)
   2) Formatter (power, versatility)
   3) File structure
   4) Support tools (spelling check, readability indices)
   5) Full features
   6) Photocomposer
   7) Additional comments
6. Data processing
   1) Language supported
   2) Program development tools
   3) Data processing packages
   4) Integration with mainframe systems

Figure 9.3. Outline of technology gatekeeper report.

the vendor corporate profile and direction, availability of products, costs, training packages, documentation, maintenance and support services should be discussed.

It makes sense to have a user-driven approach to evaluating office system vendors. This should include a framework for collecting technical data about vendor products, as indicated above, and a method of assigning weights to the criteria based on contextual data from the user. This is an application of the decision analysis technique to the process of selecting a vendor. The difference from traditional approaches is that the judgments regarding the importance of various features are derived from user data, rather than being pulled out of the air.

Over time, the organization will not only build up a comprehensive data base about systems, but also about their criteria for evaluating them.

For example, through user studies, successful implementations, and failures (sometimes called "not-so-successful implementations"), a framework for evaluating user interfaces will be constructed. Many systems are rude, intolerant, and unsympathetic to the user.[19] Through experience a criteria list can be constructed. General criteria, translatable into interface specifications, are that an interface should be forgiving, friendly, protective, easy to use, responsive, consistent, flexible, individually adjustable, reliable, stable, user-controlled, and self documenting.[20]

Chapter 10

Assessing the Organization: Cost–Benefit Analysis

He uses statistics like a drunken man uses lampposts—for support rather than illumination.

(Andrew Lang)

10.1. THE PROBLEM

The topic of cost–benefit analysis for integrated office systems has been the source of a raging debate for a number of years. Some say the issue is purely conjectural and ephemeral. That is, as office systems prove their worth over time, there will come a point where it will no longer be necessary to make a business case for them, much as few people cost-justify their use of a telephone or a swivel chair. Other cynical, yet perceptive, observers have noted that many cost–benefit analyses have served somewhat devious purposes. One is to avoid doing anything. A second is to justify what one already thinks.

The intensity and breadth of the discussion, however, indicates that this is no trivial or short-term issue.

Probably the greatest obstacle to the widespread proliferation of integrated office systems has been the inability to cost-justify them. There is substantial soft, experiential evidence that these systems can dramatically improve the efficiency and effectiveness of office workers and organizations. But until recently there has been very little proof. It has been possible to make a business case for word-processing equipment, based on time and personnel savings from increased typing efficiency. It has been much more difficult to show how more advanced, integrated office systems can improve the productivity of knowledge workers. Because the main opportunity is improving effectiveness, it is not feasible or desirable to build a cost-displacement business case, as indicated in Figure 10.1. One of the by-products of this problem is that office systems have been detoured into the limited domain of word processing, as various vendors focus on products which they can sell.

There are several main problems in integrated office system cost–benefit analysis. To begin, there is no generally accepted theory of white collar productivity or organizational performance. As indicated in Chapter 3, there are also a wide variety of conceptual frameworks regarding where the opportunities for integrated office systems lie. As a result, methodologies for cost benefit analyses are bound to lack both universality and depth.

Second, the difficulties of quantifying office productivity are enormous. There are few valid and acceptable measures of efficiency, let alone effectiveness and productivity. "Bright ideas per fortnight" is, for an extreme example, hardly an acceptable metric. Productivity measures will also, to a certain extent, be *specific* to individual organizations and based on their specific objectives. Moreover, there will likely be more than one measure of productivity for each organization or business unit. Measures will refer to different products produced for internal and external users and also to broader organizational performance. Lacking acceptable metrics of the benefits, it is somewhat difficult (to say the least) to develop the "benefit" side of the cost–benefit equation.

There is virtually no normative evidence regarding the impact of these systems. Lacking (a) valid measures and (b) evaluations of office system implementations, there is very little evidence one can point to, indicating that these systems actually do anything positive. Without such evidence the analyst cannot anticipate the effects of the proposed system, and therefore cannot project the likely benefits.

The impact of a given system will depend on local variables like (a) the nature of the system, (b) the way it is implemented, (c) the specific problems it is addressing, (d) the acceptance level of the users. Consequently, it is difficult to rely on data from other office system implementations in other very different environments as evidence of the likely impact of the proposed system. As one executive put it: "So it saved another company's managers an hour a day. My company is completely different."

The measurement problem is also compounded by the nonexclusivity of various measurable events. For example, it is possible to obtain a reading of potential time savings, but this in turn has implications for how that time is deployed. It is wrong to assume that improvements at the level of the individual user are additive. Improvements may overlap; in the case of time, savings

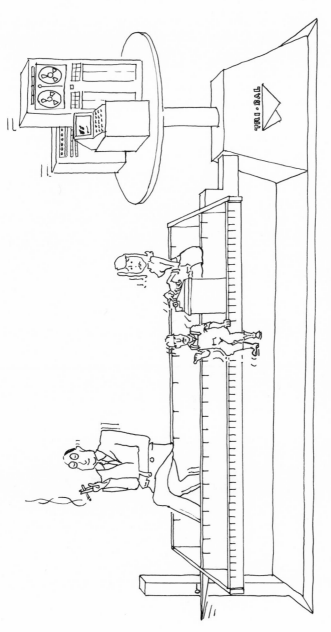

Figure 10.1 The typical cost displacement approach.

overlap with improvements in the communications process and the rationalization of procedures. Or there may be an interaction effect with such improvements, where for example time saved by individual users has a synergistic effect. In this case it would be an error to simply add up the total time savings and attempt to assign a dollar value to them.

There is also the problem of *causality*. That is, it is difficult to show a causal relationship between an office system implementation and improvements in whatever measures of organizational performance are used. If there appears to be an improvement, the question is posed: "How can you tell that the improvement was not due to some other factor, such as a wage increase, a change in the corporate executive, or a fluctuation in the business cycle?"

Another problem is that often "The First Law of Cost-Justifying Office Systems" comes to play. It states that "the probability of a chooser accepting a cost–benefit analysis is directly proportional to the degree to which s/he is favorably inclined to the technology anyway." Often if the person who makes the decision is skeptical about office systems, it does not matter how solid a business case is.

Finally, performing a cost–benefit analysis requires considerable effort. This can make the implementor vulnerable to the charge that the cost–benefit analysis itself is not cost-justifiable.

Together these problems are significant and require a strategy to deal with them.

10.2. A SOLUTION STRATEGY

A number of different approaches have been taken to tackle the problem. Each of the conceptual approaches to office system design discussed earlier contains methods for performing cost–benefit analyses.

For those taking an Organizational Communications approach the emphasis is on showing time savings through the use of office systems tools: reduction in shadow functions, media tranformations, and redundancy along with improved timing and control.[1] While much of this is useful, it fails to grapple fully with the impact of systems on overall organizational performance.

From the Functional perspective, a number of different techniques can be applied. For clerical workers, other nonprofessional work time measurement can be used. Example techniques are methods–time management (MTM), work sampling, time ladders, short interval scheduling (SIS) and systems analysis. The main problem of such approaches is their lack of applicability to the office, especially to nonclerical work. For professional work, variations on the systems analysis theme can help identify opportunities to improve procedures.[2]

Information Resource Management (IRM) approaches focus on traditional data processing or MIS techniques of cost displacement (reducing people) or subjective evaluations of the value of information. Both of these are limited when it comes to office systems. "Decision Support System" (DSS) practitioners have not given much attention to the problem of cost benefit; although it has been argued that a DSS can be an integral component of an overall management measurement system.[3]

Quality of Work Life (QWL), although in its early stages, has centered cost justification attempts at the level of overall organizational performance.

Office systems can leverage value added benefits of knowledge worker augmentation. Because of this, it makes a lot of sense to attempt to find a "bottom line" for any given organizational unit where a system is being implemented. By projecting and demonstrating the value added impact of a system on a given unit, a misplaced emphasis on cost displacement and efficiency can be avoided. The extreme case of this is *transfer pricing*. An internal market can be created for goods and services, each of which would have an internal price equal to its unit value within the company. Transfer prices can be considered as the monetary values assigned to the goods and services exchanged among the subunits of an organization. One profit center supplies and purchases goods from another.[2] The problem with this approach is that it can lead to unproductive competition and disharmony between organizational units. The high degree of independence among these units also makes planning difficult. It appears that the concept of laissez-faire capitalism within an organization is just as unfeasible as the notion in society as a whole.

The approach to conducting cost—benefit analyses for office systems outlined in this book flows from the approach to measuring user requirements already explained. It is not a rigid approach, but can be tailored to the individual situation and the requirements of the chooser. Data can be taken from whichever combination of the 12 measurement areas outlined in the previous chapter and applied to the cost and benefits equation. The approach has several strategic thrusts:

(1) Dual Foci. While the emphasis of a business case must be on how the system will (or has) affected overall *organizational performance,* it is necessary to also include improvements in efficiency in the benefits side of the equation.

Measures of organizational performance include value added, revenue generated, market share, quality of products, and other quantifications of the objectives of the organization.

Internal efficiency measures include quantifications of time savings, reduction in costs such as floor space, telephone bills, etc., reduced labor activities through streamlining procedures (and thereby freeing human resources for more useful activity), and so on.

It would be a mistake to ignore either the internal or external impacts of office systems. By including both in a *parallel* fashion a strong business case can be made. A system is implemented and the output from the office improves. If it can be demonstrated that the people in that unit are also working more efficiently, making better use of their time, etc., there is a much more convincing argument that the improvement in output can be attributed to the system.

(2) The Pilot System Strategy. Opportunities for a pilot system are identified to "choosers" (decision makers of sociotechnical systems) who are interested in learning more and perhaps experimenting with office systems. A low-risk, high-profile pilot is selected, showing costs and some anticipated benefits based on previous research and experience. It must be acknowledged, however, that it is difficult to establish a hard dollar business case for the pilot. Rather it is viewed as a relatively small investment to enable the organization to go through an experience with a new technology which appears to hold substantial opportunities for improvements in effectiveness. The pilot is implemented within a controlled evaluation framework and its impact on the organization evaluated in a detailed way. It is then possible to conduct a more convincing cost–benefit analysis for an operational system. The cost–benefit analysis is therefore based on data from an experience within the actual organization in question.

This evolutionary approach enables the user to make a small initial investment. Subsequently, more substantial investments are made on a stronger basis, using data from the pilot experience(s).

(3) Separation of Internal Benefits according to Measurability. When it comes time to conduct a cost–benefit analysis for the operational system parallel equations are presented. One shows the impact of the pilot system on overall organizational performance, projected to the operational system population. The second presents the internal efficiency benefits and separates them according to their measurability into the categories of hard quantifiable benefits, soft quantifiable benefits, and intangible unquantifiable benefits.

This removes the burden from the "chooser" of being a measurement expert. At the same time, this same person has the responsibility of deciding, on the basis of clear information, to take steps to improve the functioning of the office.

(4) Management of Potential Time Savings. Because cost–benefit analysis at this stage of the game focuses to some extent on time savings, it is necessary to integrate a plan to take advantage of such opportunities. Parkinson's law states that work expands to fill the available time. In order to translate time savings into *more* or *better* output, jobs can be redesigned and new procedures implemented. Having such a plan as part of the system design helps deal with the potential flaw of a cost–benefit analysis based largely on time savings.

The overall reinvestment strategy should be outlined in the office systems strategic plan. This plan describes the strategic objectives of office system implementations. Such objectives could include improving the quality of the organization's products, increasing market share, improving employee job satisfaction and quality of working life, undertaking a new mission, and so on. The more detailed aspects of the reinvestment strategy can be outlined in the project action plan. Projected time savings could be invested, for example, into improving department budgets, increasing contact with clients, generating more purchase orders, or a shorter workday.

The reinvestment strategy must be included in *both* the pilot and operational system cost–benefit analyses. For the pilot, the plan outlines projected reinvestment of time which will be saved. For the operational system, the plan does the same, but also includes evidence regarding the actual results of the pilot reinvestment. A reinvestment plan for the operational system can, of course, be much more ambitious because of the economies of scale involved.

(5) Top Management Education. A strategy for dealing with the problem of cost justification must have, as a central thrust, a plan to equip the "chooser" to make sound decisions regarding investments in office systems. That is, the user management can only intelligently weigh the various alternatives if it is equipped to do so.

It is not unusual for "choosers" to decide to back off from an investment in office systems because they are unable to understand the complex issues involved. In many other cases inappropriate decisions have been made because of a lack of management education.

10.3. QUANTIFICATION OF PILOT SYSTEM COSTS AND BENEFITS

The evaluation of costs and potential benefits for the pilot system follows the same outline as for the operational system. The difference is that in the former, the "benefits" are anticipated on the basis of previous research rather than on the basis of an actual experience with an office system in the user environment. Nevertheless, based on the data collected in the Pilot Systems Analysis a solid estimate of the expected impact of the system can be made. In most cases this should be adequate to cost-justify the capital costs and operating expenses of an integrated office system pilot.

10.4. COST–BENEFIT ANALYSIS FOR THE OPERATIONAL SYSTEM

As the pilot phase draws to completion, the system monitoring data is conbined with the posttest data to show the effects of the pilot. These data are used for the operational system cost-justification. However, there is not a linear relationship between the benefits found in the pilot and the projected benefits built into the operational system cost–benefit analysis. This is true for a number of reasons.

There is a substantial "economy of scale" in integrated office system design. For example, a mail system with 30 users will have a much smaller impact than a mail system with an addressable population of 5,000. Depending on the willingness of the chooser, the analyst may be able to factor in economy-of-scale considerations. This can be done by arbitrarily weighting data on the impact of the pilot system, with a correction factor generated from previous office system research.

An operational system is likely to have more, or more appropriate, functionality than the pilot. The functionality (what the system will do for the user) is often phased-in over time. As a result, benefits found in a pilot are often a subset of the benefits to be found in its operational extension.

As well, in the best of cases it is difficult to predict the profound impacts of a fully operational office system. When designed and implemented properly, the expected benefits usually turn out to have been grossly underestimated. For example, the synergy of combining a large number of people on a system with expanding functionality can yield completely unexpected, positive results. In one case, the system enabled a reduction of errors in the decision-making process in an organization. The added revenue which resulted could have paid for the system tenfold in the first 6 months. In another case, it was found that two major data-processing systems had been displaced by the office system. The users began constructing applications that more closely met their needs, and with some minor development changes it became possible to remove and sell the old DP hardware.

Finally, there is often a problem of extrapolating the results from a small pilot group to a larger organization which may have different characteristics. One cannot assume that results from a pilot group which was not randomly selected can be generalized to the rest of the organization.

Consequently, the evidence from the pilot system posttest, while critical in rooting the operational system cost-justification in reality, must also contain projections regarding anticipated benefits.

Nobody promised you that all this was going to be easy.

10.4.1. Organizational Performance Benefits

These measures will be specific to the organizational unit where the system was implemented. The unit may have a bottom line, or revenue objectives which can be measured. Other measures can be developed to quantify quality of service to the client, appropriateness of the products of the office unit, format of the product, degree to which the product was judged useful by the recipient, value added, market share, operating effectiveness, sales, ROI in human resources, etc.

10.4.2. Internal Benefits

The equation for calculating the internal efficiency and productivity benefits is shown in Figure 10.1. The model separates benefits into the three categories, and then includes *only those* benefits which are measurable (1, hard dollar, and 2, soft dollar).

(1) Hard Dollar Benefits. These are dollar savings which actually lower costs. Examples are cutting back on the use of temporary secretarial services; saving floor space which displaces other costs; reducing undesirable employee overtime; reducing mail costs; reduced equipment costs such as photocopiers, old computers, TWX or Telex, telephone, (rental or capital costs); reducing travel costs; reduced costs of paper, office supplies, etc.; and savings through slowing staff turnover (recruiting costs, training costs, etc.).

The dollar values of such cost displacements are determined using the techniques outlined in this book.

(2) Soft Dollar Benefits. These are measurable savings or improvements which can be translated into meaningful dollar values, but which are not, in themselves, direct financial savings. Examples are reductions in the time spent making unsuccessful phone calls; reduction in scheduling time; reduction in the time spent making budget and other calculations; delegation of professional and managerial activities due to time savings of subordinates; and reduction of time spent in undesirable travel.

(3) Qualitative Benefits. These are benefits which may be measurable, but which do not easily lend themselves to dollar equivalencies. Examples are reduction in the number of interruptions per day, increase in the lateral communications among persons for whom this was identified as a problem, improvement in employee morale, job satisfaction, and worker motivation as measured by the Job Diagnostic Index, and faster turnaround.

The hard and soft dollar benefits are factored into the cost–benefit equations. The qualitative benefits are added to the business case in such a way as the chooser can select which of these is acceptable.

A hard and soft dollar equation is presented in Figure 10.2. This equation is not intended to be applicable to all organizations, under all circumstances. Rather, it is presented to show one way of calculating the "internal" benefits of a system. In layperson's terms it shows benefits as being

- the total time savings per employee, summed across employees, minus
- the total time lost due to additional system related activities, plus
- the hard dollar savings.

Costs (C) = Total Hardware, Software, and other Costs over the Period D

$$\text{Benefits (B)} = \left(ND \sum_{i=1}^{n} \frac{X_iY_iZ_i}{M} \right) - \left(N \sum_{i=1}^{b} \frac{P_iQ_iZ_i}{M} \right) + (H)$$

N = Number of employees
M = Number of minutes in the work day
D = Constant (number of working days in a specified period, eg. 1 year)
X = Mutually exclusive activity, in minutes per day, per employee
n = Number of mutually exclusive activities which are measured
Y = Reduction potential for activity X, in percentage
Z = Mean daily billable rate per employee
P = Additional system related activities, in minutes per day
B = Number of mutually exclusive activities which are measured
Q = Number of days to which Z_i applies
H = Hard dollar savings

Figure 10.2 Costs and internal benefits.

10.4.3. Adding Costs to the Equation

System costs fall in two categories: capital costs and operating expenses. Naturally, the two are treated somewhat differently. In the early stages of the design process (opportunity and feasibility reports) the costs will be estimates only. As the design team gets closer to selecting the hardware and software (specification report) the vendors should produce written cost quotations. Estimates will still have to be made for operating expenses such as in-house software development, maintenance, training costs, and salaries of other support personnel.

System costs are calculated for a specified time period (e.g., one year, two years). When extending the system costs from a pilot to an operational system all costs will, in most cases, have to be entered into the equation. An example of the cost side of the cost–benefit analysis for an operational system is contained in Figure 10.3.

The soft benefits focus on the reduction of time spent in various kinds of mutually exclusive activities. Example calculations of soft benefits are contained in Figure 10.4.

Part of the equation is the calculation of "de-benefits" or *additional* soft dollar *costs* which are incurred as a result of the system. For example, there is a "learning curve" period where the employee is not working at full productive capacity. The learning period does not really result in increased dollar costs, but nevertheless has implications for overall productivity which should be factored in. An example of a de-benefit calculation is included in Figure 10.5.

Option 1—Timesharing

Employee time lost due to training	$21,899	
Training	1,250	(5 person days @ $250)
Software development	5,250	(21 person days @ $250)
Purchase 40 terminals @ $1,400	56,000	(one time)
Total initial cost	$84,399	

Monthly Charges:

Connect charges	$47,040	(2.8 connect hour/terminal/day @ $20/connect hour)
Storage charges	10,000	(10 mb. databases) (40 mb. stnds. text) (40 @ $30/month)
Modems	3,508	($87.72 × 40)
Telephone lines	1,200	(40 @ $30/month)
4 dedicated ports	1,487	(@ $346.80)
4 printers	2,745	(laser printer @ $2105/mo; 300 lines/min. @ 350/mo; letter quality @ 300/mo; matrix @ $40/mo)
Total Monthly Charges (before discount)	$65,981	
Less 20% discount	13,198	
Actual monthly charge	$52,784	

Option 2—Purchase from ABC Corporation

40 terminals @ $3,120	$124,800	
Option 2 Computer (2.48 mb. main memory; 300 mb. disk; 1 tape drive; 300 lines/min. printer)	322,000	
1 letter quality printer	6,000	
1 matrix printer	3,000	
1 laser printer	93,000	
Total Initial Capital Cost	$548,800	
Employee time lost due to training	$21,899	
Software	48,000	(WP–$18,000) (Messaging & info retrieval $12,000 (Mgmt. supp. - $18,000)
Training	1,250	(5 person days @ $250)
Software development	5,250	(21 person days @ $250)
Total Initial Cost	$625,199	

Monthly Charges:

Support staff salary	$1,250	
Hardware maintenance	1,458	
Total Monthly Charges	$2,708	

Option 3—Purchase from XYZ Corporation

XYZ Processors
    —1 mb. main memory; 202 mb. disk
    —1 mb. main memory
    —256 kb. main memory
1 300 lines/min. printer
1 160 cps matrix printer
1 letter quality printer

Software	$370,000	
40 terminals @ $2300	92,000	
1 laser printer	93,000	
Total Initial Capital Cost	$555,000	
Training Fees	$19,680	(51 people—2 days; 7 people—3 days @ $800/person/week)
Employee time lost due to training	21,899	
Software development	5,250	
Total Initial Cost	$46,829	
Monthly Charges:		
Software maintenance	$40	
Hardware maintenance	2,873	
1 Support staff salary	1,250	
Total Monthly Charges	$4,163	

Option 4—Lease/Purchase (24 months) from XYZ Corporation

Training Fees	$19,680	(51 people—2 days; 7 people—3 days @ $800/person/week)
Employee time lost due to training	21,899	
Software development	5,250	
Total Initial Cost	$46,829	
Monthly Charges:		
40 terminals	$19,790	
Laser Printer	2,210	
Hardware Maintenance	2,873	
Software Enhancement	40	
1 Support Staff Salary	1,250	
Total Monthly Charges	$26,163	

Total Outlay After 24 Months to Purchase System: $115,500

—Penalty for breaking lease is payment of remaining principal after which equipment is owned.

Figure 10.3 Example of operational system cost calculation.

1. X_i = 18 minutes (unsuccessful telephone calls)
   Y_i = .65 (% of X_i eliminated by electronic messaging)
   Z_i = \$150 (per diem billing rate for employees)
   d = 221 days (working days per year)
   m = 450 minutes per working day
   n = 40 employees

   $$\frac{ndX_iY_iZ_i}{m} = \$34,480$$

2. X_2 = 29 minutes (scheduling time)
   Y_2 = .45 (% of X_2 eliminated by admin. tools)
   Z_2 = \$150 (per diem billing rate for employees)

   $$\frac{ndX_2Y_2Z_2}{m} = \$38,440$$

Figure 10.4 Example of soft benefit calculation.

10.5. COST—BENEFIT ANALYSIS FOR SPECIAL APPLICATIONS

The approach outlined above is the general case. There are specific office system applications which require unique cost-justifications to be performed.

One example is the business case for a decision support system. Unless the impact of a system on variables such as the error rate, or the added value from improved decisions can be isolated, decision support systems must be justified on more subjective ground.

Such "soft dollar" or "qualitative" approaches are also important when investigating benefits in the areas of value of information and quality of work life.

Highly sophisticated techniques can be used to cost-justify some specialized applications. A good example is the use of Bayesian statistics to quantify the value of information. This technique is part of a broader approach which has become known as information economics (IE).[4] Other specialized tech-

p_1 = 30 minutes (daily/unproductive time)
q_1 = 25 days (during which learning takes place)
z_1 = \$150 (per diem billable rate)
m = 450 (minutes per working day)
n = 40 employees

$$\frac{np_1q_1z_1}{m} = \$1,000$$

Figure 10.5 Example of de-benefit calculation.

Assumptions

Cost of capital	15%	Discount rate—15%
Cost of debt capital	15%	
Income tax rate	50%	
Debt ratio	45%	
CCA rate	30%	
Life of equipment	– 5 years	
Study life	– 5 years	

Buy Option

Year 1

Capital

40 Terminals @ 2,300	92,000.00
1 Printer	93,000.00
Computer	370,000.00
	555,000.00

Expense

Training	41,579.25
Software development	5,250.00
Software enhancements	480.00
Hardware maintenance	34,476.00
Salary	15,000.00
	96,785.25

Year 2–Year 5

Expense

Software enhancements	480.00	
Hardware maintenance	34,476.00	
Salary	15,000.00	
	49,956.00	inflated 10%/year

Figure 10.6 Costs for buy option.

Year 1

Expense	
Training	41,579.00
Software development	5,250.00
40 Terminals and computer	237,481.00
Printer	26,520.00
H/w maintenance	34,476.00
S/w enhancements	480.00
Salary	15,000.00
	360,786.00

Year 2

Expense		
40 Terminals	237,481.00	
Printer	26,520.00	
H/w maintenance	34,476.00	
S/w enhancements	480.00	
Salary	15,000.00	
	313,957.00	inflated 10%/year from 1982

Year 3

Capital		
40 Terminals, printer & computer	115,500.00	
Expense		
S/w enhancements	480.00	
H/w maintenance	34,476.00	
Salary	15,000.00	
	49,956.00	inflated 10%/year

Years 4 & 5

Expense		
S/w emhancements	480.00	
H/w maintenance	34,476.00	
Salary	15,000.00	
	49,956.00	inflated 10%/year

Figure 10.7 Costs for rent/buy option.

	Capital	Expenses	Misc. tax	Income tax	Net cash flow
Present worth	555000	257407	1819	−363439	−450787
1982	555000	96785	888	−147408	−505265
1983	0	54952	666	−97426	41808
1984	0	60447	444	−79271	18380
1985	0	66491	222	−67104	391
1986	0	73140	0	−59240	−13901
EOS				−36356	36356

Figure 10.8 Cash flows for the buy option.

	Capital	Expenses	Misc. tax	Income tax	Net cash flow
Present worth	87335	739460	156	−405647	−421304
1982	0	360786	0	−180393	−180393
1983	0	345353	0	−172676	−172676
1984	115500	60447	154	−50696	−125405
1985	0	66491	77	−47412	−19157
1986	0	73140	0	−46129	−27012
EOS				−15441	15441

Figure 10.9 Cash flows for the rent/buy option.

Life 5	Ic 15.0%		Id 15.0%
	Rd 45.0%		Tax 50.0%
	Buy Option	Rent/Buy Option	Net
Present worth			
Net cash flow	−450787	−421304	−29483
Capital	555000	87335	467665
Expenses	257407	739460	−482054
Misc. Taxes	1819	156	1663
Income tax	363439	−405647	42208

Figure 10.10 Detailed economic evaluators.

niques which may hold some promise for office systems are utility analysis, risk analysis, sensitivity analysis, and simulation.[4]

10.6. RENT, BUY, OR LEASE

Thompson has shown how to use sophisticated economic evaluation packages to assess the merits of renting, buying, or leasing integrated office system gear.[5] This can be done by either an economic evaluation of discounted cash flow for costs, or an evaluation which also takes into account costs and value added benefits. An example of the former approach is shown in Figures 10.6. to 10.10.

Two options are compared in the illustration: "buy" versus "rent/buy." A number of assumptions have to be made and applied regarding cost of capital, cost of debt capital, life of the equipment, etc. These assumptions and corresponding capital expenditures and expenses for the "buy" option are indicated in Figure 10.6.

Figure 10.7 shows capital expenditures and expenses for the "rent/buy" option. Here the equipment is rented for the first two years and purchased in the third year. The cash flows for the two options are illustrated in Figures 10.8 and 10.9, respectively.

In Figure 10.10 the picture is put together to give the summary economic evaluators. The net present value of the "buy" option is $ − 450,787. The figure for the "rent/buy" option is $ − 421,304. As a result the "rent/buy" option is chosen.

Chapter 11

Getting Going

There is nothing more perilous to conduct or more uncertain in its success, than to take the lead in the introduction of a new order of things. Because the innovator has for enemies all those who have done well under the old conditions, and lukewarm defenders in those who may do well under the new.

(*The Prince*, Machiavelli)

The starting point for "getting going" as an innovator is to understand where you and your organization are and have come from. Organizations mature as they move deeper toward fully integrated systems.

11.1. STAGES OF GROWTH

Various "stage" theories have been developed to explain natural, social, psychological, etc., phenomena. One of the best known is Freud's theory of psychosexual development. Freud saw the development of a human being as the process of the libido, or sexual energy, being moved from and to different parts of the body. The theory (at least at the time) helped explain the process of human growth and development and also to understand problems that arose as the result of unsuccessfully completed stages.

It is useful to have a stage theory regarding the evolution of integrated office systems within an organization. Such a theory can help an organization understand the context of its activities and some of the underlying processes in its evolution.

Many writers have attempted to describe the various stages an organization goes through on its way to fully integrated operational systems. This goes back to Nolan's theory that an organization moves through four stages of growth–initiation, expansion, formalization, and maturity–in its use of information systems. Early efforts to develop a stage approach for office automation had centered on what was known at the time as the automation stage of data processing.[1-3] Zisman applied Nolan's four stages of growth to office automation.[3] One of the most useful stage theories was developed by Day under the auspices of the Diebold Office Automation program.[4] Day saw office systems evolving within an organization in five clearly identifiable phases:

(1) Conception. Individual piecemeal tools like word processing, facsimile or distributed data processing are judged to be inadequate. There is a recognition of the need to directly support knowledge workers with integrated tools.

(2) Initiation. Work is begun to go beyond cost displacement applications and implement the first value-added office system pilot. A study or studies are initiated and requirements for a pilot determined. Implementation begins.

(3) Contagion. Implementation and evaluation of integrated office system pilots to improve the work of professional, multifunction clerical, managerial, and executive personnel.

(4) Consolidation. Full operational systems are implemented and measures taken to consolidate many of the explosive developments in the contagion stage.

(5) Creative Evolution. Integrated systems are developed which are inherent in the plans of the entire organization to improve services, meet objectives, expand markets, and revise the mission of the organization.

At each stage there are technologies, organizational issues, applications characteristics, and planning needs which can be identified. It is useful to periodically evaluate what stage has been reached. Such reflection can identify problems, for example regression to a previous stage, arrest of development at a given stage, or premature projection into a future stage.

11.2. GETTING ORGANIZED

Regardless of which stage one finds oneself at, there are certain *prerequisites* for moving forward. One is top management support, somewhere on the continuum between authorization and commitment. A second is adequate cross functional involvement, where various stakeholder functions (MIS/DP, administration, Corporate Communications, etc.) are collaborating. A third is an assignment of some personnel to work on the problem. At first this may be a part-time person. After a while it will likely be an entire function itself.

Because these systems are still in their formative years, it is likely that in-house expertise will be lacking. The pitfalls are not only numerous; they are deep. Taking the wrong path in this office systems jungle can have very serious consequences. The price to pay for waiting, however, can be even greater. Given this, there may be a strong case to find the resources to get help from an integrated office systems consultant.

Selecting a consultant also has its pitfalls. With the convergence of computer, communications, and office technologies, there is also a convergence in terms of the services offered by corresponding consulting organizations. Add to this the efforts by traditional "management consulting," "organizational development," and other stripes of consultants and the picture can get confusing. In most cases, it makes sense to find a consulting organization which focuses on integrated office systems. If one hires a DP consultant, one is likely to acquire some bad baggage from the old approaches to systems. If one hires a word-processing consultant, one is likely to get help in the area of word processing—which may not be "help" at all. If the services of a management consulting organization are contracted, it is improbable that the consultants will understand the complex technical, measurement, and other issues in office system design and implementation.

An "integrated office system" consulting organization with a multidisciplinary team and a User-Driven approach is a better bet. The best of these organizations have not "migrated" from anywhere, at least recently. Rather they have been formed by individuals and groups who have had a longer-term appreciation for the way the world has evolved.

Working with a consultant is complicated by the fact that s/he will often be consulting to in-house practitioners who are (or should view themselves as) *internal* consultants. To further complicate matters, both internal and external consultants may be working with persons from the functional unit selected for a pilot study. These persons, perhaps participating on a study team, act as consultants of a third order. As a result, it is critical to spend the time to determine responsibilities and reporting relationships. More than once, internal and external consultants have tripped over each other and confused, or worse, alienated the end user in the process.[5] As part of a project plan, there should be a clear definition of who is the client and of the responsibilities of the various participants.

Moving from the conception to initiation stages, it is necessary to establish some form of integrated systems task force. It has been found useful to have this group headed by senior management. There are several parallel thrusts to align:

- Ongoing strategic planning for integrated office systems.
- Ongoing investigation of user needs and implementation of integrated system pilots.

- Ongoing extension of these pilots to operational systems.
- Ongoing vendor evaluation through a "technology gatekeeper," coupled with ongoing experimentation of new products.
- Ongoing user education.

This is depicted in Figure 11.1.

11.3. PLANNING FOR INTEGRATED OFFICE SYSTEMS

Zisman polemicizes with two extreme views on planning for office automation.[6] One group argues that office automation is "unplannable" because the concept is so volatile. It is better, they argue, to wait till things "settle down" and planning can be seriously undertaken. Planning should be postponed until the organization has had a number of experiences with office systems and can make some sense out of it all. A second group argues that because things are volatile, no implementations should be undertaken until there is a complete and comprehensive plan for office systems. Both these extreme positions are wrong. For the first group things will never settle down. For the second, planning will continue forever without any actual systems being implemented.[3] Planning *and* implementation of office systems go hand in hand. They are symbiotic. It is like the song about love and marriage: "you can't have one without the other." The concrete experiences of implementing systems feed into the planning process. On the other hand, the planning process gives some direction and coherence to the process of implementing systems.

It is important to assign resources to the office systems planning process for a number of reasons.

A significant percentage of the capital expenditures of more and more organizations is on office systems.[7] The ability of many organizations to become or remain competitive will hinge on how they incorporate use of these technologies. Planning for systems is becoming part of the overall strategic planning process.

The technology is changing rapidly. Office automation is aimed at a moving target which is unlikely to coalesce in the 1980s.[7] As a result there is a need for planning to position the organization to evolve as new technologies appear. This is especially true because of the complexity of these technologies. To avoid being led down the garden path by any vendor, the planning process should be brought to bear.

Who should drive the train? Determining organizational responsibility, for example where the office systems function should lie, requires planning and ongoing evaluation. Cooperation from the various stakeholders and commitment of resources must be secured.

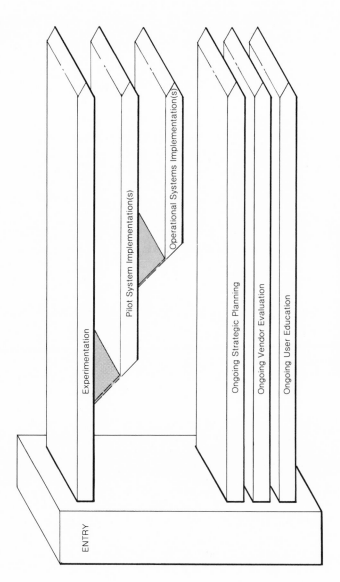

Figure 11.1. Getting going.

Office systems are also in their nascent period and are still a new topic for most people. In any organization there is likely to be a lack of homogeneity regarding perspectives, objectives, strategies, and tactics. The planning *process* is as important as the product of planning—the office systems plan. Through the process of constructing an office systems plan, a common understanding of these systems and how they should be approached can be forged.

As well, because these systems are new, one of the most difficult tasks is winning widespread user acceptance and commitment. Generalist users are often uneasy about integrating these technologies into their jobs. The planning process can help create the climate for change. A thorough office systems plan can enable the implementors to approach the users with clarity and consistency.

Implementation of office systems can have an explosive character. As the organization enters the "contagion" period, all kinds of centrifugal pressures are generated. This can be anticipated and planned for.

For these reasons a planning process should be initiated and maintained. The degree of formality of the process can vary between organizations, and likely will vary over time. This process could involve the use of a formal planning methodology conducted by an office systems function. Or it could, at the other end of the continuum, be a series of informal discussions. The degree of formality will depend on many factors such as the stage entered, the degree of top management support, and size of the organization.

Office systems planning must be based on a solid plan for the organization as a whole. Back in 1974, Louis Fried of the Stanford Research Institute said: "it is impossible to develop a long-range plan for data processing unless there is a specific long-range plan with stated goals and objectives for the corporation as a whole and for the individual users."[8] What was true for the limited data-processing systems is infinitely truer for office systems. Sometimes, however, the initiation of an office systems planning process can precipitate, aid, or help consolidate the overall planning process.

While the focus of planning should be on the process, not the final plan, it helps to understand the main topics which a final plan should contain. The content and structure of an office systems plan is not something that is standard for all organizations. A number of different cuts on it can be taken.[37] However, there are at least eight topics which should be discussed and for which approaches should be adopted.

(1) An Overall Perspective. A common understanding should be developed regarding the scope and significance of office automation in general: a conceptual framework and the main points of leverage; the main problems to be dealt with, including the human, organizational, measurement, implementation and planning issues; and a forecast of office system technologies.

(2) An Overall Opportunity Analysis. An organizational scan can provide

the data for an overall analysis of where the opportunities for improvement lie. What are the main problem areas which can be addressed? What are the key technologies which appear to be good candidates for widespread use? What is the status of current systems in comparison to this?

(3) A Charter for the Office Systems Function. More and more major organizations are establishing such a function. Issues include its mission, objectives, and policies; its line of reporting and working relationship with other stakeholder functions; the responsibilities of the function; and its size, staffing, and resources.

(4) An Educational Strategy. The issue here is how will all users and decision makers be introduced to office systems concepts and equipped to make the changes coming. This is no small matter, as many implementors have learned. Old perspectives die hard, especially when they come from the data-processing shop. A comprehensive education plan must be adopted with resources secured to set it in motion. This can include membership in office systems programs, attendance at seminars and conferences, in-house briefings and classes, audio visual materials, various publications, and in-house discussions and presentations. This will be an ongoing process, through all stages of maturity in office systems.

(5) A Design Strategy. This book is one indication of the need for new strategies for office systems design. A User-Driven Design strategy should be adopted and become the standard for building systems. A technology gatekeeper can be established to do ongoing vendor evaluation. An integration plan should be formulated to lay out how various tools will be integrated. This includes adopting an approach to local networks, external data bases, and the reliance on a single vendor to facilitate downstream integration.

(6) A Measurement Methodology. Linked to a User-Driven Design strategy, an approach to measurement should be determined. If this is mistakenly seen as a nonissue, the necessity of measurement for requirements analysis and evaluation will have to be discussed.

(7) An Implementation Strategy. What will be the approach for fostering a climate for change and managing the change itself? This includes a plan of implementation schedules, procedures, and responsibilities. A training substrategy will have to be determined. Finally there should be an approach to evaluating the implementation itself.

(8) An Action Plan. Long-range planning for office systems is not really feasible. It tends to become an exercise in forecasting and scenario building. While this can be useful, it is more appropriate, in terms of planning, to adopt a shorter-term action plan. This can be driven by data from organizational scans and also from initial pilot implementations.

A two-year plan, for example, can lay out some proposals for office systems implementations on three levels. First are systems which can be implemented organization wide, such as messaging or teleconferencing. Second are systems which are judged to be appropriate for different groupings. Examples are job types (engineers, executives, lawyers); functions (such as personnel functions in different locations); buildings (such as installation of a local network). Finally there are customized office systems necessitating a complete requirements analysis to specify. In this case, general opportunity groups can be identified for further investigation, along with time frames and resources to conduct the assessments.

11.4. UNDERTAKING THE ASSESSMENT

11.4.1. Project Management Methodology

Once an initial commitment to proceed has been established, a project management methodology (PMM) should be applied to develop a detailed project plan. Lebolt has summarized one approach to project management for office systems assessment.[9] It has seven components.

(1) Project Responsibilities. This facet of the PMM incorporates two basic concepts. With the *project triangle* concept, each project requires a clearly identified deliverer, end-product, and acceptor. If these are not clearly defined, the project can decompose. A second is *delegation and sharing of responsibility.* Responsibility cannot be delegated to an individual unless it is accepted with a *personal commitment* to deliver the associated end-project .

(2) Project Initiation. The initiation of projects for office system assessment is defined as the set of activities which precede the submission of the project plans to management and their subsequent approval. Project initiation must produce at least an outline of the criteria whereby the project is to be completed (e.g., delivery/acceptance agreement, project completion agreement).

(3) Project Delegation and Acceptance. A project manager prepares a draft initial plan which identifies end-product description, project team organization, major milestones, a work plan, a resource plan, a financial plan, and individual commitments solicited.

The initial plan makes the project manager's conditions of acceptance visible. After discussions with the project manager the initial plan, with any modifications, is accepted.

(4) Project Plan. This is prepared by the project manager. The project plan is identical to the initial plan except in the level of detail. The purpose of this plan is to facilitate the actual management of the project on a day-to-day basis. The project plan is composed of eight major components. These are delegation of responsibility for deliverables, project team organization plan,

costed milestone schedule, project work plan, resources plan, financial plan, product quality plan, and a project control plan.

(5) Project Control Tools. Various tools can be used. One is a project status report. The major purpose of the status report is to reaffirm the acceptance of the project responsibility by the project manager. It covers the current status of the project (both completion status and fiscal), accomplishments during the period, unresolved problems or obstacles to progress, and objectives for the next period.

These control tools are valuable for a project manager's personal use in measuring accomplishments against objectives.

(6) Change Control Procedures. Changes in the definition of a project's end product may occur. A mechanism to control any such changes is required. The mechanism must allow changes to be proposed, evaluated, and implemented in an orderly way. The change control procedure consists of three activities. *Change proposals* may be submitted by anyone to the project manager, who will log the proposal and arrange investigation of the impact of the change, if necessary. *Impact investigation* is scheduled by the project manager to determine the potential effect in the areas such as cost, schedule, benefits, savings, etc. of any proposed changes to the project. *Change control recommendations* are made by the project manager following an investigation into proposed changes to either accept, reject, or return the change proposal for further investigation or clarification.

(7) Project Completion. Several steps are required to formally complete the project. The consultants must receive internal approval for the delivery of the end product to the acceptor. A delivery/acceptance agreement between the project manager and the client acceptor is signed. To complete the process, a similar agreement is signed between the executive responsible and the client executive.

11.4.2. The Study Team

Once a business unit or other organization has been identified for investigation, a study team, representative of individuals from that unit, should be organized. Such a team can help bridge the gap between the office systems consultants and the client individuals. This team is more than an administrative body. Its members will act as change agents as well as leaders of the assessment. The team will work out the tactics of approaching the organization, review the measurement instruments, and in some cases conduct parts of the assessment. Eventually the team may evolve into the implementation team, and its members may find new career paths opened up by their experiences. Participation on a study team can lead to joining the office systems function down the road.

For these reasons the team should be chosen carefully. Team members should represent a good cross section of the unit being studied. This should include persons from various strata, functions, job types, and associations, as is feasible. It is especially important that representatives from unions be included. Systems properly designed will not be injurious to the users, and unions have every interest to participate in the design process to ensure that their members' interests are defended. On the other hand, the designers and choosers have every interest in ensuring that the system has the support and cooperation of the users and their organizations. Too often, the system has been "announced" out of the blue to the users and met with unnecessary resistance from a local union. Participation on a study team, while not the solution in itself, is a necessary step.

Opinion leaders are good candidates for consideration, as are innovators or persons to take the lead in changing aspects of the job. Often there is someone who has caught the office systems bug, and is delighted to see the study begin. These persons can be key to creating enthusiasm and the momentum for change. In some cases it may be prudent to include persons on the team for political reasons. Examples are a central figure who is skeptical or even hostile to the project, or someone who is in a position to jeopardize its success. Finally, the study team should have a good mix of disciplines. It should not be restricted to systems personnel, for example. Useful disciplines include education, finance, communications, methods and procedures, organization development, and the administrative and library sciences.

A team of about half a dozen members is a good size. Significantly smaller, it is likely to be unrepresentative. If larger, members are likely to end up tripping over one another.

The respondents in the assessment will eventually become the users of the system. Thus, the study is often the first step in securing user acceptance of the system. The key to winning user support is to design a system which will help them and improve their working lives. This simple fact is often overlooked. No cute tricks will convince people to accept a system which is harmful to them, or which makes their jobs more difficult and their work less productive. The experience with coercion in the office has been the same. Without genuine support and acceptance of the system by the users, it is likely to fail.

A study conducted, in part, by representatives of the user organization is likely to result in more valid data. Because of the subjectivity of many of the measures in the assessment program, it is critical that the respondents support the study. As well, it is more likely to result in some sense of ownership by the team members and users.

The central hypothesis behind the notion of User-Driven Design is that a system designed with valid data from, and the active participation of, the future users is more likely to succeed and be useful. The study team is a vehicle to ensure better respondent cooperation (and therefore more valid data) and better potential user participation (and therefore better user acceptance of the system and commitment to its success.)

Timing should be right, for introducing the study. There must be prior agreement of key parties to proceed. Also, the study should be held during a period where the respondents feel they have enough time to participate.

Greenberg, Tapscott, and Henderson found that an introductory meeting, held off-site, can help generate interest in the assessment. Such a meeting should begin with some attractive educational presentations about office systems, designed to allay fears and spark interest.[10]

In general, the consultant should creatively seek every feasible opportunity to *involve* the users and *explain* how this new and often frightening world can, with their participation, be more fulfilling and enjoyable.

11.4.3. Analysis, Iteration, and Interpretation

In most large organizations there are individuals with expertise in analyzing data. These people, often found in the research and development, operations research, general systems, or management science functions, can be a valuable resource. Data from various instruments can be computer analyzed using statistical packages which are widely available and easy to use.

As in all behavioral research, valid and reliable data—appropriately analyzed—do not necessarily result in useful information. In particular, office

Figure 11.2. Fear of technology.

system research requires careful and thoughtful interpretation of the data, given the many problems in research design which tend to undermine the validity of the data.

The client should receive no surprises at the final presentation of the findings. Data analysis and interpretation is an interactive process, where the consultant, study team, and client acceptor or chooser discuss and rediscuss the findings and their meaning. Such an approach helps ensure that the client is brought up to speed with the assessment process; that the data are interpreted with the help of client insights which a consultant would take years to develop; and that the design is coproduced with the client feeling a sense of ownership and commitment.

11.5. IMPLEMENTATION

After "User-Driven," the winning adjective to appropriately modify the word "design" would be "quick." Pilots must be constructed quickly. The climate for change can dissipate if there is a long development phase. As Meyer and Lodahl point out, reinforcement from a fast success will also solidify the user group's enthusiasm, while building the implementor's credibility. [11]

Given the continually expanding product lines of the vendors competing in the office system market, it is often feasible to use off-the-shelf technologies, at least for pilot systems. Software packages to be purchased can run on the existing in-house mainframes or minis. The only additional technologies which may have to be acquired in such cases are terminals and printers, and perhaps some additional storage or processing power. Another alternative is to select a complete system from one of the time-sharing bureaus or office system vendors. These often require no additional software development.

In cases where special applications or other features need to be programmed, the emphasis should be on building a simple, quick solution. At the same time work can begin on planning for the more extensive and reliable tools which may be required for an operational system. In all cases, systems programming should be avoided.

During the assessment process, data were collected to customize a training program. It seems obvious that training and the installation of equipment should go hand and hand. However, in countless cases terminals and printers have been installed before the training program was in place, The end result can be undue anxiety ("what is this thing on my desk going to do, once it's plugged in?") or bad experiences as untrained users lose files, get lost in the system, etc. The arrival of the equipment is a moment when interest is peaked, and when there can be actual excitement and enthusiasm in the air. The time to strike is while the iron is hot.

Chapter 12

From Pilot to Operational System

Second Law of Office Systems: The ease of a pilot implementation is inversely related to the complexity of its operational extension.

As with other phases, the design of the operational system can be driven by data from the user. These data include pilot system monitoring data and data from the pilot system posttests and the operational systems analysis.

In the posttest the original measures which led to the system design are replicated. These are coupled with additional measures to further probe user requirements for a fully operational system. In this way, the approach applied to the pilot systems analysis can be extended to the operational systems analysis.

12.1. CASE STUDY

In the late 1970s, one of the first controlled evaluations of an integrated office system was conducted at Bell-Northern Research (BNR) in Toronto.[1] An organizational assessment was conducted and a pilot system implemented to investigate the impact of these systems on knowledge workers. The pilot had such a positive impact that it was decided to extend it to a fully operational system for all of BNR's Toronto office. Data from the pilot system posttest indicated a very short payback period for the substantial investment in an operational system. However, it was found that even those data were conservative. Through exposure to and use of the system, overall organizational performance improved and the objectives and even mission of the Toronto business unit expanded.

The design of the BNR pilot research was a quasi-experimental design which was configured as follows:

$$O \qquad\qquad X \qquad\qquad O$$
$$O \qquad\qquad\qquad\qquad O$$

where O is an observation and X is the treatment.

An experimental group ($n = 19$) and a control group ($n = 26$) were pretested (observation) in August 1979. The office information communication (OIC) system (the experimental treatment) was then implemented immediately. The posttest was conducted in the following May.

Several other features of this quasi-experimental design are as follows: There were three participant observers in the experimental group. These office system project members acted as full members of the pilot, to directly observe the various facets of system use and to fully participate in learning the system and using it to help them with their jobs. Pre- and posttest measures were taken to ensure that participant observers did not differ significantly from other members of the experimental group.

(1) There was ongoing monitoring of experimental group activities on the system. Measures built into the system include log-in hours, commands used, applications used, communication patterns, etc. In fact there was a record of all activity on the system. To ensure privacy and resulting respondent trust and cooperation, the contents of messages, text, and files were not examined.

(2) Structured interviews were held midway between pre- and posttests. These interviews were used to help assess initial user progress in learning the system, to assess needed system modifications, and to continue the training process.

The measurement instruments developed for the BNR pilot included organizational scan interviews; a diagnostic Organizational Effectiveness questionnaire; an extensive survey questionnaire; a Network Interaction Analysis form asking respondents with whom they communicated in a "typical" specified time period; an Activities/Communication log; a method of system monitoring; and structured interviews.

The relationship of these instruments to the research design is indicated in Table 12.1.

12.1.1. The Sample

The test group of 19 consisted of seven managers, eight professionals, and four administrative staff. While this group cannot be said to represent

Table 12.1. Measurement Instruments

Pretest (pilot systems analysis)	Posttest
1. Questionnaire I System requirements Communication data Information use, access and problems Attitudes to technology Job design Quality of working life Demographic data	1. Questionnaire I again, plus items on attitudes towards the pilot
2. Network/interaction analysis Examined the communication network	2. Same
3. Activities/communications log A detailed account of time use and communications patterns	3. Same, plus data compared to 4 below
	4. Data generated from the system, e.g., Kinds of applications used System use over days, weeks, months Learning curve Commands used Computer communications patterns
	5. Posttest interviews of experimental group Examined problems with system training, documentation, and features desired

"typical" office workers, it did contain a variety of different kinds of employees. In the managerial group was one executive, one administrative manager, and managers involved in systems development, research, and consulting. The professional group contained a psychologist, a management science specialist, two programmers, and two engineers. Most of the administrative staff were secretaries.

A similar control group of 26 consisted of nine managers, eleven professionals, and six administrative staff.

Table 12.2 compares some demographic data for experimental and control groups.

Table 12.2. Demographic Data for Experimental and Control Groups

Variables	Experimental group	Control group
N	19	26
Job:		
Managerial	7	9
Technical Staff	8	11
Administrative Staff	4	6
Mean age	29.6	32.2
Sex:		
Male	10	18
Female	9	8
Mean length of time at BNR (in years)	1.5	1.6

The pretest data were analyzed to determine if any significant pretest differences between these two groups exist. Chi-square tests were performed on the data from the survey questionnaire. Of 236 variables, each cross-tabulated with the variable "group" (which contained the subdivisions "experimental" and "control"), only five differences were found to be significant at the .01 level ($p < .01$). This number could roughly be expected to occur by chance. It therefore appeared that the experimental and control groups are roughly equivalent, in terms of the variables measured by the survey questionnaire.

One noteworthy difference was the response to the statement "Electronic mail is cost effective." The members of the experimental group tended to agree with this statement more than those in the control group ($p < .01$). However, since this was the only variable out of 29 measuring attitudes towards office automation which showed any significant differences between groups, the possibility of pretest attitudinal differences towards office automation was judged to be quite low.

In office systems design it is not feasible to randomly sample a given population and randomly allocate subjects to control and experimental groups. Consequently, control and experimental groups were selected using other criteria. Some of these had more to do with the internal needs of the company, than with enhancing the quality of the research. Most, however, were related to both needs, as the two are generally not contradictory but complementary. That is, a good research design and system must correspond to genuine needs of the workers and organization involved to be successful.

A standard "decision analysis" was performed in which each of the criteria was given a weight. Each alternative configuration was then scored as to how well it met each of the criteria. The products of these scores by the criteria weights were summed, resulting in a total score for each of the alternative system configurations. The configuration with the highest score was then selected.

12.1.2. The System

In the pilot systems analysis, a number of requirements were identified. They fall into the categories of communications tools, information retrieval tools, document production tools, administrative support tools, and analytical tools.

An Office Information Communications System (OICS) was developed. At the time the research was conducted, there were no commercially available systems which met the requirements identified, so a unique system was designed. The system consisted of an integrated set of application programs running on the UNIX* operating system. Access was provided through terminals that were hard-wired CRTs without any special function keys or other intelligence.

A user logged onto the system by giving a unique user identification name and password. Once his or her identity had been established, the user had access to any part of the system environment through typing the command name associated with the facility desired.

For example, the user accessed the Bell and Northern corporate electronic mail system by typing "cocos," the automatic diary and to-do tool by typing "diary," an on-line bibliography by typing "library," the interactive facility to make a paper letter by typing "mkletter," and the basic calculator by typing "bc."

Early enhancements to the system enabled the user to select a user interface. For example, some users preferred a menu-based interface, and were able to select that style of interaction by changing their user profile. When the user wanted to do something on the system s/he simply typed the number associated with the menu item desired. New users or users who ran into trouble were assisted by a computer-aided instruction capability.

Some of the features of the system were as follows:

(1) Communications Tools. An electronic text messaging system enabled users to compose, send, forward, reply to, and file electronic messages. Facilities for paper correspondence were available. The user was prompted by a program which automatically generated formatted memos and letters. A "maillog" system enabled the tracking of paper mail in, out, and within the office. As well, a synchronous messaging system was provided, enabling

* Registered trademark of Western Electric.

users, if they permit it, to interrupt each other on their screens with short urgent messages.

(2) Text Processing. Several text editors were available. The most commonly used was a line oriented text editor with a terse user interface. A powerful text formatter called NROFF structured the input of the text, e.g., chapter headings, paragraphs, and the like, and outputted reports with pagination, hyphenation, justification, page numbering, point numbering, table of contents, etc. Spelling checks using three dictionaries as data bases and readability indices for examining the content of text helped with the production of documents. As well, there were tools for performing sorts, merges, text and data manipulations, along with some table, figure, and graphics capabilities.

(3) Information Retrieval. The system provided an information retrieval subsystem to maintain and query data bases of any type of information. Among the first uses of this facility in the project were a project bibliography and a conference and seminar schedule.

Also a direct linkage to numerous data bases previously only available in the company's Technical Information Centre was constructed. A special application merged a timesheet entry system with project management for project data tracking, status reporting, and milestones, etc.

(4) Administrative Functions. Among the administrative applications initially employed by users were a personal log (what was done when), to-do file, cost tracking, schedules, coming events, time reminders, phone lists, and telephone area codes and acronyms.

(5) Analytical Tools. The central analytical tool was a project control system. All financial and milestone data for company projects were included in the system. These could be accessed to assess project status. A second tool was an interactive statistics package, which enabled a variety of statistical applications with simple graphical output, ranging from calculation of means to regression analysis. The user was able to interact with the data on the screen. A basic calculator was also provided. This was used for basic arithmetic and scientific operations. As well, traditional programming and data-processing tools were available. These included tools to sort, merge, and manipulate data.

12.1.3. Limitations of the Study

The BNR study applied more rigorous scientific methods to office system field research than other studies to date. In addition, tests of selected data conducted by researchers at the University of Waterloo indicated extraordinarily high data reliability. Despite these positive aspects, there were a number of important limitations to the study which are discussed in detail in

Tapscott et al.[2] These limitations related to difficulties performing field studies in general, and office system field studies in particular; the uniqueness of the office environment where the study was conducted; and organizational changes, staff turnover, and changes in the content of work in the office environment over the 10-month period.

These problems have their greatest impact on the ability of the researchers to generalize the findings to broader populations of office workers. Consequently, while the findings of this study may well have been the most valid from office system field research to date, the researchers discouraged generalization of these findings beyond the specific experimental environment. It is best that the results are seen as an investigation into the impact of one electronic office system in a given environment. As such they serve to present more detailed and solid hypotheses for verification in other situations.

12.1.3.1. System Use

The system accounting capabilities gave a picture of the extent and character of system use. The mean log-in time per day since the end of the familiarization period for the members of the pilot group who were part of the group from the inception of the study (ongoing pilot–old group) was approximately 3.9 hours. The mean log-in time per day for the ongoing pilot group (new members added to compensate for attrition) was approximately 3.1 hours per day.

The average number of users per week climbed steadily. The overall mean number of users per week was 28 at the time of posttest.

Use of the computer messaging facility steadily increased. The average number of messages sent in the first 9 weeks of the implementation was 9.4 messages per week. The average number of messages sent by the ongoing pilot–old group in the weeks following the introduction of COCOS was 36.8 messages per week. This represents a fourfold increase in messaging over the 10-month period.

This increase can be attributed to several related factors. A more user-friendly and powerful messaging system was installed after eight months of system operation. Additions of increased functionality in the system as a whole encouraged employees to use the system more as a tool to do their jobs. Expansion of the messaging network due to the addition of new users, inside and outside the company, also increased use. As well, there was a prolonged learning curve. This was a period where employees did not simply learn the technical aspects of the system (which are relatively simple) but learned to integrate the system into the execution of their work.

There was wide fluctuation in the use of the messaging system both between users and over time. It was noted, however, that there is less individual variation between users during the last period of the study than the early period. As well, wide fluctuations over time for a given user are to be expected as some days users are out of the office, or heavily involved in face-to-face meetings, etc.

The extended learning curve of the messaging system has important implications for the introduction of such products in the marketplace. It suggests a need to couple products with training, implementation, and monitoring services.

There were several other noteworthy findings regarding messaging. Daily messaging graphs and log-in graphs do not coincide. Log-in statistics are similar to telephone use statistics, peaking in midmorning and midafternoon. Messaging statistics peak in early morning, again in late morning, decrease at noon, and then rise steadily after the lunch period until 5:00 p.m. Average message length was variable during the early weeks but stabilized at approximately 85 words per message. As well, more external messages were sent to the company than went out, as company employees became accustomed to the larger user community.

Several points regarding command usage are noteworthy. The number of commands used per user, per week fluctuated widely but showed no marked increase over the period. The number of *different* commands used per user, per week showed a slow increase as users expanded their repertoire of commands. The top 12 commands accounted consistently for 60% of all command usage. These findings suggest that a reasonably small number of commands, enabling adequate use of the system, can be learned quickly and maintained.

The main uses of the system appeared to be text editing and messaging. During the first 4 months of system operation the average user generated somewhere upwards of 400 pages of textual information. Use of the text editing tool strengthened the hypothesis that managers and professionals will use such a tool, given adequate functionality, rewards, and training.

12.1.3.2. Communications

Pretest and posttest information regarding different aspects of the process of communications were collected and analyzed. There were a number of interesting findings.

The percentage of the day spent in communications activities for the pilot group increased from 53% to 58%, while the figure for the control group decreased from 51% to 45%. The reason for the decrease in the control group is not clear. The increase for the pilot group was likely due, in part, to a reduction of time spent in administrative, noncommunication activities.

There appeared to be a reduction in the use of the telephone and also in one-on-one, face-to-face communications. These findings strengthen the hypothesis that the impact of computer messaging is not simply on replacing paper mail, but rather in substituting for other forms of communication.

There was an increase in communication among peers. In the prestudy management questionnaire, this was judged to be a desirable potential product of the office system, given the weaknesses and importance of such communication in this research and development environment.

There was an increase in the percentage of an employee's day spent in activities which were not "interruptions." These data are important for the cost-justification of office systems, for a reduction in interruptions can result in quantifiable time savings and more or better quality work.

The percentage of attempts to contact fellow workers that failed (for example, from busy phone lines) decreased. Reductions in such shadow functions carry measurable cost–benefit implications. In this case, there were average time savings of almost 10% of the employee's day–savings resulting from improvements in the communications process alone. In most cases these time savings appeared to have been "reinvested"–enabling employees to increase their output and to improve its quality.

In addition to measures of actual time savings, most employees expressed the opinion that the system had saved them time.

The results of the test group's subjective evaluations of time use were mixed. The amount of time that users judged to be "useful" increased but the amount of time they judged to be "important" did not. Both test and control groups showed an increase in the amount of time judged to be "time-effective." But attitudes towards other employees and communications with them improved for the test group only.

Attitudes towards other employees and communications with other employees improved for the pilot group only.

Hypergraph structural analysis indicated that communications within the pilot group were strengthened.

12.1.3.3. Information Access

It was hypothesized that the disparity between perceived "information needed" and perceived "information received" noted at the time of the pretest would decrease for the pilot group. This did not occur. There were a number of improvements between the pretest and posttest in the "information received." However, the perceived "information needed" also increased correspondingly. These findings suggest that as access to information improved, so did expectations regarding what is possible and perceived requirements regarding what is necessary. It is possible that improvements in information were due to a variety of system-related factors including access to the information retrieval system; on-line access to the content of previously written reports; access to previous messages; and better communications with other employees (e.g., supervisors) who had the desired information.

Employees in both groups estimated that they could save substantial time if they had access to a number of specified information topics. In some cases the estimated potential time savings were over 50% of the day. While these *projected* time savings are subjective and likely overestimated, two interesting findings stand out. Both control and pilot groups perceive they receive inadequate information and could save about half their time if they had better access to it. Surprisingly the pilot group indicated that they could save more time than the control group if they had better access to information, even though they were already using an information retrieval system. This likely reflects higher expectations regarding the impact of timely information.

12.1.3.4. Attitudes toward Electronic Office Systems

The pretest–posttest design of this study enabled the researchers to establish and validate regression equations in which the most important predictors of user acceptance can be isolated and weighted. The measures of user acceptance are not attitudes but actual behavior: use of the system. The results of these analyses are reported in Tapscott, Greenberg, and Sartor.[3] However, it is useful to examine the impact of the system on the attitudes of the users as well.

It was found that attitudes towards office system technology changed with system use. Attitudes towards the technology and its potential benefits became more positive. Preference for the use of a keyboard to compose written material increased to the point where users indicated they typed and edited 75% of written material they composed, themselves. There was a positive increase in the opinions of the *abilities* of fellow workers to use an on-line office system in their day-to-day work. Attitudes regarding the greatest potential benefits of office systems shifted from an emphasis on clerical, typing, and administrative tasks to emphasis on professional time savings and the quality of decisions.

Attitudes towards the specific BNR system were, on the whole, positive. Users tended to indicate that the system was not difficult to use. They felt comfortable typing at a terminal. They also indicated that the system was not "down" (unavailable) too much.

Users did, however, express a number of critical attitudes. They tended to agree that a better users' manual should be made available. They stated that the error messages of the system were of little value and that the system should be more tolerant of erroneous user input. Access to a printer was described as inadequate and the degradation of service during peak hours was not acceptable.

Most users felt that the system had improved their ability to do their jobs. Main benefits were seen in the areas of improved communications, better access to information, better preparation of written material, more teamwork, and better collaboration.

Most users felt that the system should be expanded, both in functionality and in the size of the user community. The added functions which received the highest scores were automatic project accounting, computer conferencing, and budgeting tools.

12.1.3.5. Job Design and Quality of Work Life (QWL)

It is often assumed that the introduction of computer systems results in a decline in job satisfaction and QWL. Posttest results of the Job Diagnostic Survey indicated that the opposite can be true. In the context of declining indices of job satisfaction for the control group, there were a number of significant improvements for the pilot group. Some improvements were in the amount of job variety, the amount of significance attributed to the job, a greater sense of accomplishment in the job, a greater desire to be creative, and a decline in the simplicity and repetitiveness of the job.

As well, the pilot group showed no change on a number of variables for which the control group registered significant declines. These were in the amount of personal growth and development, respect and fairness from one's supervisor, the degree of fair play, the degree of independent thought exercised, the quality of supervision, and the amount of job stress.

It should be noted, however, that the control group also showed improvements in the perceived opportunities for growth and perceived creativity.

It appears that the system may have had an impact in enabling pilot group employees to weather the effects of the difficult organizational changes and changes in direction of the company. As well, there is evidence that the improved communications and improved collaboration gained through system use resulted in better relationships with supervisors.

12.1.4. Transition to an Operational System

The posttest indicated that the system had had a positive impact on a number of aspects of office functioning. People were found to be wasting less time in nonuseful activities and to be enjoying their jobs more. The time savings and improvements in employee motivation were also related to improvements in the overall performance of the pilot group. The output from the group was improved dramatically. They were able to secure new clients. One of the pilot subgroups, involved in consulting activities for various clients, was able to perform so well that it quadrupled its revenue within a 14-month period, coupled with massive growth for this group. All members of the original subgroup indicated that use of the system had been the key factor in their success.

Data from the posttest were entered into a cost–benefit analysis, and it was found that on the basis of hard dollar savings and the soft dollar benefits which the BNR executive was willing to accept, there was a payback period of less than two years. This payback period did not take into account the additional revenue which would be generated through use of the system.

Data from the system monitoring were used to identify hardware requirements for the operational system. The average requirements for disc space were determined. The response time for the user group was examined over various periods of the day. Message storage behavior was examined to determine new procedures for the filing and disposition of old messages, and so on.

Data from the operational systems analysis were used to determine the required software enhancements to go fully operational. Having used a system for almost a year, the users were in a much better position to give opinions regarding their requirements than during the pretest. A long list of requests was collected and analyzed for common themes. These subjective opinions were also compared with the more behavioral data from the system monitoring and network analysis and activities/communications log. The items where there appeared to be a positive relationship were given special attention. For example time-use measures indicated that some employees spend considerable time doing budgets and analyzing numbers. Questionnaire data indicated that these users place a high priority on receiving decision support tools. It was concluded that the provision of some budgeting and modeling facilities would likely have a positive impact on the performance of these people. Given that they were managers, this was judged to have direct value added implications. The time saved could be reinvested in project work which would be billable to a client, rather than overhead.

12.2. ISSUES IN OPERATIONAL SYSTEM DESIGN

A number of new issues are raised during the transition from a pilot to an operational system. Because substantial systems resources are required, acquisition and installation of equipment is a problem of a greater order of magnitude. As well, the operational system will require hooks and interfaces to be built into existing systems in the office. Pilots can be somewhat separate from existing computer, communications, and office technologies in a given organization. However, an operational system will expand to incorporate other technologies. For example, the operational system may reach out and include a PBX which previously was used for switching only voice. It may have interfaces to corporate data bases so that knowledge workers can access such information directly. It may include or replace the stand-alone word processors on site. It may involve computer pointers to microform or paper files. This process of pilots evolving into operational systems which devour broader office technologies is depicted in Figure 12.1.

Corresponding to this expansion of technologies will be expansion on a number of other levels. The system will expand geographically, raising technical issues (such as wide area networks) and organizational issues (such as staffing, training, and system support). Organizational expansion will also occur as the system spreads into various functions like personnel, finance, marketing, research and development, and operations. As the capabilities of the system grow it will also expand deeper into the jobs and working lives of the users. Links to teleconferencing, home terminals, public data bases, and videotex are examples.

Such expansion points to the need to situate operational system implementation within an overall strategic plan for systems. Cross-functional systems require cross-functional responsibilities. Who owns the system? Who has responsibility and authority for making changes to it? Who is responsible for training? Who does a user call when s/he has a problem? The overall responsibility for the system must fall within the executive. New organizational structures may be necessary. An office automation function led by a senior executive can help coordinate the integration of office technologies. In addition, support groups will have to be established for areas such as training, needs assessment and evaluation, support and maintenance, user education, technology gatekeeping, and ongoing design and enhancements.

While pilot systems have manual systems to fall back on, operational systems must be reliable. When the system goes down the organization cannot function. This points to the need for fail-safe systems and also for the provision of adequate systems support and maintenance. If mechanisms are not in place, for example, to repair or replace a broken terminal, there will be an unproductive, and likely unhappy employee. The often leisurely approach to maintenance for previous generations of computer systems may die hard. It is part of a broader culture in which the users were judged to be necessary, but undesirable components of computer systems.

With the addition of the personnel departments, finance, and top executive, security issues gain not only importance, but visibility. User commitment to an operational system can be brought into question by a single incident—for example one unauthorized user obtaining the superuser password. In one case a system was seriously jeopardized when, because of a network error, a user

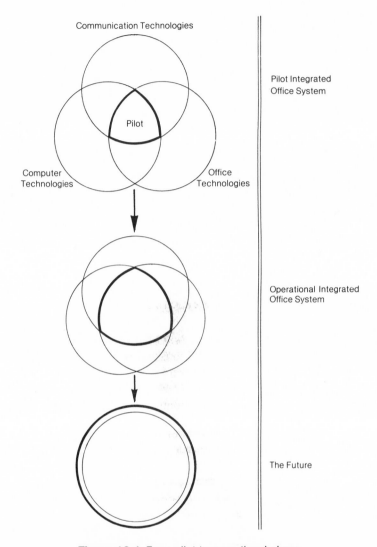

Figure 12.1 From pilot to operational phase.

entered the messaging system and found himself assuming someone else's identity including access to all that person's files.[4]

With evolution to operational systems the planning process can be brought to bear on the problem of systems integration. No one vendor will supply the most appropriate systems in all these areas. Moreover, the office system must be integrated with external systems, to enable communication with suppliers, clients, external data bases, and so on. This requires a complete organizational strategy for computer, communications, and office technologies.

Chapter 13

User-Driven Design, Work, and Society

The convergence of computers, communications and office automation should lead to better ways of working on those tasks that require human organization. It is my hope that the smaller world we find ourselves in as we connect more closely with others will be a better one.

(Howard Morgan, 1979)

Office automation is beginning to change the nature of work, the composition of the workforce, labor–management relations, and the social organization of the work place. In doing so, it has begun to raise some profound issues regarding the values, character, and directions of Western society.

Where is this information technology revolution heading? What will be its impact on society as a whole, and the people within it? These are important questions for those charged with the design and implementation of integrated office systems. These questions arise during many office automation programs. An appreciation of the broad societal framework is the final requirement for a complete strategy for User-Driven Design. While an exhaustive discussion of this topic is not possible within the framework of this book, some of the main issues and their implications are discussed. As office systems technology has developed, there has been an understandable attempt to anticipate the likely consequences for job loss. There has also been deep concern about the technology's impacts on the quality of work life in the office.

13.1. IMPACTS ON THE ORGANIZATION AND WORK LIFE

The recent discussion about the impact of office systems on the quality of work life and on the organization itself took a giant leap forward at an international symposium on QWL held in Toronto in August/September 1981. At it, the world leaders in QWL and sociotechnical systems theory joined with leaders from the office automation community, the labor movement, governments, and business to debate and discuss integrated office systems.

One of the clear themes emerging is that many of the problems of the past flowed from the nature of many of the previous generations of computer (data processing) systems. These systems often resulted in poorly designed jobs, employee dissatisfaction, alienation and turnover, and in general, poor quality of work life. Traditional systems focused on efficiency rather than effectiveness, resulting in greater structuring, streamlining, and rigid controlling of work. Jobs were often deskilled or eliminated in the search to avoid or displace costs. Traditional systems were often designed and implemented by technologists, who had little appreciation of the many complex human and organizational issues their systems would provoke. The users were rarely involved in, let alone driving, the design process. All the problems of "technology-driven systems" discussed in Chapter 2 came into play.

On the other hand, the new generation of integrated office systems can result in dramatic and measurable *improvements in the quality of work life.* There is nothing inherently negative about the technology. If systems are designed and implemented properly, users become not only more productive, but enamoured and addicted.[1]

13.2. OFFICE SYSTEMS AND UNEMPLOYMENT

For several years a raging debate has reviewed the likely impact of office automation on employment. This discussion has involved not only politicians, labor leaders, journalists, and academics, but office workers—ranging from clerks to managers—who wonder if their jobs may change or disappear because of the new technology. The debate really goes back a couple of centuries, perhaps to the invention of the power loom and the Luddite rebellion, when the spectre of technology replacing human labor was first introduced. The discussion really exploded during the 1950s and 1960s as fear about massive unemployment because of automation became widespread. When the data processing of the 1960s and early 1970s failed to generate a balance sheet of job loss, the debate appeared to subside, only to be regenerated with the advent of the microprocessor and the introduction of word processing with its clear cost-displacement orientation.

What will the effect of the new generation of integrated office systems be on employment?

Zeman and Russel, in an excellent article, describe two positions which they call the "optimists" and the "pessimist."[2] These two schools have also been referred to as the "structuralists" and the "expansionists." [3] Essentially the "optimists" are those who argue that the overall impact of chip technology will be to generate prosperity and employment. The "pessimists" see this technology as a killer of jobs, which will result in massive, structural unemployment. The authors conclude that it is prudent to tread the "middle ground" as the overall impacts are difficult to determine and will largely depend on unknown factors such as the state of the economy, government policy, and so on.

13.2.1. New Jobs and Prosperity?

There is a strong case that the impact of integrated office systems will have a positive effect on employment. The backdrop to this is a 1966 report published in Washington by the National Commission on Technology, Automation, and Economic Progress entitled "The Outlook for Technological Change and Unemployment." The report drew heavily on statistical material which devastated opponent views in the United States and elsewhere.[2] Automation, judged as similar to other technological change, was seen to produce greater demand and economic growth. Since then this has been the general trend.

However, data processing did displace many clerical positions, despite its overall positive impact. The first successor of data processing–word processing–has not done the same to secretaries. While the marketing strategies of word-processing vendors has tended to focus on the cost-beneficial tradeoff between their machines and secretaries, it has become clear that such alleged benefits have not materialized. Russel, in a study of office automation in Canada, noted that the installations of word-processing equipment which were studied had either increased employment or maintained it at current levels. While specific cases of job loss can be cited, especially when word processors were installed in production environments, these have not been the norm.[4]

In a study on the strategic impact of microelectronics in the United States and Western Europe between 1977 and 1987, Arthur D. Little Inc. (ADL) concluded that many billions of dollars of new wealth and corresponding jobs are being generated. Like the 1966 Washington report, ADL argued that the impact of microprocessor technology is not fundamentally different from the impact of other technological innovations. All tend to result in a net gain, rather than decline in employment. ADL says that within the decade $30 to $35 billion additional wealth is being created in United States, West Germany, Britain, and France alone. New products and industries are coming forth and jobs that otherwise might have been lost are being gained.

A typical "positive" attitude is summarized by Gardiner:

> . . consider that new technologies while destroying some jobs tend to create other more challenging jobs. Just as the internal combustion engine made the hansom cab driver obsolete but provided jobs for people manufacturing, maintaining and selling cars, so the computer makes assembly jobs obsolete but creates more challenging jobs.[5]

As technology enables organizations to expand their services and products, new jobs can result. For example, there were fears that the introduction of computers in the banks would sharply reduce jobs. But in the case of the Royal Bank of Canada the number of employees actually swelled from 24,000 to 36,000 as the new technologies enabled it to expand its customer services over the 1970s.[7]

Similarly, J.A. Mark, writing as the Assistant Commissioner of the U.S. Bureau of Labor Statistics, writes:

> There is . . . abundant evidence in our experience over the last three decades that as long as the economy is expanding and demand is increasing, steady technological advance is compatible with rising employment. Between 1950 and 1978, a period of technological change, employment of all persons in the nonfarm business sector grew 67 percent from about 44 million workers to 78 million workers. During this same period, output increased some 163 percent.[7]

A key assumption behind the above-cited examples is that the new technologies are not qualitatively different from previous innovations. This assumption is being challenged by many who argue that it is precisely the unprecedented *character, power,* and *scope* of microelectronics which creates the potential for massive widespread unemployment.

13.2.2. Massive Unemployment?

Some writers argue that the *character* of microelectronics is different. For example, Rabeau makes the case for a "new industrial revolution" by outlining three different periods of industrial innovation.[8] The first industrial revolution (1750–1870) and the second industrial revolution (1870–1970) involved the substitution of mechanical capital for human labor, decreased demand for some kinds of labor, and increased demand for others. However, the third industrial revolution, which began around 1970, involves the substitution of information capital for human labor with a resulting decrease in demand for both skilled and unskilled labor. The entire gamut of white collar workers will be affected ranging from low-level clerks through middle management to top executives.

In *The Collapse of Work* Jenkins and Sherman of the Association of Science, Technical and Managerial Staffs—Britain's largest white collar union—also conclude that the impact will be on a wide spectrum of office workers. They estimate that five million people will be out of work in Britain by 1990 as a result of microprocessor technology.[9] Other writers have stressed differences in the *speed of innovation* brought about by the chip:

> While even mainframe computer technology diffused relatively slowly, the miniaturized computer—the chip—is diffusing 7 to 10 times faster than any other previous technology. Consequently, within the last two or three years we have observed, especially in European countries and lately to a lesser extent in the U.S. and Canada, a revival of the employment debate. The people who propose that technological unemployment is a serious emerging problem say that the predictions of the 1950s will come to us in the 1980s and that they will come to us with vengence because we have not prepared for the upcoming wave of automation.[2]

Some writers have emphasized the *scope* of the microelectronics revolution. Valaskakis and Sindell argue that the changes provoked by "infomediation" are structural, not sectoral. "They do not just relate to the telecommunications field or even to the information sector but rather to the entire economy." [3] Unlike data processing, office automation and its industrial counterpart robotics hold the potential for profoundly affecting nearly every conceivable aspect of work.

However, most of those who see office automation as resulting in widespread unemployment have emphasized the impact of systems on highly structured and routine work. For example, in a report published by the government of France, Nora and Minc estimate that 800,00 secretaries, large numbers of clerks in the insurance industry, and 30% of bank workers could loose their jobs by the end of the 1980s.[10] The giant German based electronics company Siemans says that by 1990 integrated office systems can take over about 40% of office work.[2]

13.2.3. The Heart of the Matter

Where is the truth?

To begin, it is generally agreed that office automation will result in the loss of many specific jobs and even job types. Office system technology provided the opportunity to improve the efficiency of office work and to displace or avoid the costs of human labor. This fact is behind much of the resistance to automation programs in the office. That computer technology may have generated some new jobs somewhere is of little consolation to the employee who loses a job, or who sees his/her peer group declining through attrition, or who finds him/herself less marketable because of shrinking requirements for a particular vocation.

For many applications of computer technology, the issue of job loss is not central. For these, the primary effect of automation will be to increase effectiveness through adding value to labor and improving the output of products of office work. This kind of application has been discussed at length in the previous chapters. There are other examples, however, where increasing efficiency by labor cost displacement can be a central function of system implementation. There are three examples of this type of application:

(1) The Completion of Traditional Data Processing. The target here are those workers who do highly routine and structured pocessing, filing, and retrieving of information. Most of these workers are women. Heather Menzies, who writes that women account for 90% of employment in these occupations, says "... women are on a collision course between their continuing concentration in clerical occupations and the industry's diminishing requirements in that line of work." [11] These positions take up, very roughly, about one-tenth of the white collar workforce in Canada and the United States. There are a number of outstanding jobs which can be automated. One is clerks in information intensive sectors of the economy such as government, insurance companies, banks, corporate head offices, etc. Applications include accounts payable, accounts receivable, payroll, general ledger, and other various book-keeping and information processing activities. A second category of jobs concerns activities associated with previous generations of data processing. For example, the need for key punch operators will decline as information is entered directly into a given system through interactive terminals by distributed users.

(2) Application of Office Systems To Other Structured Work. Here the possibility exists to cause major changes in the composition of the work force. Again, women would tend to be affected most by changes in these sectors. Examples of sectors which could decline dramatically are the following:

- Bank tellers. Computerized personal banking devices could obviate the need for tellers and clerical support in the banks.
- Telephone operators. For example, in 1969 the Bell Canada bargaining unit contained 13,600 telephone operators employed in Ontario and Quebec. With the impact of successive technological advances this figure dropped to 7,400 ten years later. It is expected that videotex will eliminate paper telephone directories and drastically reduce the need for information operators. Computerized switches will also reduce labor costs. [12]
- Retail clerks. Interactive point of sale systems, optical character recognition in

supermarkets, and videotex-based shopping at home will undoubtedly reduce the proportion of the workforce involved in such retail activities.
- Letter Carriers. Electronic messaging is often the backbone of an integrated office system. Paper mail and mail delivery will become more and more redundant as organizations and individuals choose to send information at the speed of light.

(3) Application of Office Systems to Unstructured Knowledge Work. Direct support of the majority of office workers—professionals, managers, executives—can result in large productivity gains. As with other categories of workers, the objectives of productivity improvements can be either reducing labor costs or improving the output of these employees (or a combination of these). Attempts to cut costs have to date been relatively unsuccessful. For example, Citibank (one of the first to experiment with office systems) cost-justified its initial pilots through projected reduction in the number of managers needed. It was thought that the system would improve a manager's span of control from seven to nine employees, resulting in opportunities for cost avoidance. Such benefits did not materialize and the objectives of the program were changed. Nevertheless, as the difficult human and organizational issues become better understood, there is every reason to think that labor costs to perform a wide range of unstructured and complex office activities could be reduced. Some examples are as follows:

- Middle managers spend the majority of their day in various communications activities. A sharp improvement in the communications process through electronic mail, computer conferencing, teleconferencing, voice messaging, intelligent telephones, etc., could make the Citibank objective a reality.
- Insurance Salespersons. On-line systems can reduce many of the administrative, communications, and unproductive information processing and retrieval activities of a variety of sales professions. A good example is the real estate salesman who has all available properties and clients in an integrated data base. Time savings, compared to the old way, are enormous. Or taking the example further, what will happen to that salesman when his clients can advertise and search properties using their home or office videotex terminal?
- The professions. It can be expected that improvements in the effectiveness of professionals could lead to a decline in employment, given the absence of a corresponding improvement in the demand for their services. What will happen to rural veterinarians when farmers can diagnose livestock problems using interactive television? Or to paramedical personnel in the family practice clinic, as physicians begin to use computer-assisted diagnosis, treatment, and scheduling? Or to teachers as computer-aided instruction becomes widespread?

These then are some of the jobs that are most likely to be the target of labor cost-cutting applications of office automation. This is where we may see significant job dislocation due to office system implementation. It is clear that the number of those potentially affected is quite large. What does this augur for our society?

The "optimists" would argue that while there may be short-term dislocation, the expanding employment opportunities created by the microchip revolution, as well as the growth generated by the natural workings of the economy to reallocate labor efficiently, will eliminate the long-term job loss
problem. Lamberton castigates the "optimist" view as

> simply the old notion that the future will take care of itself; that resources will
> always have prices that ensure their proper use. It presupposes a great deal more
> knowledge of the future than we, in fact, have. . . . [Looking only at long-term
> consequences] leaves room for a serious gap between displacement and genera-
> tion. It assumes that one kind of labour can be transformed into another kind of
> labour. It assumes also that the sharing of rewards of technological progress raises
> no insuperable problems. These are big assumptions. The all-pervasive nature of
> information technology suggests that the gap between displacement and genera-
> tion could be very wide. Nor can we be confident that the sharing of benefits will
> proceed smoothly. Social costs are not a myth; negative impacts of computers on
> working life have been frequent.[2]

The recent performance of all of the economies in the industrialized
nations gives further cause for concern about adequate creation of alternative
jobs. There is clearly good reason to be at least skeptical of the "optimistic"
scenario.

How much of a problem of longer-term dislocation is there likely to be,
therefore, and what does this imply for the technology's future? Much clearly
depends on how the key players in the game behave: the extent to which
those currently in control of office system implementation opt for labor-
saving applications; the degree to which those directly affected by job loss act
to resist the implementation of these systems or force their adoption in a
manner that minimized dislocation. But the most important factor is likely to
be the overall political and social response our society makes to the key issue
raised by the adoption of this technology: on what criteria and through what
mechanisms are the net benefits of the microchip revolution to be distributed? The stance taken on this question will fundamentally affect the perceptions and actions of those directly involved with the implementation of office
systems; and in doing so will determine the extent to which we capture the
potential benefits which the technology has to offer. If, for example, we
choose to continue to "let the chips fall where they may," the technology will
be (quite rightly) perceived by many as a potential threat rather than an
opportunity. Those affected can be expected to take whatever action they
deem appropriate to defend themselves against having to individually bear
the consequences of dislocation, including action to prevent implementations. If, on the other hand, a clear social commitment is made to share
equitably the benefits and burdens of the technology's implementation, it is

much more likely that those applications of the technology which offer overall benefits will indeed be adopted.

13.3. WHITHER WESTERN SOCIETY?

Alvin Toffler concludes *The Third Wave* with an appeal to reorganize
Western society, to bring it into tune with the new third wave reality. He calls
for the building of new political institutions, based on minority power,
semidirect democracy, and decision division:

> Above all it means starting this process of reconstruction now, before the further
> disintegration of existing political systems sends the forces of tyranny jackbooting
> through the streets, and makes impossible a peaceful transition to Twenty-first
> Century Democracy.
>
> If we begin now, we and our children can take part in the exciting reconstitu-
> tion not merely of our obsolete political structures but of civilization itself.[13]

While Toffler's theoretical underpinnings are flawed, in his plea he is
raising some important issues regarding the new technology on the one hand,
and western economic and political institutions on the other. These are issues
which not just the leaders of our society, but also the designers and implementors of integrated office systems are well advised to consider. That is, as
the proliferation of office system becomes more widespread, an appreciation
of the limitations of the political and economic backdrop will help equip the
implementor to avoid the most frequent pitfalls.

When it comes to employment and the quality of work life, computers
are a double-edged sword. To date they have resulted in a net growth in jobs,
and a net improvement in the interesting, creative, and skill-demanding positions available in the work force. Yet, they have also destroyed many specific
jobs and even occupations in the process, while at the same time creating
some very tedious and alienating positions. Unfortunately, people, when
discussing the problem, often look at only one edge or the other.

We have entered a period where the nature of work and social organization is beginning to change, and a question is posed. What will be the roles
and objectives of users, governments, business, and labor in this process? Of
many complex issues which flow from this question, several stand out. How
will the benefits of the new technologies be distributed? Who will control
office automation and through what process? What kinds of economic planning are required?

13.3.1. Distribution of the Benefits

Integrated office systems, properly designed and implemented, can be liberating. There is nothing inherently injurious in the technology. Elimination of a tedious job is not, of necessity, an evil. Some authors go even further:

> Anyone who could be replaced by a machine, should be replaced by a machine. Let machines do the mechanical things and thereby set us free to do the human things. The shift from considering machines as labor-saving devices to considering them as labor-replacing devices is a fine example of our great capacity to turn solutions into problems. Machines have saved many of us from drudgery and are now accused of stealing our jobs.[5]

However, with no formal mechanism to enable effective social distribution of the benefits of information technology, it is likely in the short term and even in the long term that large numbers of people will only see the negative edge of the sword. These people are confronted with a glaring contradiction: the magnificent potential of the technology versus a reality in which they are the victims of technological progress.

There are several (not mutually exclusive) variants of how the benefits of this "third wave" can be distributed.

(1) View: It'll All Come out in the Wash. This is simply the discredited extreme position of Zeman and Russel's "optimists." There is no reason to expect that a major reorganization of the work force will happen spontaneously, and with negligible detrimental impacts.[14]

(2) View: Enlightened Corporate Management Will Ensure a Smooth Transition. This theory holds that management, out of social enlightment or wise self-interest, will guarantee jobs and seek to implement systems such that quality of work life is improved. There have been such cases but this has certainly not been the norm.[15]

(3) View: Office Workers Will Demand to Benefit from Office Automation. This view, held by conflict theorists, holds that the users and the user's organizations (associations, unions, etc.) will close ranks to ensure that the technological change is beneficial, rather than injurious. The broad public discussion regarding trends towards white collar unionization is symptomatic of this process.

(4) View: Distribution Is the Responsibility of Government. This view holds that the issues raised are too large to be resolved at the individual corporation level, and that legislation and economic planning are required. Corporations are expected to use new technologies to improve their efficiency, productivity, profitabiltiy, and competiveness. Reduced labor costs, streamlined and structured work, etc., are generally judged to be desirable outcomes of technological innovation. It is only at the broad governmental level that appropriate guidelines, standards, and planning can be applied.

Which one, or combination, of these variants will come to the fore remains to be seen. Those designing and implementing office systems would do well to consider the alternatives as they formulate objectives for an office automation program.

13.3.2. Control of the Technology

It is questionable if traditional North American approaches to technological change will be able to handle the transformation of work indicated by integrated office system. Typically, the users are informed of change at the time of "installation" of the new system. As one computer company executive is quoted as saying "(office workers) will respond when we break their arms, and we're in the twisting stage now."[16]

Recently there has been much discussion about involving the users in the process of design and implementation.[15] But this discussion skirts the issue of actual *control* of the technology.

The experiments with worker participation in corporate decision making conducted in Europe over the last decade have not been repeated in North America. In some European countries, workers have a form of veto over automation programs. Examples are the agreements between the British civil servants union and the British government; and agreements between the Norwegian Federation of Trades Unions and the Norwegian Employees Confederation (employing 90% of the workers in the country). The European experiences have received considerable criticism from both sides. Militant unionists view such participation as a form of co-option which undermines their independent strength and resolve. Some managers have regarded participation as a violation of their management prerogative to run their organization.

In 1979, the Communications Workers of America held a special conference on the topic of technological change in the workplace. At it, there was considerable discussion about the need for "workplace democracy" to involve workers in the process of change. Invited speakers, including Jackson Grayson (founder of the American Productivity Center), Richard Miller (Vice President of the Diebold Group), Starr Roxanne Hiltz (coauthor of *The Network Nation*), and D.L. Lander, (Director, General Motors) were all advocates of the notion.

Again it remains to be seen how far management will go to give control; users will go to take away control; and governments will go to legislate standards and guidelines for control of office system technology.

Some writers have argued that the technology has inherent effects on the centralization of organizations. Many left wing authors emphasize the dangers of microelectronics as a tool for social control and centralization. However, among these, there is a growing trend to see the potential of the technology to facilitate more democratic work: As the CSE Group on Microelectronics put it:

> Engineers and designers like to tell us that they make design choices on technical grounds. Experience and training teach us that this is not true. The typical hierarchy of control set up in modern applications of computer systems is not technically necessary.... In fact as microelectronics can control a piece of equipment independently of other machines, the technical structure of work could be made more democratic, less centralized and less hierarchical.[17]

In a summary article, Cherns points out that the microprocessor removes the limits to both centralization and decentralization at all levels of the organization.[18] He goes on to argue:

> Since the new technology has the capacity for both, it could very well be that societies or governments with a preference for centralization will use it to strengthen their tendency to centralize, while those that prefer decentralization will decentralize further. The questions then are: Which is likely to turn out to be the more efficient? What are the long-term consequences of one or the other choice? What are the likely difficulties?

13.3.3. Economic and Social Planning

There are a number of other issues which cannot be adequately dealt with at the individual corporate level by designers and implementors of office systems, but which more and more are posed. This hierarchy of issues and corresponding scope or sphere of change is indicated in Figure 13.1. At the top of the hierarchy is the issue of economic and social planning.

At the lowest level of the hierarchy is individual job design. Jobs must be redesigned as part of the implementation of an integrated office system. The design of jobs must be user driven—based on information from the user and involving the user in the process. Office workers will all have to acquire new skills, both technical and also having to do with new work activities and responsibilities. Training and retraining are ongoing and iterative processes. As the technology and its functionality grow the user learning process will continue. Whether the transition is smooth and positive for the office workers involved will depend largely on the planning and strategy of the designers and implementors.

At a higher level, the reorganization of the workplace must be a well-thought-out and highly planned undertaking. New structures to deal with office systems (the office automation function, steering committees, etc.,) and new structures for the entire organization must be user driven as well. How will the users and user organization such as unions be involved? How far will workplace democracy be granted, or taken?

At one level higher, the shape and composition of the entire national

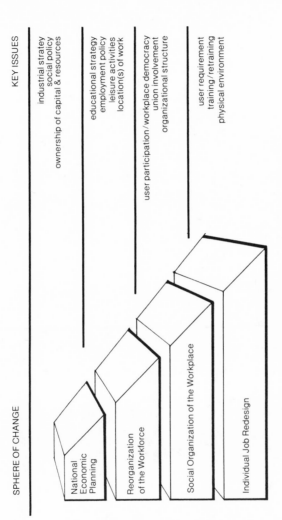

Figure 13.1. Integrated office systems: social issues.

workforce is beginning to change. What will be the values and policies which will drive the transition to the information era, or third wave? Educational institutions must make the turn and begin equipping students with at least some of the basic knowledge and skills which they require. Is the much heralded "information marketplace" or the development of cottage industries really feasible and/or desirable? [19] What will be the impact on masses of users working at home? What should happen to the workweek and should this be an issue for those driving the office automation train?

Finally, these systems raise the need for broad economic and social planning. One of the hottest topics has become industrial strategy, as Western nations attempt to grapple with the centrality of information technology to their international competiveness, balance of trade, and success as nation states. McLean argues for a coherent government policy designed to exploit every conceivable point of leverage. [20] This would include direct public support for the manufacture of key electronic products, support for government and industrial research and development, a planned government procurement policy, and planning of a communication infrastructure.

However, issues are arising which go beyond even that. As the shape of the economy begins to change, national economic planning is becoming a necessity in order to avoid the social dislocation which the technology can cause to ensure that improvements in productivity and wealth result in improvements in the quality of life of working people. Will the new technology increase the gap between social classes, between men and women, between skilled and unskilled, or will it help do the opposite?

The answer is not simply "blowin' in the wind." Nor will it depend simply on the extent to which users are involved in the process of change. It will depend, in the final analysis, on the actual control which users have in shaping their own destiny in the office. Control includes decision making and a share in the ownership of capital and its technological fruits. The ultimate question is to what degree will such control be granted or taken.

References

REFERENCES FOR CHAPTER 1

1. Englebart, Douglas C. Toward Integrated, Evolutionary Office Automation Systems, in *Proceedings of the Conference on Engineering Management in the Computer Age* pp. 63–64. Denver Colorado (1978).
2. Toffler, Alvin. *The Third Wave.* Bantam Books, New York (1980).
3. Hindin, Harvey J. Will atomic particles communicate? *Electronics* 51(17), 73–74 (August 17, 1978).
4. Strassman, P.A. Stages of Growth, *Datamation* 22(10), 46–60 (October, 1976).
5. Zisman, Michael D. Office Automation: Revolution or Evolution, *Sloan Management Review* 19(3), 1–16 (Spring, 1978).
6. Purchase, Alan, and Carol F. Glover. Office of the Future, *Stanford Research Institute Business Intelligence Program Guidelines* (1001). Menlo Park, California (April, 1976).
7. Zisman, Michael D. The Holy Incantation, *Computer Decisions* 12(10), 124–125 (October, 1980).
8. Bridel, Robert J. From his introductory remarks to the Office of Tomorrow Conference, sponsored by Canadian Office magazine. Toronto, Ontario (1979).
9. Burns, J. Christopher. The Evolution of Office Information Systems. *Datamation* 23(4), 60–61 (April, 1977).
10. Keen, Peter G., and M. S. Scott Morton. *Decision Support Systems: An Organizational Perspective.* Addison-Wesley Press, Reading, Massachusetts (1978).
11. Morgan, Howard Lee. Decision Support Systems: Technology and Tactics, *Proceedings of AFIPS Office Automation Conference.* Houston, Texas (March 23–25, 1981).
12. Mintzberg, Henry. *The Nature of Managerial Work.* Harper and Row, New York (1973).
13. Tapscott, H. Donald. Investigating the Office of the Future, *Telesis* 8(1), 2–6 (1981).
14. Poppel, Harvey L. Information Resource Management (IRM)—A New Concept, a paper given to the 1976 N.C.C. Cited in McNurlin, Barbara C., The Automated Office: Part I, *EDP Analyzer* 19(5), 1–19 (May, 1981).
15. Harris, Louis, and Associates, Inc. *The Steelcase National Study of Office Environments: Do They Work?* 1978. Available in Canada from Steelcase Canada Ltd. P.O. Box 9, Don Mills, Ontario M3C 2R7.
16. Tapscott, H. Donald, Morley Greenberg, Michael Collins, Del Henderson, Ingrid Lebolt,

David Macfarlane, and Loris Sartor. *Measuring the Impact of Office Information Communication Systems*, Vol. III. Unpublished report. Toronto, Ontario (December, 1980).

17. Kenney, George C., et al. An optical disk replaces 25 mg tapes, *IEEE Spectrum* 16(2), 33–38, (February, 1979).

18. Anderson, Howard. *Cost Effective Office Automation for Today's Management.* Presentation to the National Conference on the Office of Tomorrow, Toronto, Ontario (February 13–15, 1979).

19. Carlisle, James. *Evaluating the impact of office automation systems.* Proceedings of the N.C.C., Dallas, Texas (1977).

20. Bair, J. H. Communication in the Office of the Future: Where the Real Payoff May Be. Paper given to the International Computer Communications Conference. Kyoto, Japan 2–3 (August, 1978).

21. Meyer, Dean. The Conceptual Growth of the Diebold Automated Office Program. Report by the Diebold Group, Inc. New York (1981).

22. Meyer, Dean. Computer-based Message Systems: A Taxonomy, *Telecommunications Policy* 4(2), 128–133 (June, 1980).

23. Turoff, M., and S. R. Hiltz. Meeting Through Your Computer, *Spectrum* 14(5) 58–64, (May, 1977).

24. Uhlig, Ronald P. Human Factors in Computer Message Systems, *Datamation* 23(5), 120–126 (May, 1977).

25. Hammer, M., and M. D. Zisman. Design and Implementation of Office Information Systems, *Office Automation. Infotech State of the Art Report.* Series 8, No. 3. Infotech Limited, Maidenhead, Berkshire, England (1980).

26. Tapscott, H. Donald. Research on the Impact of Office Information Communications Systems, in *Proceedings of the IFIP TC-6 International Symposium on Computer Message Systems.* Ottawa, Canada (April 6–8, 1981) edited by Ronald P. Uhlig. Amsterdam: North-Holland Publishing Company.

27. Burns, J. Christopher. The Office in the 1980's, in *Information Systems in the 1980's*, pp. 21–34. Arthur D. Little. Inc., Acorn Park, Cambridge, Massachusetts (1978).

28. McCallum, R. Good Secretaries Are Hard to Find as Jobs Call for More Management Skills. *Globe and Mail.* Report on Business section, p. B1, Toronto, Ontario (March 5, 1979).

REFERENCES FOR CHAPTER 2

1. Anderson, Howard. *Cost Effective Office Automation for Today's Management.* Presentation to the National Conference on the Office of Tomorrow, Toronto, Ontario (February 13–15, 1979).

2. Carlisle, James. *Evaluating the impact of office automation systems.* Proceeding of the N.C.C. Dallas, Texas (1977).

3. Bair, James H. *Avoiding Working Non-Solutions to Office Communications System Design.* Invited paper at the COMPCON Conference, San Francisco, California (February 25–28, 1980).

4. In *Teleinformatics 1979*, IFIP International Conference, Amsterdam: North-Holland Publishers, 1979, pp. 201–208.

5. Lodahl, T. M. Designing the Automated Office: Organizational Functions of Data and Text, *Emerging Office Systems*, edited by Robert Landau, James H. Bair, and Jean H. Siegman. Ablex Publishing Corp., Norwood, New Jersey (1982).

6. Tapscott, D., Morley Greenberg, and David Macfarlane. Researching Office Information Communications System. *The Canadian Journal of Information Science* 5 (May, 1980)

REFERENCES FOR CHAPTER 3

1. Conrath, D. W. *An Investigation of Organizational Communications Needs, and a Study of the Impact of a Business Communication System (SLI) on Meeting these Needs.* Bell Canada Restricted Document. Toronto, Ontario (1976).
2. Barnard, Chester I. *The Functions of the Executive.* Harvard Press, Cambridge, Massachusetts (1938).
3. Deutch, Karl W., On Communication Models in the Social Sciences. *Public Opinion Quarterly* 16(3), 356–380 (Fall, 1952).
4. Goldhaber, Gerald M. The ICA Communication Audit: Rationale and Development. In *Proceedings of the Academy of Management Convention*, Kansas City, Kansas (August, 1976).
5. Greenbaum, H. H., and R. L. Falcione. *Organizational Communication 1977: Abstracts, Analysis, and Overview.* Joint publication of the American Business Association, Champaign, Illinois, and the International Communication Association, Austin, Texas (April, 1979).
6. Likert, R. *The Human Organization: Its Management and Value.* McGraw-Hill, New York (1967).
7. Likert, R., and D. Bowers. Organization Theory and Human Resources Accounting, *American Psychologist* 24(6) (1969).
8. Likert, R. Human Resource Accounting. *Personnel* 8–19 (May–June, 1973).
9. Hain, T., and R. Widgery. *Organizational Diagnosis: The Significant Role of Communication.* Unpublished manuscript delivered to the International Communication Assoc. Convention, Montreal, Quebec (1973).
10. Dennis, H., G. Richetto, and J. Wiemann. *Articulating the Need for an Effective Internal Communication System: New Empirical Evidence for the Communication Specialist.* Unpublished manuscript delivered at the International Communication Assoc. Convention, New Orleans, Louisiana, (1974).
11. Hain, T., and S. Tubbs. Organizational Development: The Role of Communication in *Diagnosis, Change, and Evaluation.* Unpublished manuscript delivered to the International Communication Assoc. Convention, New Orleans, Louisiana (1975).
12. Burhans D. *The Development and Field Testing of Two Internal Communication Measuring Instruments.* Unpublished manuscript, California State University, Los Angeles, California. Later delivered at the 1972 Int. Communication Assoc. Convention. Atlanta, Georgia (1971).
13. Jain, H. Employee Knowledge of Hospital Compensation Policies and Supervisory Effectiveness. Unpublished manuscript delivered to the International Communication Association Convention, Atlanta, Georgia (1972).
14. Goodnight, G., D. Crary, V. Balthrop, and M. Hazen. *The Relationship Between Communication Satisfaction and Productivity, Role Discrepency and Need Level.* Unpublished manuscript delivered to the International Communication Association Convention, New Orleans, Louisiana (1974).
15. Hazen, M., and V. Balthrop. *A Casual Analysis of the Relationship between Communication Satisfaction and Productivity, Role Discrepancy, Need Level and Organizational Position.*

Unpublished manuscript delivered to the International Communication Assoc. Convention, Chicago, Illinois (1975).

16. Hiltz, Starr Roxanne. The Impact of a Computerized Conferencing System on Scientific Research Communities. *NJIT Computerized Conferencing and Communication Center*, Research Report 15. NSF-MCS-77-27813 (June, 1981).

17. Hiltz, Starr Roxanne. Communications and Group Decision-Making: Experimental Evidence on the Potential Impact of Computer Conferencing. *NJIT Computerized Conferencing and Communication Center Research* Report, Vol. 2 (1975).

18. Hiltz, S. R. A Social Scientist Looks at Computer Conferencing. *Proceedings of 3rd Intern. Conference Computer Communications (NJIT), pp. 203–207 (1976)*.

19. Hiltz, Starr Roxanne. The Human Element in Computerized Conferencing Systems. *Computer Networks* 2 (1977).

20. Turoff, Murray. OEP, Delphi Conferencing: Computer Based Conferencing with Anonymity, *Technological Forecasting and Social Change* 3(2), 159–204 (1972).

21. Turoff, Murray. Conferencing via Computer, *Proceedings of IEEE Information Networks Conference* pp. 194–197 (1972).

22. Turoff, Murray. The State of the Art: Computerized Conferencing, *Views from ICCC 1974*, pp. 81–86 (N. Macon, ed.) (1975).

23. Hiltz, Starr Roxanne, and Murray Turoff. *The Network Nation*. Addison-Wesley Publishing Company, Reading, Massachusetts (1978).

24. Bair, James H. Productivity Assessment of Office Information Systems Technology. *Trends and Applications: 1978: Distributed Processing, IEEE* pp. 12–24 (May, 1978).

25. Bair, James H. Communication in the Office of the Future: Where the Real Payoff May Be. *SRI International.* Menlo Park, California (August, 1978).

26. Bair, James H. A Communications Perspective for Identifying Office Automation Payoffs. *SRI International* pp. 1–8. Menlo Park, California (May, 1979).

27. Bair, James H. *Productivity Assessment of Office Automation Systems* (two volumes). Report prepared for National Archives and Records Service, SRI project 7823. Menlo Park, California (March 1979).

28. Conrath, David W. *Measuring the Computer's Impact on Organizational Structure.* Proceedings of the First International Conference on Computer Communication, pp. 68–73, Washington, DC (October, 1972).

29. Conrath, D. W. Communications Patterns, Organizational Structure, and Man: Some Relationships. *Human Factors* 15(5), 459–470 (October, 1973).

30. Conrath, D. W. Communications Environment and Its Relationship to Organizational Structure. *Management Science* 20(4), 586–603 (December, 1973).

31. Conrath, David W. Organizational Communication Behavior: Description and Prediction, in *Evaluating New Telecommunications Services* pp. 425–442. Plenum Press, New York (1977).

32. Conrath, D. W., and James H. Bair. The Computer as an Interpersonal Communication Device: A Study of Augmentation Technology and its Apparent Impact on Organizational Communication. *International Computer and Communications Conference*, Stockholm, Sweden (August, 1974).

33. Engelbart, D. C. *Augmenting Human Intellect: A Conceptual Framework.* Summary Report, Stanford Research Institute, Menlo Park, California (1962).

34. Engelbart, D. C. *Human Intellect Augmentation Techniques.* Final Report, Stanford Research Institute, Menlo Park, California (1968).

35. Engelbart, D. C., R. W. Watson, and J. C. Norton. *The Augmented Knowledge Workshop*, presented at the National Computer Conference. New York, (1973).

36. Edwards, Gwen C., Organizational Impacts of Office Automation. *Telecommunications Policy* 2(2), 128–136 (June, 1978).
37. Hammer, Michael, and Michael Zisman. *Design and Implementation of Office Information Systems.* Published by the Exxon Enterprises Incorporated, pp. 1–43 (May, 1979).
38. Hammer, M. and Marvin Sirbu. What is Office Automation? published in *Proceedings of the First Office Automation Conferences.* Atlanta, Georgia (March, 1980).
39. Hammer, M., and M. D. Zisman. Design and Implementation of Office Information Systems, *Office Automation. Infotech State of the Art Report.* Series 8, No. 3. Infotech Limited, Maidenhead, Berkshire, England (1980).
40. Tsichritzis, D. Form Management, *Omega Alpha.* Computer Systems Research Group, University of Toronto, Toronto, Canada (1981).
41. Hogg, J., O. M. Nierstrasz, and D. Tsichritzis. Form Procedures, *Omega Alpha.* Computer Systems Research Group, University of Toronto, Toronto, Canada (1981).
42. Hammer, M., and J. S. Kunin. OSL: An Office Specification Language–Language Description, *Office Automation Group Memo OAM-024* (December, 1980).
43. Kunin, J. OSL: An Office Specification Language/Reference Manual, Office Automation Group Memo OAM-021 (October, 1980).
44. Ellis, Clarence A., R. Gibbons, and P. Morris. Office Streamlining. *Integrated Office Systems,* edited by N. Naffah. North-Holland Publishing Company, Amsterdam (1979).
45. Sirbu, M., S. Schoichet, J. Kunin, and M. Hammer. OAM: An Office Analysis Methodology. MIT Laboratory for Computer Science, Office Automation Group Memo, Cambridge, Massachusetts (1981).
46. Booz Allen Hamilton. The Booz Hamilton Multiclient Study on Office Productivity. New York (1980).
47. Tapscott, H. Donald. Investigating the Office of the Future, *Telesis* 8(1), 2–6 (1981).
48. Whaley, Charles P. How Many Multifunction Workers are Working In Your Office?, *Telephony* 200(18), 80–82 (May 4, 1981).
49. Holmes, F. W. IRM: Organizing for the Office, *Journal of Systems Management* 30(1), 24–31 (January, 1979).
50. Oplinger, J. Information Resource Management. The Diebold Automated Office Program. Working Session 80-1 (January 8–9, 1980).
51. The Diebold Group. IRM Planning for 1980–1982. The Diebold Research Program. New York (June 20–22, 1979).
52. Martin, James. Application Development Without Programmers. Savant Research Studies, Carnforth, England (1981).
53. Shah, Bharat. Perspectives on the Value of Information, Unpublished paper, Bell-Northern Software Research, Toronto, Canada (1979).
54. Oplinger, J. Information Resource Management. The Diebold Automated Office Program. Working Session 80-1 (January 8–9, 1980).
55. Connell, J. J. IRM vs. the Office of the Future, *Journal of Systems Management* 32(5), 6–10 (May, 1981).
56. Connell, J. J. The Fallacy of Information Resource Management, *Infosystems* 28(5), 78–84 (May, 1981).
57. Keen, P. C. W., and C. B. Stabell. Mason, R. O. and E. B. Swanson, *Measurement for Management Decision,* Forward by P. C. W. Keen and C. B. Stabell. Addison-Wesley Publishing Company, Reading, Massachusetts (1980)
58. Carleton, G., and B. Shah. *Decision Support Systems Tools,* unpublished report, Toronto, Ontario (September, 1979).
59. Keen, Peter, G., and M. S. Scott Morton, *Decision Support Systems: An Organizational Perspective.* Addison-Wesley Press, Reading, Massachusetts (1978).

60. Gessford, J. E. *Modern Information Systems.* Addison-Wesley Publishing Company, Reading, Massachusetts (1980).

61. Alter, Steven. *A Study of Computer Aided Decision Making in Organizations.* Ph.D. Dissertation, Sloan School of Management, MIT, Cambridge, Massachusetts (June, 1975).

62. Alter, Steven. How Effective Managers Use Information Systems, *Harvard Business Review* 54(6), 97–104 (November–December, 1976).

63. Carlson, Eric D. Decision Support Systems: Personal Computing Services for Managers. *Management Review* 66(1), (January, 1977).

64. Alter, Steven. *Decision Support Systems: Current Practice and Continuing Challenges,* Addison-Wesley Publishing Company, Reading, Massachusetts (1980).

65. Mason, R. O., and E. B. Swanson. *Measuring For Management Decision.* Addison-Wesley Publishing Company, Reading, Massachusetts (1981).

66. Johnston, Carl P., Mark Alexander, and Jacquelin Robin. Canada, Ministry of Labour, *Quality of Working Life—The Idea and Its Application.* Supply and Services, Ottawa, Canada (September, 1978).

67. Taylor, James C. The Human Side of Work: The Socio-Technical Approach to Work System Design. *Personnel Review* 4(3) (Summer, 1975).

68. Trist, E. L., and K. N. Bamforth. Some Social and Psychological Consequences of the Longwall Method of Coal-Getting, *Human Relations* 4(1), 3–38 (February, 1951).

69. Davis, L. E., and R. R. Canter. Job Design Research, *Journal of Industrial Engineering* VII(6), 275–282 (November–December, 1956).

70. Pava, Calvin. Socio-Technical Design for Advanced Office Technology—A working paper. Harvard Business School, Cambridge, Massachusetts (To be published in 1982).

71. Davis, L., and E. L. Trist. Improving the Quality of Work Life Experience of the Sociotechnical Approach, in *Work in America*, Department of Health, Education and Welfare, Government Printing Office, Washington, D.C. (1972).

72. Bair, James H. *Evaluation and Analysis of an Augmented Knowledge Workshop.* Report for the Rome Air Development Center, Number RADC-TR-74-79, also published as NTIS microfiche AD-778835. Griffiss, New York (April, 1974).

73. Vallee, Jacques, Robert Johansen, and Kathleen Spangler. The Computer Conference: An Altered State of Communications?, *The Futurist* 9(3), 116–121 (June, 1975).

74. Hiltz, S. R., Research on the Impact of Computer Conferencing Systems. from a verbal presentation to Bell Northern Research, Ottawa (August, 1979).

75. Hackman, J. Richard, Greg Oldham, Robert Janson, and Kenneth Purdy. A New Strategy for Job Enrichment. *California Management Review* 17(4), 57–71 (Summer, 1975).

76. Tapscott, H. Donald, and David D. R. Macfarlane, Perspective for the Office of the Future, in *Proceedings of the Seventh Annual Conference of the Canadian Association of Information Science*, Banff, Alberta (May, 1979).

77. Cherns, Albert B., and Louis E. Davis. Assessment of the State of the Art, in *The Quality of Working Life*, Vol. I. Macmillan, New York (1975).

78. Jansen, Robert. The Transformation of Job Enrichment and the Emergence of Motivational Work Design. Roy W. Walters & Associates, Internal Report. Dallas, Texas (January 25, 1977).

79. Burke, W. Warner (ed.). *Current Issues and Strategies in Organization Development.* Human Sciences Press, New York (1975)

80. Lawler, E. E., D. A. Nadler, C. Cammann. *Organizational Assessment: Perspectives on the Measurement of Organizational Behavior and the Quality of Working Life.* John Wiley & Sons, New York (1980).

81. Van de Ven, A. H., and D. L. Ferry. *Measuring and Assessing Organizations.* John Wiley & Sons New York (1980).
82. Proceedings of the International Symposium on Quality of Working Life. Toronto, Ontario (1981).

REFERENCES FOR CHAPTER 4

1. Kerlinger, F. N. *Foundations of Behavioral Research.* Holt, Rinehart and Winston, New York (1964).
2. Lawler, E. E., D. A. Nadler, and C. Cammann. *Organizational Assessment: Perspectives on the Measurement of Organizational Behavior and the Quality of Working Life.* John Wiley & Sons, New York (1980).

REFERENCES FOR CHAPTER 5

1. Bair, James H. Productivity Assessment of Office Information Systems Technology. *Trends and Applications: 1978 Distributed Processing, IEEE* 12–24 (May, 1978).
2. Bair, James H. Communication in the Office of the Future: Where the Real Payoff May Be. *SRI International.* Menlo Park, California (August, 1978).
3. Bair, James H. A Communications Perspective for Identifying Office Automation Payoffs. *SRI International,* pp. 1–8. Menlo Park, California (May, 1979).
4. Bair, James H. *Productivity Assessment of Office Automation Systems* (two volumes). Report prepared for National Archives and Records Service, SRI Project 7823. Menlo Park, California (March 1979).
5. Strassman, Paul A. Organizational Productivity—The Role of Information Technology. *Informationl Processing 77, IFIP,* North-Holland Publishing Company, Amsterdam (1977).
6. Conrath, D. W., Communication Patterns, Organizational Structure, and Man: Some Relationships. *Human Factors* 15(5), 459–470 (October, 1973).
7. Conrath, D. W. Communications Environment and Its Relationship to Organizational Structure. *Management Science* 20(4), 586–603 (December, 1973).
8. Norman, R. G., and S. Bahiri. *Productivity Measurement and Incentives.* Butterworths, London, England (1972).
9. Osborn, Robert. Measuring Programmer Productivity, *BNSR, Proprit. Report.* Toronto, Ontario (August, 1979).
10. Keen, Peter, G., and M. S. Scott Morton. *Decision Support Systems: An Organizational Perspective.* Addison-Wesley Press, Reading, Massachusetts (1978).
11. Weinberg, Gerald M. *The Psychology of Computer Programming.* Van Nostrand Reinhold Company, New York (1971).
12. Kujawa, E. N. Effectiveness and Efficiency, AFIPS 1981 Office Automation Conference Digest, Houston, Texas, pp. 119–123 (March 23–25, 1981)
13. Gale, Bradley T. Can More Capital Buy Higher Productivity? *Harvard Business Review* 58(4), (July–August, 1980).
14. Dahl, Henry L., and K. S. Morgan. Return Investment in Human Resources, in *White Collar Productivity*, edited by R. N. Lehrer. McGraw Hill, New York (1982).

REFERENCES FOR CHAPTER 6

1. Van de Ven, A. H., and D. L. Ferry. *Measuring and Assessing Organizations.* John Wiley & Sons New York (1980).
2. Lawler, E. E., D. A. Nadler, and C. Cammann. *Organizational Assessment: Perspectives on the Measurement of Organizational Behavior and the Quality of Working Life.* John Wiley & Sons, New York (1980).
3. Goodman, P. S. *Assessing Organizational Change: The Rushton Mine Experiment.* John Wiley & Sons, New York (1979).
4. French, W., and C. Bell. *Organizational Development*, pp. 84–85. Prentice Hall, Englewood Cliffs, New Jersey (1973).
5. Maedke, W. O., et al., *Information and Records Management.* Benzinger, Bruce and Glencoe, Beverly Hills, California (1974).
6. Ackoff, Russel L., and Patrick Rivett. *A Manager's Guide to Operations Research.* John Wiley & Sons, New York (1967).
7. Lawler, E. E., D. A. Nadler, and C. Cammann. *Organizational Assessment: Perspectives on the Measurement of Organizational Behavior and the Quality of Working Life.* John Wiley & Sons, New York (1980).
8. Havelock, R. G. *Planning for Innovation through Dissemination and Utilization of Knowledge.* Ann Arbor, Michigan: Institute for Social Research (1969).
9. Hult, Margaret, and Sven-Ake Lennung. Toward A Definition of Action Research: A Note and Bibliograpy, *The Journal of Management Studies* 17(2) 241–250 (May, 1980).
10. McNurlin, Barbara C. Programming by End Users, *EDP Analyser* 19(5) (May, 1981).
11. Martin, James. *Application Development Without Programmers.* Savant, Carnforth, England (1981).
12. Engelbart, D. C. *Augmenting Human Intellect: A Conceptual Framework.* Summary Report, Stanford Research Institute, Menlo Park, California (1962).
13. Meyer, Dean N., and Thomas M. Lodahl. Pilot Projects: A Way to Get Started in Office Automation, *Administrative Management* XLI(2), 44–50 (February, 1980).
14. Tsichritzis, D. The Architects of System Design, *Datamation* 26(9), 201–202 (September, 1980).

REFERENCES FOR CHAPTER 7

1. Cook, Thomas D., and Donald T. Campbell. The Design and Conduct of Quasi-Experiments and True Experiments in Field Settings. In *Handbook of Industrial and Organizational Psychology.* Rand McNally College Publishing Company, Chicago (1976).
2. Hiltz, S. R., K. Johnson, and M. Turoff. The Quality of Group Decision Making in Face-to-Face Vs. Computerized Conferences. Presented at the annual meeting of the American Sociological Association, Toronto, Canada (1981).
3. Hiltz, Starr Roxanne, and Murray Turoff. *The Network Nation.* Addison-Wesley Publishing Company. Reading, Massachusetts (1978).
4. Campbell, Donald T., and Julian C. Stanley. *Experimental and Quasi-Experimental Designs for Research.* Rand McNally College Publishing Co., Chicago (1963).
5. Tapscott, H. Donald. Investigating the Office of the Future, *Telesis* 8(1), 2–6 (1981).
6. Bair, James H. Experiences with an Augmented Human Intellect System: Computer Mediated Communication, *Proceedings of the Society for Information Display Journal* 14(2), 42–51 (Spring, 1973).

7. Conrath, D. W., and James H. Bair. The Computer as an Interpersonal Communication Device: A Study of Augmentation Technology and its Apparent Impact on Organizational Communication. *Interpersonal Computer and Communications Conference*, Stockholm, Sweden (August, 1974).

8. Bair, James H. *Evaluation and Analysis of an Augmented Knowledge Workshop*. Report for the Rome Air Development Center, Number RADC-TR-74-79; also published as NTIS microfiche AD-778835. Griffiss, New York (April, 1974).

9. Edwards, Gwen C. Organizational Impacts of Office Automation. *Telecommunications Policy* 2(2), 128–136 (June, 1978).

10. Vallee, Jacques, Robert Johansen, and Kathleen Spangler. The Computer Conference: An Altered State of Communication?, *The Futurist* 9(3), 116–121 (June, 1975).

11. Lewin, K. Action Research and Minority Problems, pp. 34–36. *Journal of Social Issues* 2(4), 34–36, (1946).

12. Papanek, Miriam Lewin. Kurt Lewin and His Contributions to Modern Management Theory, *Academy of Management, Management Proceedings*, 317–321a, (August 19–22, 1973).

13. Brown, L. Dave. Action Research: Hardboiled Eggs out of Eggheads and Hardhats, in *Academy of Management, Management Proceedings* 549–555 (August 19–22, 1973).

14. Baker, H. Kent, and Ronald H. Gorman. Diagnosis: Key to O.D. Effectiveness, *Personal Journal* 55(10), 506–510 (October, 1976).

15. Cunningham, Bart. Action Research: Toward A Procedural Model, *Human Relations* 29(3), 215–238 (March, 1976).

16. French, W., and C. Bell. *Organizational Development*, pp. 84–85. Prentice Hall, Englewood Cliffs, New Jersey (1973).

17. Lind, E. Delano. Building Community-Wide Networks, *Public Management* 59(4), 15–16 (April, 1974).

18. Moore, Michael L. Assessing Organizational Planning and Teamwork: An Action Research Methodology, *Journal of Applied Behavioural Science* 14(4), 479–491 (April, 1978).

19. McGill, Michael E. Action Research Designs for Training and Development, *Academy of Management, Management Proceedings* 542–549 (August 19–22, 1973).

20. Kirkhart, Larry, and Neely Gardner, A Symposium Organization Development, *Public Administration Review* 34(2), 97–98 (March–April 1974).

21. Small, James F. The Structured Group Interview, *Training and Development Journal* 24(9), 26–32 (September, 1971).

22. Lui, Michel. Putting the Job Satisfaction Debate in Perspective, *Management International Review* 13 4–5, 27–36, (1973).

23. Trist, Eric L., Gerald I Susman, and Grant R. Brown. An Experiment in Autonomous Working in an American Underground Coal Mine, *Human Relations* 30(3), 201–236 (1977).

24. Susman, Gerald I., and Roger D. Evered. An Assessment of the Scientific Merits of Action Research, *Administrative Science Quarterly* 23(4), 582–603 (December, 1978).

25. Lawler, E. E., D. A. Nadler, and C. Cammann. *Organizational Assessment: Perspectives on the Measurement of Organizational Behavior and the Quality of Working Life*. John Wiley & Sons, New York, (1980).

REFERENCES FOR CHAPTER 8

1. Bair, James H. *Tracking Organizational Performance*. Presentation to the Diebold Office Automation Program, Kissimmee, Florida (1981).

2. Lawler, E. E., D. A. Nadler, and C. Cammann. *Organizational Assessment: Perspectives on the Measurement of Organizational Behavior and the Quality of Working Life.* John Wiley & Sons, New York, (1980).

3. Chronbach, L. J., and P. E. Meehl. Construct Validity in Psychological Tests, in *Psychological Bulletin* 52(2), 281–302 (July 1955).

4. Campbell, D. T., and D. W. Fiske. Convergent and Discriminate Validation by the Multitrait–Multimethod Matrix, *Psychological Bulletin* 52(4), 281–302 (July, 1955).

5. Van de Ven, A. H., and D. L. Ferry. *Measuring and Assessing Organizations.* John Wiley & Sons, New York (1980).

6. Webb, E. J., D. T. Campbell, R. D. Schwartz, and Sechrest, *Unobtrusive Measures: Non-Reactive Research in the Social Sciences.* Rand McNally, Chicago (1966).

7. Nie, Norman H., C. Hadlai Hull, Jean G. Jenkins, Karin Steinbrenner, and Dale H. Bent, *Statistical Package for the Social Sciences*, 2nd ed. McGraw-Hill, New York (1975).

8. Goldhaber, Gerald M. The ICA Communication Audit: Rationale and Development. In *Proceedings of the Academy of Management Convention*, Kansas City, Kansas (August, 1976).

9. McLean, R.J. Organizational Structure as Viewed by Intra-Organizational Communication Patterns. Ph.D. thesis, University of Waterloo Management Sciences Department, Waterloo (1979).

10. Sartor, L. A Program for Analysing Human Communication Network Data. Unpublished manuscript. Toronto, Ontario (1981).

REFERENCES FOR CHAPTER 9

1. Bair, James H. Communications in the Office of the Future: Where the Real Payoff May Be. *SRI International.* Menlo Park, California (August, 1978).

2. Tapscott, H. Donald. Investigating the Office of the Future, *Telesis* 8(1), 2–6 (1981).

3. Martin, James. *Distributed File and Data Base Design Tools and Techniques.* Savant Research Studies, Carnforth, England (1979).

4. Martin, James. *An End User's Guide to Data Base.* Prentice-Hall Inc., Englewood Cliffs, New Jersey (1981).

5. Lowenthal, E. I. Data Base Systems and Office Automation: The Perfect Corporate Merger, *In Depth.*

6. Goldhaber, Gerald M. The ICA Communication Audit: Rationale and Development. In *Proceedings of the Academy of Management Convention*, Kansas City, Kansas (August, 1976).

7. Graham, Mark. *Decision Support Analysis*, Unpublished manuscript, Bell-Northern Research Report, Toronto, Canada (1981).

8. Henderson, D. A. *Document Production and User-Driven Design*, Unpublished manuscript, Bell Northern Research, Toronto, Canada (1981).

9. Diebold Group. Measurement and Evaluation Techniques, *Report from the Diebold Office Automation Program.* New York (1981).

10. Sirbu, M., S. Schoichet, J, Kunin, and M. Hammer. OAM: An Office Analysis Methodology. MIT Laboratory for Computer Science, Office Automation Group Memo, Cambridge, Massachusetts (1981).

11. Ontario Ministry of Labour, The Evolution of Socio-technical Systems: A Conceptual Framework and An Action Research Program, by Eric Trist. In *Issues in the OWL* Occasional paper No. 2 (June, 1981).

12. Hackman, J. R., and G. R. Oldham. Through the Design of Work: Test of a Theory, *Organizational Behavioural and Human Performance* 16(2), 250–279 (August, 1976).
13. Van de Ven, A. H. and D. L. Ferry. *Measuring and Assessing Organizations*, John Wiley & Sons, New York (1980).
14. Pava, Calvin. Socio-Technical Design for Advanced Office Technology—A working paper. Harvard Business School, Cambridge, Massachusetts (To be published in 1982).
15. Tapscott, H. Donald, Morley Greenberg, and Loris Sartor. Predicting User Acceptance of Integrated Office Systems. Unpublished report. Toronto, Ontario (1981).
17. Opening Up Data Files to Laymen, *Business Week* (2700) (August 10, 1981).
18. Macfarlane, D. R. D. Evaluating Integrated Office Systems. Paper presented to the Diebold Office Automation Program. Washington, D.C. (1981).
19. Morgan, Howard Lee. *Research and Practice in Office Automation*, in Proceeding of the IFIP Congress, Tokyo, Japan. North-Holland Publishing Company, Amsterdam (1980).
20. Rohlfs, S. *Guidelines for the Interface Design of Interactive Systems.* Unpublished manuscript. Ottawa, Ontario (1981).

REFERENCES FOR CHAPTER 10

1. Uhlig, R. P., D. J. Farber, and J. H. Bair. *The Office of the Future.* North-Holland Publishing Company, Amsterdam (1979).
2. Sirbu, M., S. Schoichet, J. Kunin, and M. Hammer. *OAM: An Office Analysis Methodology.* MIT Laboratory for Computer Science, Office Automation Group Memo, Cambridge, Massachusetts (1981).
3. Mason, R. O., and E. B. Swanson. *Measuring for Management Decision.* Addison-Wesley Publishing Company, Reading, Massachusetts (1981).
4. Kleijnen, J. P. C. *Computers and Profits: Quantifying the Financial Benefits of Information.* Addison-Wesley Publishing Company, Reading, Massachusetts (1980).
5. Thompson, G. Office Automation: Rent, Buy or Lease? Unpublished manuscript. Toronto, Ontario (1981).

REFERENCES FOR CHAPTER 11

1. Strassman, P. A. Stages of Growth, *Datamation.* 22(10), 46–60 (October, 1976).
2. Shepard, J. M. *Automation and Alienation: A Study of Office and Factory Workers.* MIT Press, Cambridge, Massachusetts (1971).
3. Zisman, Michael D. Office Automation: Revolution or Evolution, *Sloan Management Review* 19(3), 1–16 (Spring, 1978).
4. Day, Lawrence. Stages of Growth in Office Automation, Presentation to the Diebold Office Automation Program. Boca Raton, Florida (1979).
5. Brown, L. D. Approaching the Client Organization, Presentation to the Diebold Office Automation Program (1981).
6. Zisman, Michael D. Planning for Office Automation, *Computer Decisions* 12(12), 30–31 (December, 1980).
7. Diebold Group. Planning for Office Automation. Report from the Diebold Office Automation Program. New York (1981).
8. Fried, Louis. Stanford Research Institute Report. Menlo Park, California (1974).

9. Lebolt, I. T. Project Management: User-Driven Design of Office Systems. Unpublished manuscript. Toronto, Ontario (1981).
10. Greenberg, A. M., H. Donald Tapscott, and Del Henderson. Conducting Studies to Determine User Needs for Electronic Office Systems: Some Practical Guidelines. Unpublished manuscript. Toronto, Ontario (1980).
11. Meyer, Dean N., and Thomas M. Lodahl. Pilot Projects: A Way To Get Started in Office Automation, *Administrative Management* XLI(2), 44–50 (February, 1980).

REFERENCES FOR CHAPTER 12

1. Tapscott, H. Donald, Investigating the Office of the Future, *Telesis* 8(1), 2–6 (1981).
2. Tapscott, H. Donald, Morley Greenberg, Michael Collins, Del Henderson, Ingrid Lebolt, David Macfarlane, and Loris Sartor. *Measuring the Impact of Office Information Communication Systems*, Volume III. Unpublished report. Toronto, Ontario (December, 1980).
3. Tapscott, H. Donald, Morley Greenberg, and Loris Sartor. Predicting User Acceptance of Integrated Office Systems. Unpublished report. Toronto, Ontario (1981).
4. Sartor, L. Security Issues in Implementing Electronic Office Systems. Unpublished manuscript. Toronto, Ontario (1981).

REFERENCES FOR CHAPTER 13

1. Greenberg, Morley. *Integrated Office Systems and the Quality of Working Life.* Presentation to QWL '81. Toronto, Ontario (1981).
2. Zeman, Zavis, and Russel, Robert. The Chip Dole: An Overview of the Debate on Technological Unemployment, *CIPS Review* 4(1) (January–February, 1980).
3. Valaskakis, Kimor, and P. Sindell. Industrial Strategy and the Information Economy: Towards a Gameplan for Canada, Gamma Paper No. I-10, Montreal, Quebec (1980).
4. Russell, P. A. *The Electronic Briefcase: The Office of the Future.* Occasional Paper No. 3, Institute for Research into Public Policy, Montreal, Quebec (1978).
5. Gardiner, W. L. *Public Acceptance of the New Information Technologies: the Role of Attitude.* Gamma Paper, No. I-9 (1980).
6. Silversides, Ann. Women's Traditional Jobs Predicted to Suffer Most in Technological Revolution, *Globe Mail.* Report on Business section (January 17, 1981).
7. Mark, J. A. Impact of Technological Change on Labor. Proceedings of the Conference on the Impact of Technological Change on the Workplace. St. Louis, Missouri (June 1979).
8. Rabeau, Y. Tele-Informatics, Productivity and Employment: An Economic Interpretation, Report by Gamma Group, Montreal, Quebec (1980).
9. Jenkins, C., and Sherman, B. *The Collapse of Work.* Methuen Eyre, London, England (1979).
10. Nora, S., and Minc, A. *L'information de la Societe.* Paris, La documentation francaise (January, 1978).
11. Menzies, H. Women and the Chip. The Institute for Research on Public Policy. Montreal (1981).
12. Mather, Boris. Computerization and Employment: A Labour View, *Communication Workers of Canada*, Saskatchewan, Canada (1980).
13. Toffler, Alvin, *The Third Wave.* Bantam Books, New York (1980).

14. Tapscott, H. Donald, Morley Greenberg, and Loris Sartor. Predicting User Acceptance of Integrated Office Systems. Unpublished report. Toronto, Ontario (1981).
15. Greenberg, A. M., H. Donald Tapscott, and Del Henderson. Conducting Studies to Determine User Needs for Electronic Office Systems: Some Practical Guidelines. Unpublished manuscript. Toronto, Ontario (1980).
16. Hoard, B. Automation Viewed as Threat to Workers. *Computerworld* XIV(22), pl (June 2, 1980).
17. CSE Microelectronics Group, *Capitalist Technology and the Working Class*, CSE Books, London, England (1980).
18. Cherns, A. B. Speculations on the Social Effect of New Microelectronics Technology? *Management Labour Review* 119(6), 705–721 (November–December, 1980).
19. Thompson, Gordon B. Memo from Mercury: Information Technology is Different, Occasional Paper No. 10. Institute for Research on Public Policy, Montreal, Canada (1979).
20. McLean, R. J. Organizational Structure as Viewed by Intra-Organizational Communications Patterns. PH.D. thesis, University of Waterloo Management Sciences Department, Waterloo (1979)

Index